CONTEMPORARY CONCERNS

CONTEMPORARY CONCERNS

Strategic, Economic, Cyber, Gender, and Beyond

Editors

Sitakanta Mishra
Neeta Sinha

Foreword by

Prof. Nigam Dave

KALPAZ

First Published, 2018

Published by

Kalpaz Publications
C-30, Satyawati Nagar,
Delhi – 110052
Ph.: 011-47034999, 9811692060
www.kalpazpublications.com
E-mail: kalpaz@hotmail.com

Printed at: G. Print Process, Delhi

Cataloging in Publication Data—DK
Courtesy: D.K. Agencies (P) Ltd. <docinfo@dkagencies.com>

Contemporary concerns : strategic, economic, cyber, gender, and beyond / by Sitakanta Mishra, Neeta Sinha.
pages cm
Contributed articles.
Includes bibliographical references.
ISBN 9789386397737 (hardback)

1. Information technology—Social aspects—India. 2. Information technology—Economic aspects—India. 3. Corporate culture—India. 4. India—Economic policy—1991- 5. National security—India. 6. Asia—Strategic aspects. 7. Women—Legal status, laws, etc.—India. I. Mishra, Sitakanta, editor. II. Sinha, Neeta, editor.

LCC HM851.C66 2018 | DDC 303.4833 23

Contents

Strategic Discourse

Gender Typecast

Preface

Has the world become awful; if yes, why; and since when? The answer is obvious. Is it possible to make it better; can the untoward happenings be bunged, and the damages already unleashed be alleviated? The answer is inconclusive. While the idealists would still vouch for corrective measures and emphasize moralistic human behaviour, pessimists paint an apocalyptic scenario. Phenomena like climate change, nuclear weapons, population explosion, pervasive immorality and hatred among humans, etc. are indicative of the slippery slope that the world is moving on. On the other hand, the humanity has achieved phenomenal success in the sphere of health, shelter, communication, etc. which should make the world a better place for all. But this seems a misnomer.

In the name of modernity and civilization, the kind of 'growth and development' model we have devised and embarked on during the last few centuries has overlooked the intrinsic connect between human civilization and the nature. While every species in the globe attach to, and accommodate with, the nature, only the humanbeings manipulate the nature for survival, instead of adjusting to it. By now, the face of the earth has malformed to the extent of no return. Today, global concerns, largely man-made, are manifold and leading the globe towards dooms day.

Contemporary Concern is a thematic interlace of research papers on pressing issues that the humanity is confronting with at present. With intriguing analyses on areas like cyber/social media, corporate issues, fiscal policy, strategic, and gender issues, the volume brings forth the veracity of concerns with which we have not been able to come to term with, even though they are persisting for the last couple of decades. Scholars and practitioners from various strands have delved into specific concerns by deconstructing their culmination, to suggest out of box solutions while acknowledging the fact that these would continue to exasperate the humanity with their mutated nomenclature.

In the first section, "Virtual Vicissitude", three eminent authors, Binod C. Agrawal, Pradeep Mallik, Nidhi Arora, dwell upon the concerns emanating from the increasing use of virtual / digital medium through which consent or dissent can be manufactured. Agrawal analyzes some salient features of digital media influences and concerns in national and international perspectives. Digital media greatly influences the process and functioning of democracy in the world; more importantly digital media has been entrenched into the societal fabric germinating many transformations in social fabric, including gender equations, sexual orientation, violence, etc. The 'social media' revolution what we are undergoing today is born out of the communication revolution unmindful of its socio-cultural impact. As far as India is concerned, Agrawal finds the concern critical since digital media is being utilized and promoted in a hierarchically separated, multi-lingual and multi-religious society having vivid "world views".

Nidhi Arora enquires into the criticality of 'big data' which is evolving as a new type of corporate asset forming a strong basis for competition among companies. In this digital age, 'data' would be precious like crude oil. Information and analysis of individual pattern of use of digital information can be value for business. Capturing, storing, retrieving and analyses of information or data in a timely manner are vital issues for business houses. With increasing access to faster communication and digital technology, there is an explosion of data and the organizations require to enhance their capability to aggregate and analyze the voluminous data from multiple sources.

Professor Pradeep Mallik brings out the flipside of social media use and its lasting impact on behavioural and social interaction which is increasingly getting worrisome. Undoubtedly, the social media has proven to be an effective vehicle for organisation and mobilization as it encourages contributions and feedback from everyone who is interested. It blurs the line between media and audience. The platform is useful for its openness, prompt feedback, and participation. With ease of sharing of information, there are rarely any barriers to accessing and making use of content. However, social media platform has been a place for manipulation, bully, trolling and hyperbole for which many of us would be far happier without the artifice of it.

The second section discusses the concerns relating to urbanization and the corporate world which has engulfed the modern day-to-day life. Rampant urbanization with rising population, particularly in the developing countries, is becoming pandemic. It stresses upon availability of resources, capability to provide basic amenities, thus creating a widening hiatus between the urban demand and supply of resources. Rising urban population along with depleting resources and environmental concerns have brought the issue of sustainable urbanism for serious discussion. It manifests in widespread urban poverty, unbridled growth of slums, environmental degradation, social insecurity, and so on. In pursuit of addressing all these, 'sustainable urbanism' has become central to urban policies and has influenced theories and practices of urbanism in different parts of the world. Mihir Bholey explores how the concept of Smart City is a timely response to all urban problems. Harmik Vaishnav, Neeta Sinha, and Supriya Pal have examined the human resource concerns that the corporate world is confronting today.

Dr Harmik Vaishnav categorically emphasizes that lucid and unambiguous language or communication for professional prudence is absolute necessity in the corporate world. The contemporary trend of Globalization in the field of business, technology, international relations, and cross-cultural interaction and experiences play a crucial role especially the English language. When the contemporary world has defied geographical detachment and cultural barriers for the sake of business, science and inter-mingling of people, language has to bring them to certain intellectual and emotional level, rather than separating them. Therefore, as Dr Vaishnav rightly concludes, brevity with simple words and structure with clarity and precision is the key. Dr Neeta Sinha and Supriya Pal have delved into the millennial generation or the Generation Y related human resource concerns. This generation known as echo boomers, facebook generation, generation next, net generation; so have unique characteristics necessitating special management set up.

Any change or alteration in the fiscal policy has larger socio-economic implications. One such example is the globalization process coupled with IT revolution that has eased the movement of man and material worldwide. It is debatable if the world is a better place after globolisation. Swati Gupta and Nausheen Nizami have studied at length Indian current fiscal policy and the IT industry to find the socio-economic repercussions. Swati Gupta enquires about the financial planning and portfolio management for retail investors in the post-demonetization phase in India. As she rightly points out, if one looks into the bright side of demonetization, it has curbed mindless spending and has made a lot of investment avenues affordable. One needs to take advantage of the current subdued market conditions, review the current investment status and the possible investment avenues, and take a leap towards financial growth through effective portfolio management.

She advises to start investing early and create a portfolio that helps maximise and optimise one's returns.

Dr Nausheen Nizami, on the other hand, examines decent work provision to IT employees, their own self-assessment on the indicators of decent work. The IT industry in India is significantly different from the labour market found in agriculture and manufacturing sectors. The IT services offer employment opportunities for white-collar, educated labour-force in a relatively clean and standardised office environment. Indian society has quickly accepted the IT related industry and in a short span India became the global leader in IT. Fast growth of the IT sector attracted major chunk of workforce, which has strong implications on other sectors of Indian economy. Meanwhile, the retrenchment rate in this sector is equally high. The challenge, therefore, is to provide a decent work environment with stability and security of work to make the employee happy while being productive.

The section dealing with strategic discourse critically evaluate the phenomena like 'right wing' upsurge, illegal migration, Chinese strategic inroads into important places, nuclear security and nonproliferation regime, etc. No easy solution can be found to address the concerns emanating from these issues. All the authors have raised pertinent questions in their search for appropriate answers. Shilpa Parasrampuria asserts that the liberal global order upswing for last few decades faces a great challenge today as new nationalist chants echo across continents. Is this an offshoot of domestic disarray that the political leadership found themselves, and in their attempt to look for salvation by deftly turning public attention towards contentious foreign policy issues? Reshmi Kazi objectively assesses whether Pakistan has addressed effectively nuclear proliferation concerns that it was involved in. She concludes by raising essential questions on the efficacy, legitimacy, and implications of the Nuclear Suppliers Group (NSG) exemption for Pakistan. Manisha Chaurasia explores the possibility of an Indo-Pak collaborative framework on nuclear security which is the biggest concern of the world so far. Safety and security of nuclear assets has risen to the fore front of the global agenda during the last few decades, given the intent and capability of non-state actors and disastrous consequence in case of misuse of nuclear material and technology.

Beside hardcore issue areas, three other phenomena have attracted global attention in recent times: the migration and refugee crisis, China's global presence through inroads into strategic places of the world, and gender-based discrimination/stereotype. In the case study on South Asia,

Sitakanta Mishra examines the negative implications of unresolved illegal migration in the region on the regional peace and stability. The regional grouping SAARC, suppose to tackle the issue through mutual cooperation, is handicapped and illegal migration has culminated in a strategic concern for the linkage between terrorism, smuggling, trafficking. etc. E. Dilipraj attempts to fathom the asymmetric relations between China and Latin American countries and consequent geopolitical implications. Parvathy Poornima and Aanchal Jha have critiqued the gender-based discrimination pervasive in the world which needs urgent attention.

Suffice it to say, there is no end to the list of concerns that the humanity is facing today. Here an attempt is made to ponder over some of the pressing concerns to contribute to the larger intellectual debate. The volume does not provide or advocate any lasting solution to all these concerns except highlighting them for greater public discourse and understanding.

In pursuit of editing this book, we sincerely thank the School of Liberal Studies (SLS) of Pandit Deendayal Petroleum University, and Director Professor Nigam Dave, who have been our constant support and source of inspiration. Our colleagues in SLS have always been supportive in times of toil. We hope this attempt will be a worthy addition to the existing pool of literature and deliberations on respective issue areas.

Sitakanta Mishra

August 2018 **Neeta Sinha**

Foreword

Every epoch is entangled with varieties of concerns which are "mostly caused by a too rapid speed of advances, so that the side-effects of a predominantly positive evolution (progress) become difficult to control", as rightly says F. Heylighen, a research professor at the Free University of Brussels. The epoch in vogue has undoubtedly inimitable concerns which require humane interdisciplinary responses. The edited volume by Dr Sitakanta Mishra and Dr Neeta Sinha aptly amalgamates and ponders over some of the critical contemporary concerns that the humanity is confronting with, as we all nervous which mode it would culminate in. Many are equally busy suggesting or devising innovative approaches/methods to arrest and reverse the trend which is welcome. However, we need to be realistic to accept that there can be no panacea for all the concerns, but tiny steps with determination by every individual would contain and slowdown the deterioration unset around us – be it in the environment, social harmony, humanity, so on and so forth. Chaos theory testifies that a tiny butterfly flipping its wings on one side of the ocean can bring high tide on the other side, so we do we have hope.

At a time when the humanity is passing through a critical juncture and its complete annihilation is not unthinkable, only a combination of spiritual, civic, and family virtues should be our ethical guide, which comes from an indomitable individual and collective will, for building a strong society to reverse the disastrous trend. Civilizations across people have tried to ponder over three pathways – logic, ethics, and aesthetics: *Satyam, Shivam, Sundaram*. Many great thinkers have pondered over the challenges of mankind and advised right direction by applying both realist and idealist approaches. One greatest thinker of this epoch Mahatma Gandhi has rightly insisted to discard seven social sins or behaviours that cause lasting harm to society: politics without principles, business without morals, well-being without work, education without character, science without humanity, fun without responsibility, religion without sacrifice; all these go against the ethical code and thereby weaken the society and humanity at large. These seem to be the most desirous paths for the current times if the human civilization has to sustain.

It is in this context that Dr Mishra and Dr Sinha have compiled this volume giving us a peep into the flipside of 'modernity' in this epoch for which, to quote Wordsworth, "the world becomes too much with us".

This volume is a must read for anyone and everyone interested in current global and national public discourse.

Nigam Dave
Director/Dean, School of Liberal Studies
Pandit Deendayal Petroleum University,
Gandhinagar, Gujarat

August 2018

Virtual Vicissitude

Chapter - 1

Concern for Human Future in Digital Media Era of India

— Binod C. Agrawal

Introduction

Several millennia old Bharat that is India continues to fault and flourish with anomalies, conflicts and constrictions that has survived as an interdependent cultural mosaic through its meandering and checkered past. India has withstood multiple onslaughts of numerous foreign, intra, and internal invasions, political upheavals and serious ideological crises. The cultural characteristics in all periods of turmoil were strong. In the changing situation, familial fabric, family focused politics and social structure continues to dominate society well reflected in the current socio-political process. The process of social, economic and linguistic transformation interwoven within religious and external and internal invasions created a socio-religious flux of perpetual evolution, enrichment and continuity of the Indian Sub-continent.

Continuous military encounters, migration of population and inter-state human movement gave rise the emergence of strong bond of family and marriage with a distinct non-verbal and symbolic communication. It helped evolve multiple tongues that provided a fertile ground for internal ideological intrusions and inner strength to remain an integrated having ability to absorb like a sponge and re-configure distinct political, economic and cultural and social entities from mountain covered North and ocean bound South over time in an unbroken "history".

The global unbarred communication revolution along with other cultural, economic, political, social and technological, interventions in human history is continuously bringing about rapid changes with unimaginable and accelerated pace in all walks of human life. Digital media has enhanced human ability to become "talking head" which was until recently a "tight lip" bound by cultural norms within the subcontinent and elsewhere in the world. The net result, it seems, is emergence of new kinds of inter-personal, familial and gender conflicts leaving unknown and unimaginable ripples.

Hence, the objective of the paper is to briefly describe and analyze some salient features of digital media influences and concerns in national and international perspectives. More especially the following aspects of digital media influences will be analyzed:

1. Technology Perspective of Digital Media
2. Digital Media in Euro-American Context
3. Digital Media and Democracy in World and national Perspective
4. Digital Media and Social Transformation
5. Digital Media and Man-Woman Relationships
6. Digital Media, Pornography and Violence
7. Social Media for Peaceful and Just World

In the concluding section, brief futuristic concerns will be expressed. Digital media has often been interchangeably thought of and referred to as "social media" in several parts of the world. In India, digital media has been born out of communication revolution, its growth and development has created virtual world and released a tsunami while there has been little realization of digital media socio-cultural impacts. The changes are eminent in the cultural ethos. Hence, it is argued that social media likely impact must be serious a concern and must be assessed, studied and understood. It must form analyzed for better appreciation and to design protective measures for the future of India.

The concern in the context of India is critical since digital media is being utilized and promoted in a hierarchically separated, multi-lingual and multi-religious society having vivid "world views". The fear is that digital media may be imposed by the dominant minority over poor majority. In the process, digital media will slip from the hands of ordinary citizens and politically powerful, outspoken and economically dominant few who will begin to apply digital media as a weapon of exploitation and suppression of the poor by robbing their legitimate human rights. Studies have cautioned about growing gulf between poor and rich, urban and rural and media owners and non-owners as a result of digital media especially satellite broadcasting in India (Agrawal 2015). Earlier Agrawal (1993: 231) observed "The satellite broadcasting has reduced the possibility of people's participation, thereby, weakening the democracy". An alternate view is that digital technology by itself does not create any necessary condition for strengthening or weakening the social fabric of the culture and society rather the digital media users would determine its social outcome, direction and process of change. A brief technological perspective is essential to elaborate the communication technological implications for understanding the social concern.

Technology Perspective of Digital Media

Digital media has often been interchangeably and popularly referred to as "social media" in many parts the world as digital media was born out of rapid growth and development of information and communication technology. A whole host of new digital and satellite technology applications have been invented, accelerated and promoted by international market forces. The market is flooded by Euro-American by electronic consumer products globally. Digital media today is like hurricane that has crossed the time and space boundaries. There are three information and communication technology perspectives of digital media. These could be "techno-positivism", "techno-neutralism" and "techno-negativism" perspectives. The techno-negativism perspective is that it will lead adverse social influences that would drastically divert the direction of socio-political changes that may jeopardize the human welfare. Serious thoughts must be given within the cultural domains in order to divert the path of human devastation and survival while keeping ecological balance in mind. On the other hand "techno-positivism" views digital media to contribute in the political and emotional integration, freedom to express opinion, stimulate one to one and to many horizontal exchanges of information. The "techno-neutralism" view of digital media in the larger social context. According this view digital media by itself does not create any necessary condition for strengthening or weakening the social fabric of the culture and society rather the digital media users would determine its social outcome, direction and process change (Hamclink 1986).

Digital Media in Euro-American Context

In United States of America, France, and other European countries, the digital media also known as "new media" has become a catch word. After the turn of the century, and by 2008 AD digital media significantly has altered the sources of political information, methods of elections campaign and seemed to have influenced human participation. Digital media has also influenced individual, familial and community interaction. The most visible change could be observed is in the social democratic process. "No doubt over the past decades, the landscape of the politics has drastically changed with mass adaptation of digital technology."[1] India is not left behind and within five years India has been sailing in the digital media boat.

In order to assess, examine and understand the relationships between digital media and democracy in the United States of America at the University of Wisconsin-Madison, a dedicated Social Media Research Group (SMRG) has been setup. SMRG focuses on the study of "user-created digital media and its political and social implications,"[2] "...Internet for participatory engagement and political conversation, with particular attention to the political blogs and web news sources, social networking systems, and peer-to-peer interactions in online settings."[3] SMRG explores possible interplay and connection "between digital media and civic and political life and consequences of these interactions.[4]...They have also explored "Online incivility and formal features of political blogs to understand how these factors influence perceptions and judgments."[5]

Digital Media and Democracy in World Perspective

Unwin (2012) among few who has emphasized that digital media and for that matter any information technology is not an autonomous power that can inherently be used for good or bad whereby "existing structures and political process can be fundamentally changed.There is no simple answer to this."[6] On the contrary, Storsul (2014) observed that young people were hesitant about using digital media for political deliberation in Norway (Storsul 2014: 26).[7]

In context of India, Parmar (2014) reported extensive use of digital media for political campaigning in Parliamentary Elections of 2014.[8] In a two phase parliamentary national opinion poll survey that covered 13428 and 15267 voters from all major States, among other questions, enquired about the use of digital media in the election as source of political information. The two-phase survey was carried out in April-May 2014 among voters of both genders. These opinion surveys reported that in first phase, 1.3 percent voters and in second phase, 2.2 per cent voters used internet for receiving election related political information.[9]

Other media and communication scholars have concluded remarkable effects of digital media. Digital media according to some of them has brought about major "shift" in almost every aspect of human life. The prediction is that digital media will lead to irreversible socio-political and economic changes in almost all spheres of human life. So in future, humans will make informed decisions though such conclusions have limited empirical research support, especially in India. However, research study carried out in the capital of India, New Delhi during August 2014, indicated that as much as 78.8 per cent respondents did not use digital media to have any political information or use digital media for informed political decision making. At the same time, it should be mentioned that though as much as 15.5 per cent adult voters of Delhi used Facebook, 2.4 per cent Twitter, and 1.8 per cent What Sapp and 0.5 per cent used other social media.[10]

The acceptance and expansion of digital media and consequent developments pushed India to catch up with Euro-American cultural, political, socio-economic and technological realities. The rest of the world including China without much serious thought of their cultural, economic, political and socio-technological history have embarked to introduce digital media without realizing social and economic consequences. Today, the largest number of digital media users lives in Asia. While political governance in democratic India remained stable, digital media has invaded socio-cultural, economic and political world of India in big way. The political leadership and economic compulsions have made digital media all pervasive, and continues to penetrate every passing second across all social classes, religious groups and linguistic regions both in rural and urban India and among poor and rich alike. The intelligent guess is that increased penetration and use of digital media may bring an age of high-tech feudalism and control.

In this context, it should be mentioned that digital media seems to becoming a new and instantaneous source of quick information for broadcast media in India. Digital media is being recklessly used by political leaders, ordinary digital media users and corporates to exhibit and display, share views, express sorrow and happiness; pain and pleasure. The notion of individual privacy is in great jeopardy. Hence, concern is expressed for the future of the Indian society.

Digital Media and Social Transformation

Digital media is believed to have many unprecedented transformational effects on the youth. Today, several million men and women have migrated abroad and are living away from their cultural roots of from across India in which Gujarat has appreciable share. First time these youth are facing strange language, food, religion and host of social patterns of interaction alien to them having little understanding of conservation and meaning of peaceful co-existence for survival. It has loosened moral, ethical and familial norms and values of conservation. The family structure, institution of marriage, family responsibilities and whole host of interpersonal obligatory social networks are under strain. It has created serious moral and personal conflicts between self and family, self and village. The new situation has added challenges of negotiating other cultures without realizing that their future could be in jeopardy. Are these observable challenges and conflicts having latent influence on the "left behind family", extended household and village remains in the realm of speculation?

Digital media and mobile smart phones on the face of it have provided remarkable connectivity among friends and foes, relatives and neighbors, parents and children, employers and employees. Digital media has created time and space neutral exchange and sharing of intimate, personal and professional information with great ease. Today, young men and women and old living abroad are in touch with their parents, relatives, friends, children and professional colleagues, if not on an hourly basis at least on daily basis. This interaction in no way should be construed as increased human communication and interaction to enhance bonding of family and household. Increased digital media and mobile phones in no way ensure improved sensitivity of environment and mutually satisfying human communication and relationships.

The lure of the migrants creates an aura of "present orientation" and imitative desire to live independently in material comfort. For many it has infused self-imposed conditions for avoiding parents, relatives and neighbors. A case of Western India may be sighted especially of Gujarat and Maharashtra where there has been appreciable west ward is continuing in search of better life remunerative jobs and improved quality of life. The migrating youth have to struggle for survival in the new environment often with limited money. Without sharing their problems and in lure of "better" living "left behind family" having high expectations form their children suffer both emotionally and often financially. It is very pronounced especially among the youth living in Europe and North America and to some extent in mega cities of India. This situation will continue to escalate and family may face perpetual brunt and crisis in which both the young and old will suffer from a variety of familial, social and economic trauma. The resultant influences can be observed in growing family tension, alienation and growing distances within the family.

Digital Media and Man-Woman Relationships[11]

The digital media has begun to influence socio-economic, linguistic and socio-cultural domains of human life and consequently man-women relationships. In a recent article Cabanes and Acedera (2012: 917) have examined "…the role of the mobile phone in the exercise of conjugal power between left-behind fathers and migrant mothers from families separated by labor migration" with special focus on selected. Asian countries like Indonesia, Sri Lanka and Vietnam. The researchers have found mobile phones or smart phones as most preferred digital media especially in Philippines and also in India. The researchers pointed out that in engaging mobile telephony the users found them equally entrenched within realm of new media and world of everyday. "As a consequence, people find themselves having to negotiate with the pluralized relationships that these colliding spaces bring about. There is no doubt that this idea has firmly superseded the once poplar supposition that the online world is a space that is completely detached from the offline world" (Cabanes and Acedera 2012: 919-920). They concluded "the mobile phone thus tends to build resentment in many of the left-behind fathers. This certainly contributes to increasing the strain present in the already difficult relationships between the spouses in mother-away families. "So while, it is true that the technology can mitigate some of the effects of migration by providing more frequent and instantaneous communication, it cannot shield of the fathers and mothers from the tremendous difficulties of having to deal with two opposing forces: the changed realities in a transnational Filipino family and the traditional expectations of Philippine society" (Cabanes and Acedera 2012: 928). It may be noted that there was no concern expressed or discussed as to how in the change circumstances, digital media could help or assist in altering the transformation of language use in the Philippine society.

In India, Agrawal (2014) reported positive role of digital media in creating reciprocal and symmetrical communication between husband and wife in family and public discourse that may lead to structural changes in man-women relationships and use of language due to extensive use of mobile telephone among migrant workers with their left behind wives and families. Agrawal (2014) observed that while in the past, migrant husband could speak to his wife in privacy, once in six to eight months or even after a year when he returned to home. Now, a migrant worker is in touch almost instantaneously every day as if he is talking to his wife from another room of the house.[12] The case study of two male migrant workers from Uttar Pradesh and Rajasthan clearly supported the view that oral means of communication was not barrier for non-English low literate couple living long distances from each other. Regular mobile calls from either side have helped strengthen the familial bond between spouses and family. New communicative code of language has been evolved to save time and money. In the process wives, have felt a sense of equality that was not heard or used within the cultural norms earlier or experienced by the wife. The response of the husbands was not adverse and was accepted with ease by the spouses. The analysis trends to supports the techno-neutralism view along with the views of Unwin who argued that user determines the nature of use of digital media and its resultant effects.

The brief analysis in the context of India tends to support the view that at familial level, the digital media has helped create reciprocal and symmetrical men-women relationships and new form of communication between husband and wife, family, siblings and others in personal and public discourse. This may lead to structural changes in language use due to extensive use of mobile telephone in India (Agrawal 2014).

Digital Media, Pornography and Violence

The other arena of digital media effect could be experienced in a largely patriarchal family structure that relates to growing anti-social criminal tendencies and destructive outlook of life and disregard for keeping ecological balance. Media reports have indicated increasing, criminal tendencies, international terrorism and experimentation with sex and excessive miss use of human body. These anti-social and criminal activities today are being facilitated by perceived privacy and anonymity by digital media. From this perspective, digital media has contributed in anti-social activities that may lead to increase socio-psychological dissonance, social anomie and birth of new kinds of crimes. For the first time in human history, digital media has permitted uninhibited and unchecked public exhibition of normal, abnormal and obnoxious sexual acts in most pervert and devious ways. These are viewed by several million adults and adolescents. It all started, though in small way, in India with large scale arrival of ½" Video Cassette Recorder (VCR) more than thirty years ago (Agrawal *et al.*, 1989). A question has been raised by psychologists, sociologists and anthropologists whether such unrestricted viewing would influence human sexual behavior and promote sexual violence.

Social Media for Peaceful and Just World

Digital media has invaded human privacy and freedom apart from professional and technical life. It has further begun to influence techno-social development, social structure and religious beliefs. The primordial human behavior has evolved over a period of several millennia without perceptible discontinuity that continues to persist as "Humans are among the world's most adaptable animals...are unique in also having cultural means of adaptations" (Kottak 2011: 4-5). Intervened by historical, external military invasions and inter-continental migration, the process of cultural adaptation and evolution has continued. Digital media interventions, in a very short period, has very rapidly accelerated the process of techno-social change all round with exceptionally high speed without any past precedence. The changes are being felt and speculated without giving any clear direction of change. At the same time, the core of the human behavior though dynamic in nature is fairly insulated from minor technology perturbation of digital media, at least, in India.

There are at least three aspects of primordial behavior in which digital media could make dent to bring about changes that can be postulated. These are observable at the social and cultural surface. These changes can be noticed in individual, household and village or *Mohalla* or even an urban ward which is difficult to separate or discern that may bring about irreversible changes. Research studies carried out from time to time has indicated continuous interaction of digital media and culture by a symbiotic process in influencing observable surface changes without any long term irreversible effects. One of the plausible explanations for such an uncertainty to establish discernable impact or effect is that digital media as a technological innovation remains within the realm of "social exhibitionism" for spreading mindless and ephemeral information with little or no conviction or social consequence that could lead to fundamental change in the primordial behavior though perturbation can be felt and observed. Digital media, however, in the bargain has squeezed the poor who are diverting their scarce resources, social capital of time and money to fall into trap of increased perpetual poverty (Agrawal 2015). So, digital media influence is yet to be understood that is a social concern in India.

Conclusion

Based on the foregoing analysis presented so far, it could be said that while there is a concern both in India and globally about the social future and possible adverse influence of digital media, it is too early to draw any definitive conclusion. In case of India, in its long and meandering socio-cultural history, no major structural changes are expected resulting from the penetration and use of digital media.

Given the linguistic diversity and hierarchal division of the Indian society and in absence of any pan Indian patterns of digital influence, uniform digital media impact and any irreversible social change, in short term, is not pre-empted. The family structure being dynamic, contrary to static images described by social scientists having long history of inter-state and international migration while continue to evolve without tempering the deep rooted patterns of family and marriage will remain largely intact. Observable minor reversible surface changes might be visible as cyclic changes in India without any irreversible impact. If digital media impact is examined within this frame, the chances are that minimal evolutionary and continuous emerging changes could be experienced that is what the analyses have indicated. The tentative conclusion is that digital media for present should not be major social concern.

Notes

1. "Undertaking the Development Data Revolution: Social Media Data and Research" organized by U.K. Economic and Social Research Council and Indian Council of Social Science Research scheduled held on January 9, 2015, Doubletree (Hilton) hotel, West End London, U.K. (Newton Bhabha Fund Initiative).
2. http://smad.journalism.wisc.edu/, accessed on January 15, 2014.
3. *Ibid.*
4. *Ibid.*
5. *Ibid.*
6. Tim Unwin, "Social media and democracy: critical reflections", http://www.cpahq.org/cpahq/cpadocs/Unwin%20CPA%20Social%20 media%20 and%20democracy.pdf
7. Tanja Storsul, "Deliberation or Self-presentation? Young People, Politics and Social Media", Nordicom Review 2.4, Vol. 35, No. 2, 2014, pp. 17-28.
8. A Case Study on Use of Social Media in Indian General Election-2014",http://www.academia.edu/7676021/Case_Study_on_Use_of_Social_ Media_in_ General_Election_India_2014
9. For detail see two phase reports on Lok Sabha Elections 2014 conducted by TALEEM Research Foundation for Zee News in the months of April and May 2014.
10. For detail see unpublished report on "Electoral Politics in Forthcoming Delhi Vidhan Sabha Election: An Opinion Survey" conducted by TALEEM Research Foundation, Ahmedabad (2015).
11. Adopted from "New Media Turned Tight lip into a Non-Stop Talking Civilization: An Analysis for Language Transformation in Family Discourse", Keynote Address by Binod C Agrawal presented in National Seminar on 'Emerging Languages in Public Discourse and New Media' organised by CIIL in collaboration with AMIC held at CIIL Mysore, March 15-16, 2014

12. Ibid; Julia T. Wood, "Gendered Media: The Influence of Media on Views of Gender", http://www.udel.edu/comm245/readings/GenderedMedia.pdf

References

1. Agrawal, Binod C., 2017, "Media and Dynamics of Change in Democracy of India", paper presented in the plenary session of the International Conference of EFCS held at Lucknow, March 3-5, 2017.
2. "Growing Social Inequality in the Wake of Communication Globalization: Is There Way to Arrest Poor Becoming Pauper in South Asia?" Revised, enlarged re-written paper presented earlier in the Symposium on "Resisting Inequality/ Enabling Inclusion: An India-Canada Comparison" held on June 8-10, 2015 at York University, Toronto, Canada.
3. "New Media Turned Tight lip into a Non-Stop Talking Civilization: An Analysis for Language Transformation in Family Discourse", Keynote in the National Seminar on 'Emerging Languages in Public Discourse and New Media ' organized by CIIL in collaboration with AMIC at CIIL Mysore, March 15-16, 2014.
4. "Human Future and Communication Revolution: Can there be a Peace and Co-Existence on the Planet Earth", paper presented in National Workshop on 'Communicating Science of Conservation of Planet Earth to the People for Peaceful Co-Existence and Just World' held at Jawaharlal Nehru University, New Delhi on March 22-24, 2013.
5. "Communication Technology and Democracies of South Asia: The Danger of Curbing Freedom", in *Communication and Democracy*, Eds., Slavko Sphichal and Janet Wasko, 1993, pp. 221-232. Norwood, New Jersey: Ablex Publishing Corporation.
6. Agrawal, Binod C., *et al., Communication Revolution: A Study of Video Penetration in India*, Ahmedabad: DECU, Indian Space Research Organisation, 1989.
7. Alexander Hanna, Chris Wells,Peter Maurer, Dhavan V. Shah, Lewis Friedland and Jorh Matthews.
8. "Partisan Alignments and Political Polarization Online: A Computational Approach to Understanding the French and U.S. Presidential Elections", in 'Politics, Election and Data Workshop (PLEAD)', San Francisco, CA. November 1, 2013.
9. Anonymous, Delhi *Vidhan Sabha* Elections 2015, Ahmcdabad: TALEEM Research Foundation 2015.
10. C.J, Hamclink, "Is Information Technology Neutral?", in J.Becker, G. Hedebro and L. Palden, eds., *Communication and Domination: Essay to Honour Herbert I Schiller*, Norwood NJ: Ablex Press, 1986, pp. 16-24.
11. Conard Philip Kottak, *Cultural Anthropology Appreciating Cultural Diversity* (Fourteenth Edition), New York: McGrow Hill, 2011.
12. Tanja Storsul, "Deliberation or Self-presentation? Young People, Politics and Social Media", *Nordicom Review 2.4*, Vol. 35, No. 2, 2014, pp. 17-28.
13. Unwin, 2012, http://www.cpahq.org/cpahq/cpadocs/Unwin%20CPA%20Social%20media %20and%20democracy.pdf

Chapter - 2

Big Data Analytics: A Prospective Solution to Business Hitches

— *Nidhi Arora*

Introduction

In past few years, business people have seen tremendous explosion in data that is being generated through daily transactions. Corresponding to this, the heterogeneity in data volumes have grown by an even larger amount. Organizations with high-performance computing infrastructures and data centers are finding ways to deal with the voluminous data. Various tools are also used to bring in significant benefits in data mining, machine learning and knowledge discovery but still there is a big hole.

Many traditional data centric applications lack in their ability to handle the most important aspect that is data. In this chapter, our focus is on emerging trends in computing with possible solutions of business problems through big data analytics. Although there are many obstacles in dealing with the huge amount of data, big data analytics tools have potential to reform the data analytics. Big data analytics comes to the rescue for business problems by deploying, integrating and operationalizing big data environment required to realize the value of their existing business resources.

Recent innovations in technology and affordable price of electronic gadgets have taken over the charge of data explosion. In today's age of big data, the variety and amount of digital data generated is quite high and it is too big to process conventionally or to transport anywhere. Over a period of time, big data may be seen evolving as a new type of corporate asset forming a strong basis for competition among companies. In that case, companies should seriously start thinking about whether they are organized to exploit big data's potential and to manage the possible threats it can pose. Success will demand not only new skills but also new perspectives on how the era of big data could evolve—the widening circle of management practices it may affect and the foundation it represents for new, potentially disruptive business models.[1] (Brown, et al. 2011)

Data creates value for business. Effective utilization of data can bring better results for business people. With this fact and the prevailing scenario, business people have understood the significance of managing the data. This has given rise to conscious intentions of managers to derive insights from information to take more realistic and better decisions. These intentions from business in turn have raised the need of tools and technologies for extracting hidden knowledge from pool of data.

A business runs on its day-to-day transactions governed by data which is generated as a result of transactions. The data hence generated brings along with it variety and veracity which makes it difficult for business people to deal with the enormous amount of data. With huge amounts of information generation, common database management systems cannot adequately support data management and analysis in business related problems.[2] (Barkhordari and Niamanesh 2015) The problems may range from business intelligence, querying, reporting, and searching from day-to-day transactions or exploring trends on Google, monitoring social media, health care management and dealing in commodity market. When Big data was first conceptualized, it may not have been anticipated that gradually it will span out to almost all interdisciplinary systems. This combination has given rise to a specialized field of data analytics called big data analytics. Capturing, storing and retrieving information in a timely manner are vital issues in these systems and to solve such kind of problems big data analytics forms the ideal solution.

Big Data Defined

Big data is described as extremely large datasets that have grown beyond the ability to manage and analyze them with traditional data processing tools. In other words, big data defines a situation in which data sets have grown to such enormous sizes that conventional information technologies can no longer effectively handle either the size of data or the scale or the growth of big data.[3] (Ohlhorst 2012) Big Data can be characterized on the basis of its unique features:

- When the data is gathered with a precise goal, only a specific type of data is collected by applying certain types of conditions or filters while big data is data collected without any goal; whatever data comes is recorded. Due to this reason, the volume of big data is very large with a good degree of noise accumulation as compared to the regular data.

- When the data is collected from a particular source, it forms regular data whereas big data is not limited to particular file or computer or network. Big data constitutes data collected from multiple sources irrespective of their location. This is why big data is heterogeneous in nature.
- The structure of big data is not properly organized. Our data-driven world is experiencing explosion in quantity of data in all domains ranging from science and medicine to business and entertainment. The historical records of patients, the business data in the form of marketing, production & sales, stock market transactions, the census data and the data generated continually on the Internet like images, videos files and documents are all the reasons of large-sized databases.

Hence, data comes in three flavors viz structured data, semi-structured data and unstructured data with distinctive characteristics as shown in figure 1.

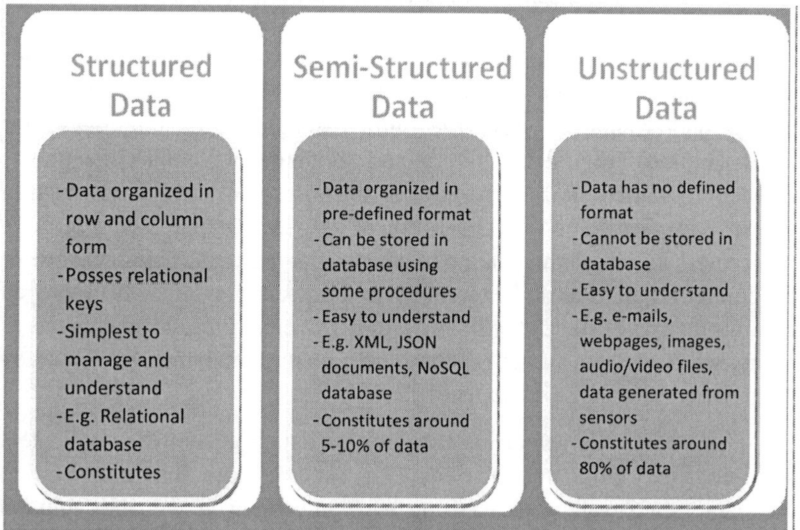

Figure 1: Types of Data

Data is collected sometimes in the form of comments in social media, it sometimes is captured through automatic sensors while some other times it is the historical data fetched from logs of an organization. So, is it the volume only that makes the data it big? If no, what constitutes big data? Three basic characteristics which make big data what it is today are 3Vs viz. volume, velocity and variety as presented in figure 2.

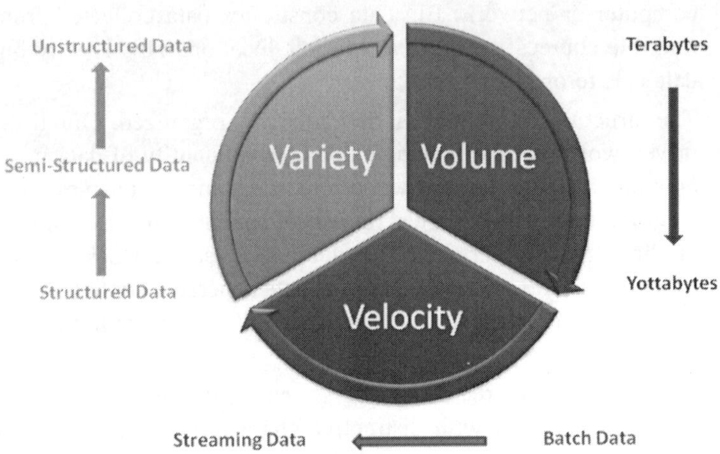

Figure 2: Big Data Characteristics

Volume is the primary characteristic of enormous data which defines the big data. In fact, the sensors and automatic devices collect data every millisecond around the world. We, human beings, are a major contributor to this volume of digital data. Every mail exchange, twitter message, photos and videos shared via Internet adds to the volume of data. This situation did not exist five years back. Invention of new technologies and electronic devices has increased the volume of data to a large extent. This data volume is actually required to do better analysis. For example, an analysis carried out on a dataset of size 500 will allow drawing more precise conclusions as compared to dataset of size 100. Hence, many companies have already started archiving large amounts of data.

The second V is Velocity with which the data is generated or collected. It is due to this V that volume of data has become larger than ever. Earlier, companies used to analyze data using batch processing but with the evolution of big data technology the analysis can be done on the fly. It means that data analysis can be carried out while it is being generated, without need of storing it into database.

The third V is variety of the data which is collected. It is quite rare to have data in a form that is perfectly relational that can be directly used for processing. Most of the data generated by organizations is unstructured and extracted from diverse sources in contrast to the traditional data available mostly in the form of excel sheets and databases. With the variety of new applications used by organizations, data is not available in pure structured form. It may be in formats like text, images, audio, video, relational databases, logs, historical documents in various forms, sensor data, etc.

How Big is Big Data?

The three Vs are the driving dimensions of big data and at the same time they are open-ended. There is no specification that limits the volume, velocity, or variety of data that defines it to be big. Some people define volume based on the number of interesting pieces of information for each occurrence or the columns in a table or the number of features or dimensions while some other people volume consider it to be the combination of depth and width.[4] (Minelli and Dhiraj 2013) For a small company, few terabytes of data may be considered as big, for a multinational company terabytes may be small and for a government organization data may scale up to exabytes. In general, data is considered to be big data when the data we have to process is bigger than what we can process in the given time with available techniques.

The bigness of big data depends on its location in the stack. At the data layer, it is not unusual to see petabytes and even exabytes of data.[5] (Barlow 2013) At the analytics layer, you're more likely to encounter gigabytes and terabytes of refined data. By the time you reach the integration layer, you're handling megabytes. At the decision layer, the data sets have dwindled down to kilobytes, and we're measuring data less in terms of scale and more in terms of bandwidth. At the top of the stack, size is considerably less relevant than speed.

Many companies are collecting and warehousing a lot of data through their routine business activities. If we look around, purchases at department/ grocery stores, transactions at banks, buying and selling at e-commerce websites and of course social networks are experiencing huge amount of data. The size of data is increasing exponentially. Yesterday's big data was of some Terabytes, today's big data is in petabytes or exabytes and tomorrow its size may increase to hundreds of zeta bytes. Roughly, when the data is too large and too complex to classify using traditional methods, it is considered as big data. Some of the examples of explosion are: Google processes approximately 100 petabytes per day, Facebook has 2.5 petabytes of user data + 15 terabytes per day, Twitter generates approximately 12 terabytes of data per day, eBay has 6.5 petabytes of user data + 50 terabytes per day and NSE exchange 1 terabytes of data every day. The speed at which the data is generated on social media, it is prominent that by the time this chapter will be published, these numbers would certainly differ. Obviously, to be able to store such huge data storage capacity has doubled roughly every three years since the 1980s.

In addition to three Vs which define main characteristics of big data, there are many additional features out of which the two commonly accepted are Value and Veracity. Value refers to benets obtained by the user from the big data and Veracity refers to the quality of big data[6] (Sharma & Mangat 2015). McKinsey Global Institute report 2011 highlighted Big Data as data sets whose size is beyond the ability of typical database software tools to capture, store, manage and analyze.[7] (Manyika et al. 2011) Big data enables us to see those things which we could not see before; with the evolvement of big data analytics we are able to analyze massive amounts of data for better business outcomes. Deriving insights from data is not a new problem from traditional relational databases that contain organized data. Storage is relatively cheaper these days and it is possible to store more data in unstructured form. It is important to have intelligent ways to distill large amounts of data in different formats to actionable knowledge. Big data is different normal data in many ways. Some of the characteristic differences are listed in table 1 below.[8] (Hu *et al.* 2014)

Table 1: Difference between Regular Data and Big Data

Characteristic	Regular Data	Big Data
Data Generation Rate	per hour or per day	per millisecond
Data Structure	Structured	Semi-structured/ unstructured
Data Source	Centralized	Distributed/ Variety of sources
Data Integration	Easy	Difficult
Data Access	Interactive	Batch or real-time

Big Data Analytics

Big Data analytics facilitates in transforming complex and unstructured data into useful information. It not only requires perception and planning by a human expert but also leverage advanced computational tools, which have developed in other fields, to reveal trends and correlations within and across large data sets that would otherwise remain undiscovered. Above all, it requires human expertise and perspectives. Analytics in business is the practice of iterative, methodical exploration of an organization's data with emphasis on statistical analysis. Analytics is used by many companies to achieve precision in business decisions and to possibly optimize their business processes. Data for such companies is like a corporate asset which if utilized properly can be used in leveraging the competitive advantage. Having quality data is not sufficient; success of data analytics need experienced analyst who can understand the data well and apply appropriate tools and technologies to extract knowledge from available data.

Analytics is not new; there are various existing techniques for carrying out data analytics such as statistical analysis and machine learning, predictive modeling etc. The choice of tools and techniques depend on the underlying goal of data analytics. With the increase in the volume of data the choice of methodology is very important. Whatever data is available many not be required in analytics because at the time of data acquisition no conditions were applied. Hence the data in hand may be noisy, may contain missing data or some undesirable data. At this stage, data preprocessing plays an important role during the ETL (Extract, Transform, Load) procedure. Big data can be considered to be categorized into analytical use and enabling new products. Big data analytics can reveal insights hidden previously by data too costly to process, such as peer influence among customers, revealed by analyzing shoppers' transactions and social and geographical data.[9] (O'Reilly 2012)

Data Analytics refers to the science of investigating raw data by applying procedural rules or algorithms to derive insights. The process of data analytics becomes more useful when it comes to examining big data containing some useful information. The focus of Data Analytics lies in inference, which is the process of deriving conclusions that are solely based on what the researcher already knows. It can be used in almost all domain enabling business managers and decision makers to take better decisions. Traditional data world of business transactions is now beginning to merge with new commercial opportunities. With the increase in variety and complexity of data, now the goal of businesses has transformed to model the business to take best advantage of available data for better productivity and revenues. Figure 3 shows the increase in scope of applications with the data explosion.

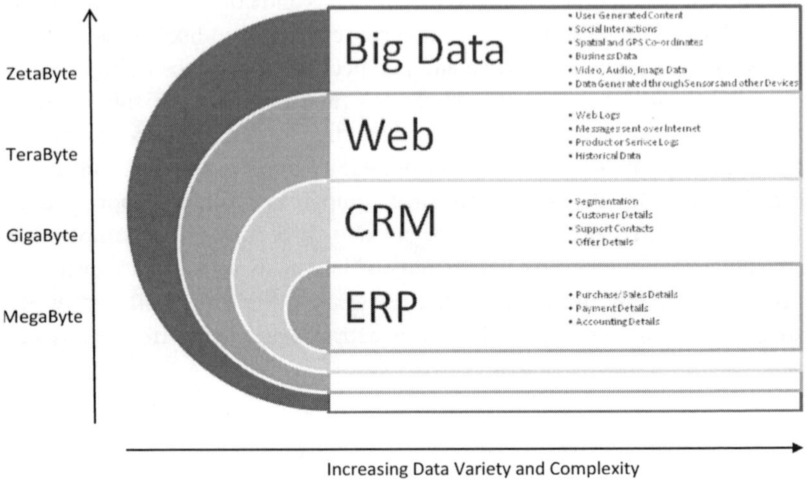

Figure 3: Data Explosion

The companies who have understood the importance of data analytics have either adopted or are in the process of adopting it. This has given them the ability to analyze heterogeneous data including the weblogs, customer/vendor data, daily transactional data, social media data, financial data and prospects data which was otherwise difficult to deal with in routine. Data analytics can lend them a hand to stay in the game and to be competitive to serve their customers better. Big Data Analytics act as a driver in optimizing the primal processes and functions for the organizations. It involves aggregating all types of data whether internal or external. The use of big data tools allows organizations to supervise massive data, manage risk, satisfy stakeholder's expectations and improve their overall performance by transforming data into information, information into knowledge and knowledge into intelligence. In short, the main objective for any organization for using big data analytics is to improve the efficacy decisions taken by business people. A schematic of big data analytics process is shown in figure 4.

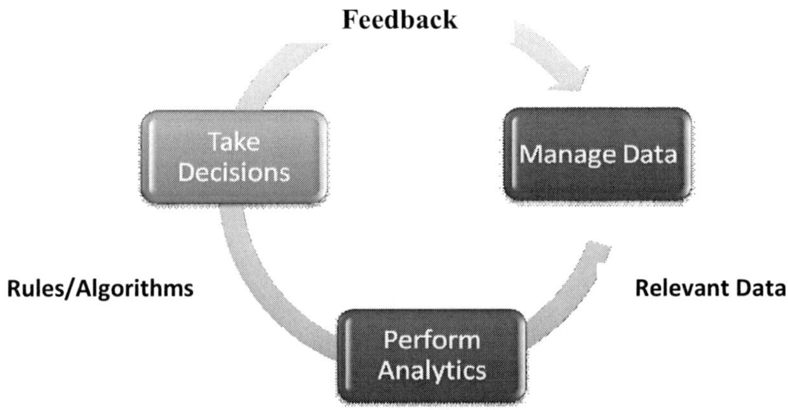

Figure 4: Big Data Analytics Process

Big data analytics can also be classified[10] (Vashisht & Gupta 2015) in categories like: Text analytics, Audio analytics, Video analytics, Social media analytics and Predictive analytics. Text analytics refers to the process of analyzing unstructured text to extract relevant information by using statistical analysis, computational linguistics, and machine learning. E.g. Extracting textual information from social network feeds, emails, blogs, online forums, survey responses, and news. Audio analytics are used to analyze and extract information from unstructured audio data like call centers and healthcare companies. It can be used in various video surveillance applications. Social media analytics includes the analysis of structured and unstructured data from various social media sources including Facebook, Linkedin, Twitter, YouTube, Instagram, Wikipedia, and others. Predictive analytics includes techniques for predicting future outcomes based on past and current data using NNs, SVMs, decision trees, linear and logistic regression, association rules, and scorecards.

Big data can bring about considerable cost reductions and substantial improvements in the time required to perform a computing task because of existing technologies. These technologies allow organizations to achieve an edge over the competitors. Big data allows capturing data from various sources to understand their severity by simplifying the historical patterns for providing visualizations for possible actions. Nothing better than the real-time applications of big data let us understand the penetration and need of analytics in variety of business domains. Some of the big data applications are depicted in figure 5.

Figure 5: Applications of Big Data

It can be luring to know about benefits of big data analytics and believing that it has solution to all your business hiccups, but in addition to bringing in big data analytics tools, companies also need skilled manpower and full-proof analytical planning. Analytic tools can be chosen depending on the size of company and its data analytics requirements. There are varieties of tools available in the market ranging from spreadsheets with statistical functions to complex data mining. Think of a scenario where a company acquires another company and both follow different ERP systems. This can be a great challenge for the company to manage overlapping or redundant databases. Inability to manage such data properly may result into dissatisfaction on the part of customers or annoyance for employees. Either the acquiring company can analyze all the data beforehand to determine which information from both the company's is to be clubbed to avoid any mis-match and loss of information; or to fetch the information only when it is required.

A lot of information may be overlooked due to lack of insight into how much information is to be captured from acquired company's ERP system. With no concrete provision for the disposal of unnecessary information, the company may end up keeping all the data resulting in wasteful expenditure on infrastructure and upholding costs. So, what is the solution? With proper planning for data handling and procedures for data mining in place, big data analytics can come to the rescue. Through data analytics companies can set up required tools and technologies to understand value of incoming data in addition to existing data and to improve quality of data management procedures. Gradually such companies will experience better managed data and freedom from inconsistent information.

Big Data Challenges

Those who rightly understand the fact that anything which cannot be understood, cannot be analyzed will definitely target to manage their data by accepting its challenges and transforming them into opportunities. Emergence of new data sources are generating huge amount of unstructured data with lot of business opportunities. This confluence has created the current interest and opportunities in big data analytics. One of the major challenges lies in analyzing unstructured data available in the form of e-mails and documents. This has given rise to yet another facet of big data analysis viz. data science which covers the tools and techniques along with some new processes for making sense out of big data.

Data analysis is noticeably more challenging than locating, understanding and extracting the data. All of these steps should be performed programmatically and at the end of each cycle the system should be able to provide explanation on how the result was derived. Ultimately, the decision-maker has to interpret the results and take decisions on the basis of reports generated. Some of the challenges perceived by a group of prominent researchers[11] (Agrawal et al. 2012) are as shown in figure 6.

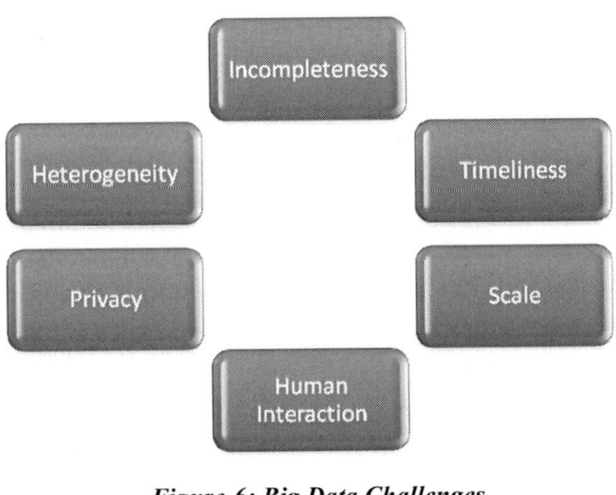

Figure-6: Big Data Challenges

Big data analytics algorithms consider homogeneous data but it is in variety of formats being captured using different instruments from diversified sources. The captured data may not be complete or free from errors and may contain noise. If the data is to be used in most effective manner, it has to be available in most precise, accurate and complete form which is too far from expectations. The flood of data itself forms a huge challenge, some processes should be defined to validate which data is to be captured otherwise the situation will be more complex than business people have ever thought of. Another key challenge is data privacy. Whether big or small, every company finds data privacy to be a big challenge. Big data security challenges lie in: (1) Data is extremely large in volume, channeling the protection approaches. (2) Security workload is much heavy. In general, big data is stored in a distributed environment; therefore, there are security threats from networks.[12] (Chen & Zhang 2014)

Business Hitches and Big Data Solutions

Managers often find themselves surrounded by data, but they are not able to efficiently utilize the information that is offered by ocean of data. They need to understand that data is no longer simply records lying in the database; it is much more than that. In addition to structured data, lot of useful information can be extracted from text, audio and video files. Correct approach with specialized tools can lend significant information to them to drive their business in right direction. Tools for natural language processing can provide valuable insight using text mining, sentiment analysis etc. No business can experience a stable phase as cyclical ups and downs are undetachable fact of business. If there are business hitches, there are ways out of it with the right tools in place to recognize specific data patterns based on predefined measures.

Inefficiency in Data Management

There is a significant amount of data which cannot be captured in digital form e.g., data on paper or data accessed from other sources or search results. This includes those already stored in company databases, from external third-party sources, the Internet, social media and remote sensors. Studied have revealed that upto 25 per cent of the effort goes in searching for data and then transferring it to another location. The other reasons for inefficient data management could be improper recording of data or careless storage of data. Convinced with the advantages of data analytics, business people who wish to utilize substantially large data sets start capturing transactional data with the hope of getting valuable business insight also face the problem of limited data storage.

Solution: The biggest advantage of using big data is its strength in integration of both structured and unstructured data. Managing, merging and governing variety of data have become easier with big data tools for which many organizations still struggling. Big data makes it possible to integrate massive volumes of data in variety of formats providing real-time analytics from the view-point of business. To deal with data storage problems, business people can consider third-party cloud service providers which offer storage and computing power required for data crunching. Cloud storage lets them analyze huge amount of data sets without significant investment in infrastructure.

Inability to Carry out Data Analysis

Organizations have to put lot of effort to carry out data analysis because their data comes from various sources and in different formats including text in PDFs, Word documents, attributed data in excel spreadsheets, CSVs, in graphical forms like charts and graphs and images etc. This gives way to problem of integrating massive data to meet the objective. Companies see their competitors investing in big data storage and analysis, they feel compelled to do so without having any knowledge of rationale behind using big data analytics.

Solution: Big data has capability to integrate and analyze data coming from various sources across the organization in an efficient and flexible manner. Additionally, high-speed data movement, such as data replication and changed data capture tools for rapidly moving large data sets. The companies which are looking for business solutions with ability to find, acquire, extract, manipulate, analyze, connect and visualize data, big data is the right choice. Big data employ collaborative tools for data analysis implementing massive parallel processing for both data distribution and parallel computation.

Failure to Perform Risk Analysis

Risks in business may appear any time in any shape and size. Organizations many a times fail to conduct risk analysis due to lack of focus, lack of skilled manpower or not understanding the need of risk analysis. But the most important reason is unawareness of best technique for risk analysis. Business people are not sure whether they can perform well knowing the inherent risk.

Solution: Big data can mitigate risk by optimizing the complex decisions of unplanned events more rapidly. If risk analysis is done before hand, it can help business people to estimate the optimum resource allocation thereby reducing the overall cost to the organization. A good risk manager must ensure that he communicates such patterns by viewing identified vulnerabilities to the management for timely decision. In actuality, managers are expected to challenge their own capacity in the interest of the company so that they can learn new ways of solving a particular issue which was earlier approached using traditional methods. Hence, the push within the organizations is to constantly upgrade themselves, change existing practices and think innovatively rather than sticking to the same old methods.

Ill-effect on Cost Balance

One of the reasons for reluctance of organizations to switch to big data technologies and big data analytics is the perceived increase in their overall cost for bringing in big data infrastructure. Setting up Big Data environment is considered by many companies as increase in their maintenance costs and this reason is seen as a limiting factor.

Solution: Big data cost is spread upto cost of getting required software, infrastructure and human resources. Setting up Big Data environment may initially count you on your budget but the benefits realized will be countless. It is very important for decision makers to have an understanding to align technology-related objectives with business objectives. Organizations can hire specialized Big Data experts to better understand the data and appropriate methods to control the data. These experts can also have understanding of specialized tools for capturing, storing, searching and analyzing the data in a way that can add value to the organization. Once the data is studied pattern-based analysis tools can be used by organizations.

Inaccuracy of Data

Although it's true to point out that many companies have started collecting big data, but not all of them are using Big Data in a way to benefit the organization or to provide true value. This may be because of inaccuracy of the data collected or the inherent noise or missing values which makes the companies unable to utilize big data correctly.

Solution: If the companies accept the fact that data will never be available in the form they want, their life can become easier. Collecting accurate data ready for analysis is absolutely a dream with increase in volume of data. The solution is simple too. Data preprocessing techniques can be applied to deal with noisy and missing data without the loss of generality.

Inability to Take Business Decisions

Managers often find themselves in a situation where they are surrounded by variety of data but are either unable to understand what to do with this data or they are inefficient to draw conclusions out of it. They don't know how to utilize this data to take further decisions. Even if they do, it is no longer enough for companies to simply understand operations of their company from the big data viewpoint of improving what already exist.

Solution: It is quite clear that identifying significant information for the company can improve its decision quality. Companies which have started making use of big data analytics have noticed improved decisions than before. Big data analytics allow organizations to keep themselves ready for unforeseeable incidents based on the data obtained from historical and real-time data. This allows organizations to join the dots and identify vulnerabilities, critical areas or unexplored opportunities for possible growth.

Only Data, Where are the Business Opportunities?

Business people many times complaint that their company is generating too much data and they are unable to realize its advantage to the fullest. They only end up managing the data with the available tools and their actual focus has shifted from creating and generating new business opportunities to data management.

Solution: With the development of big data analytics tools, business people of data-driven enterprise have realized its competitive advantage. This fact has to be accepted that data analytics tools can only offer computational ease but it is to be effectively planned. It is upto the decision makers to determine what information they need, how much information is sufficient to get down to a decision, what to do with the additional data etc. Information regarding their prospective customer's preferences, their requirements, likes and dislikes is critical than other information. Social media sites have been identified to generate opportunities for the business people. How those opportunities can be grabbed depends on the planning and vision of managers.

Everyone is Not a Technical User

While we talk so much about technicalities, this is not to forget that everyone who own or runs a business is not a technical user. For them it is a dream to get the advantages of Big Data analytics tools even if they are aware of it. They can hire data analytics experts, but would they be able to understand what exactly is happening with their business data? Such non-IT business users are looking to manage data if they can have access to charts, graphs, dashboards, etc.

Solution: The business intelligence market is coming up with data visualization tools with the help of which data can be demonstrated in the form of charts, graphs and slideshows. Considering the non-IT business users' perspectives, some of the vendors have switched their focus to offer analytics model allowing non-IT business users in the driver's seat. These applications will also let the users query and manipulate information easily expanding their reach beyond charts and reports.

Summary

Data is exploding day by day possibly scaling faster than the computational tools. The name "Big data" itself signifies that data is seeing no limits for its size. Obviously, the time required to analyze such huge amount of data is also shooting up not proportionately, but exponentially. With rapidly increasing volume of data, more time is required not only to preprocess the data but also to manage it in subsequent stages of data analysis possibly applying complex parallelization algorithms with more computational effort. Despite of the fact that we are surrounded by IT-enabled compute-intensive systems for data management, but the process of data analysis is incomplete without interaction with human experts.

The rate at which data is being generated in organizations requires their capability to aggregate and analyze the voluminous data from multiple sources. Big data allows doing so by capturing and storing vast amounts of data in the business and help them to remain in the competitive market through distinctive operations. It also allows data integration by linking, matching, cleansing and data transformation across heterogeneous systems. The necessity to connect and correlate relationships, hierarchies and multiple data linkages which is otherwise out of control is realized by big data. Companies that invest in proper technology will definitely have advantage over their competitors leading to a prominent performance gap compared with those which are not utilizing big data analytics.

Notes

1. Brown, B., Chui, M., Manyika, J., "Are you ready for the era of Big Data?", *McKinsey Quarterly*, McKinsey Global Institute, October 2011.

2. M. Barkhordari, N. Niamanesh, "ScaDiPaSi: An Effective Scalable and Distributable MapReduce-Based Method to Find Patient Similarity on Huge Healthcare Networks", *Big Data Research*, Vol. 2, No 1, 2015, pp. 19-27.
3. Ohlhorst, Frank J., Wiley and SAS Business Ser. *Big Data Analytics: Turning Big Data into Big Money*, John Wiley & Sons, 2012.
4. Minelli M., Dhiraj A., *Big Data, Big Analytics, Emerging Business Intelligence and Analytic Trends for Today's Businesse*s, John Wiley & Sons Inc., 2013.
5. Barlow M., *Real-Time Big Data Analytics: Emerging Architecture*, 2013, O'Reilly Media Inc.
6. Sharma S, Mangat V., Technology and trends to handle big data: A survey, in 2015 fifth international conference on Advanced Computing and Communication Technologies, pp. 266–71.
7. Manyika J., Chui M., Brown B., Bughin J., Dobbs R., Roxburg C., Byers A.H., "Big Data: The Next Frontier for Innovation, Competition, and Productivity", McKinsey Global Institute, May 2011, https://bigdatawg.nist.gov/pdf/MGI_big_data_full_report.pdf
8. Hu H, Wen Y, Chua T-S, Li X., "Toward scalable systems for big data analytics: A technology tutorial", *IEEE Access*, Vol. 2, No. 14, 2014, pp. 652–87.
9. O'Reilly Media I., Big Data Now: 2012 Edition, 2012, O'Reilly Media Inc.
10. Vashisht P., Gupta V., "Big Data Analytics: A Survey" in 2015 international conference on Green Computing and Internet of Things, 2015.
11. Agrawal D., Bernstein P., Bertino E., Davidson S., Dayal U., Franklin M., Gehrke J., Haas L., Halevy A., Han J. et al., "Challenges and opportunities with big data", a community white paper developed by leading researchers across the United States, 2012.
12. Chen C.L. P., Zhang C.Y., "Data-intensive applications, challenges, techniques and technologies: A survey on Big Data", *Information Sciences*, Vol. 275, 2014, pp. 314-347.

Chapter - 3

Social Media: Muscular Limbs, Worrisome Belly

— ***Pradeep Mallik***

Social media, a mirror to society, is living multiple roles: the dual role of agent as well as index of free exchange of ideas and information in a society; tool of social and political mobilization leading to overthrow of benign rulers as well as dictators; platform for carrying out business and tracking one's sales and marketing; vehicle for political campaigns and governance, and many others. While their intelligent uses make social media look like the proverbial *Kalpa Vriksha* which offers everything to everyone, it has an underbelly, too. This chapter attempts to underline some of the undesirable and sometimes unpleasant and scary aspects of social media.

So, First of All: What is Social Media?

Advancement in science has given us Information Communication Technology (ICT), which, in turn, is a convergence of microelectronics, computing, telecommunications, broadcasting, and optoelectronics. Social media, as we describe them, are essentially western in origin. The term refers to the wide range of internet-based and mobile services that allow users to participate in online exchanges, contribute user-created content, or join online communities.

Social media networks (SMNs) are a subset of ICT and defined as "online tools and utilities that allow communication of information online and *participation and collaboration*" (Newson, et al. 2008: 03) (accent added).

Often referred to as Web 2.0, the kinds of internet services which are commonly associated with social media are blogs, wikis, social bookmarking, social networking sites, status update services, virtual world content and media sharing sites (Dewing 2012).

There is some overlap in the nature of the individual tools of social media. Blog is short form of weblog which can be hosted on websites like Wordpress, Blogspot, Weebly, Tumblr, etc; Wiki is a collective website where participants can create, edit and host content, the most prominent example being Wikipedia; bookmarking sites allow users to organize and share links to websites, examples being Reddit and Digg; social networking sites allow participants to constructed a public profile and also allow articulation of a list of participants with whom they are connected, the most popular being Facebook and Linkedin; status update services allow users microblogging so that they can tell others about their status or an event and follow such posts by fellow users; virtual world content sites offer game-like virtual environment for users to interact in, example being Second Life in which users create an "avatar" of themselves and interact with others through those avatars (OECD, 2007); media sharing sites enable users to post audio, video, photographs, etc. popular examples being YouTube, Instagram and Pinterest.

The enormity of social media tools can be understood by taking the example of the popular site called Facebook. Launched in 2004 as a social networking website exclusively for Harvard students, Facebook as of January 2017 has more than 1.86 billion monthly active users which is a 17 per cent increase year over year.[1] In other words, if facebookers were to be treated like a nation, then "facebook nation" will be larger than China and the US combined. Peoples of a few European countries will have to join them to outnumber the "facebookans". Facebook users interact with other users, or Facebook friends, by updating their status, writing on other members walls or sending direct personal messages. Users are able to create and join interest groups, "like" pages, import and search for contacts, and upload photos and videos.

The Significant Other

There is another significant platform: WhatsApp. Instant messaging platform WhatsApp, which has been acquired by Facebook, has grown to 1.2 billion worldwide. It is extremely popular in India and has more than 70 million active users.[2] The instant messaging platforms are built around the notion of private communication. Nevertheless the easy availability of

WhatsApp on most phones, its easy interface, and group features that allow bulk messages to be sent, has made it one of the hottest tools of communication. WhatsApp is being used to disseminate messages, engage with fellow users, be they college group, a cultural collective, a scientific group or voters. WhatsApp allows people to send text and multimedia messages using mobile data or Wi-Fi networks free of charge, thus avoiding costly SMS messaging. A user doesn't need to create profiles or add friends, the app links directly to his contact list so that someone can send a message to anyone in his phonebook. In the last couple of elections in India, the volunteers or social media coordinators of the political parties worked with the campaign's main WhatsApp channel to send out image posts and messages in hope that the receivers will forward them to others and create a "human chain" of communication.

Democratization of Media Space

The examples and discussions above make it clear that social media tools are (i) online utilities, (ii) are about flow of information and communication, (iii) involves participation of people, and (iv)collaboration among them for co-creation of content. These utilities are nothing but the websites that not only interact with the users, but also allow users to interact among themselves without the interference of the hitherto powerful gatekeepers: the editors of the traditional media houses which owned newspapers, radio or television. Like the traditional mass media tools, they too inform, educate, entertain people and work as a platform to being consumers and manufacturers and service providers on a common platform. Media consumers use social media to gratify their needs just as the consumers used and are still using the traditional media.

Indeed, social media have emerged as a great leveler. They are contributing in a big way in blurring the distinction between the two distinct groups of people who were seen as media content producers and media content consumers. The two are rapidly catching up with each other's production and consumption. It would not be an exaggeration to say that the media space is getting rid of hierarchy and getting democratized.

Uses of Social Media

Little wonder, social media are used by individuals and groups in different ways and for varied purposes. Individuals have exploited every avenue these media offer them: to like, follow, share, connect, comment, feel good, pump up their self-esteem, and create an aura around them.

I shall discuss in detail the last mentioned in the next few pages. Individuals have also used social media to come together to take on dictators, fan uprising and throw the high and mighty out of power. This too shall be discussed in the subsequent pages.

Corporate and petty businesses use social media to prop up their brand and sales, and jack up their bottom line; politicians use them to connect to their constituencies, voters and electors. Both these groups, that is, businessmen and politicians also use these media to track their competitions. Governments use them for better governance. There are examples galore of the good work that the social media have enabled.

Let us begin expanding them in the reverse order. First, the governance; a cursory look at the websites of various ministries of our federal government leaves one awed. So many initiatives are being taken to help people connect with the government through social media platforms. Intended direct beneficiaries of government schemes as also other citizens can connect to the officials concerned and even ministers by logging on to websites or simply by tagging them to their Twitter and Facebook posts. Victims of crime, at the hands of state (read the police, the bureaucrats), semi-state actors (read the politicians and their cronies) and non-state actors (read the society goons), can tag officials concerned to air their grievances. There are several cases of justice being served thanks to people taking to the social media.

Of course the tools are heavily skewed in favour of digital-haves. The digital have-nots in the population tend to be left out, but conditions are changing fast as internet penetration in Indian increases and the tariffs fall like the mercury in the winter. Internet is indeed becoming more and more affordable. Look at the price war between major telecom companies these days.

Social media platform providers sustain themselves by enabling other businesses make money. Technology architects create models using which corporates and petty businesses can promote their products and services online. Statisticians and programme writers create online measurement tools that help these businesses track their progress as well as their competitions'. Analysts provide analytics that help them take strategic decisions and prosper.

India's 2014 parliamentary elections will be remembered for many reasons but of more importance to us today is the use of social media platforms in political campaigning. It saw large-scale use of open-access internet platforms to connect, build conversations, share, mobilize opinion and citizen action. The then prime ministerial candidate of the BJP (and hence of the National Democratic Alliance) Narendra Modi exploited social media to the hilt to reach out to India's huge youth demographic. He ran the campaign like a US presidential election and occupied the centre stage in the great dance of Indian democracy.

In various studies about citizen's voting behaviour ever since the classic Lazarsfield investigation in the 1940s[3] results have shown that voting decisions are not usually based on one-step communication (Melkote and Steeves 2015). Rather two-step and multi-step communication dynamics play more important role in framing opinions of the voters, which means conversation with opinion leaders, peer group, colleagues, friends and all acquaintances who ever can shape, impact, consolidate, challenge, or weaken the voter's opinion. Therefore, online social networks providing endless possibilities of exposure and connectivity seem to assume much importance in the present times.

A 2013 study by the IRIS Knowledge Foundation, which was supported, by the Internet and Mobile Association of India (IAMAI), 'Social Media and Lok Sabha Elections'[4] indicates that there are 160 high impact constituencies out of 543, where social media will not only influence the voter turnout but also sway poll results by 3-4 per cent. This impact is not limited to the metros and Tier I cities, because a third of India's social media traffic comes from towns with population of less than five lakhs. Triggers are always an essential part of social media engagement. The on-ground activity results in heightened online activity.

Now the last two or the first two that I mentioned in the previous section: These show the two extremes of what an inspired group of individuals and do with social media and what social media can do to individuals.

Egyptian Uprising

It began with an individual and then a whole lot of people joined in not so distant past to throw out a dictator. For example, Hosni Mubarak and millions of Egyptians who rose against him and in a span of 18 days of uprising, the president of more than 30 years was gone, and cooling his heels behind bars. (He has walked free after six years in prison.)

The role of social media has been beautifully explained by quite a few authors. Johnny West is one of them:

A young Internet executive called Wael Ghoneim helped organise a call for a demonstration for 25 January in Cairo's Tahrir Square through a Facebook page entitled We Are All Khaled Said. Fifty thousand people came, not just the dedicated hard core, but fresh faces, old and young. They came back the next day, and the next and the next, swelling to millions, and the rest is history. (West 2011: 145)

(Khaled Said, a young blogger, was brutally beaten and killed after he is said to have posted an incriminating video of police officers. Wael Ghonim was the Middle East marketing director for Google.)

The uprising began on 25 January 2011 when protesters gathered in Cairo's Tahrir Square by the thousands, and 11 February 2011 when President Hosni Mubarak stepped down from power. The first large-scale protest on 25 January 2011, dubbed the "day of rage" by protesters took place on Egypt's National Police Day, a national holiday that commemorates the policemen who lost their lives in the 1952 revolution. For the activists, the Egyptian police force represented "repression by the state, the problem of torture and arbitrary arrest symbolizing the corruption and sense of a loss of dignity that cast a shadow over Egyptian society throughout Mubarak's presidency."[5]

It must be mentioned here that though the deposition of Mubarak took a mere 18 days, the oppositional movement that brought him down was a product of a much longer process of planning and buildup, a product of years of repression and disenfranchisement that fomented political mobilization.[6]

The use of social media as an effective vehicle for organisation and mobilization can be explained by several established theories of communication, which are provided in the following section. Though Lasswell's functionalist theory of the media and Granovetter's theory of weak ties are both based on sociology rather than International Relations, and were developed before the advent of social media, these theories can be adequately used to explain why the Egyptian activists in this example chose social media as their form of communication.

Social Media as an Alternative Press

With its low entry barriers, social media tools provide an accessible platform for citizen journalism, defined as the use of digital media tools to "report on events on the ground, uploading text and videos directly to the Internet or feeding the information and videos to media outlets."[7] The dialogue taking place via Facebook, Twitter and other SMNs was used by the mainstream media as a source during the height of the protests. Al-Jazeera in particular relied on reputed bloggers and Twitter users during the uprisings for real-time coverage of events, by using Sharek, a citizen's media platform that received and filtered through submissions by citizen journalists.

Blogging requires merely Internet access and typing skills, and these low-cost barriers have led to personal blogs proliferating worldwide. There were 35,000 active blogs in the Arab region in 2009, growing to 40,000 by 2010. This number has increased dramatically since the 2011 uprisings, speculated at 600,000 blogs today, according to the Arabic Network for Human Rights Information.

Of course, this was not the first time a technological innovation has been used as a tool for change. The advent of Gutenberg's printing press in the 15th century played a crucial role in weakening the power of the medieval church and led to the Renaissance, and later the Reformation and Scientific Revolution. In fact, "Roughly during the first century after Gutenberg's invention, print did as much to perpetuate blatant errors as it did to spread enlightened truth."[8]

However, the rampant and happy use of social media kind of romanticized the uprising. Someone said, "Democracy is just a tweet away."[9] Google executive Wael Ghonim famously said, "If you want to liberate a society, just give them the Internet."[10] *New York Times* columnist Nicholas Kristof labeled the "quintessential 21st-century conflict," in which "on one side are government thugs firing bullets…[and] on the other side are young protesters firing 'tweets'."[11] It was aptly summed up by an anonymous of activist: "We use Facebook to schedule the protests, Twitter to coordinate, and YouTube to tell the world."[12]

Essence of Social Media

To sum up the phenomenon called social media let us first discuss the issue of 'participation': Social media encourages contributions and feedback from everyone who is interested. It blurs the line between media and audience. On openness, most social media services are open to feedback and participation. They encourage voting, comments and the sharing of information. There are rarely any barriers to accessing and making use of content – password-protected content is frowned on.

On conversation: Whereas traditional media is about "broadcast" (content transmitted or distributed to an audience) social media is better seen as a two-way conversation. On community, social media allows communities to form quickly and communicate effectively. Communities share common interests, such as a love of photography, a political issue or a favourite TV show. On connectedness, most kinds of social media thrive on their connectedness, making use of links to other sites, resources and people.[13] So far, so good.

Social media have an underbelly too. And it is scary. Psychologists, sociologists, communicators, have all expressed concern over what they see social media creating a false identity. Let us begin with this small three-line exchange between two friends:

"Quick, go like my picture," said a girl to her friend.

"Oh, I must have missed it, when did you post it?"

Her friend replies: "Just now."

This exchange of words is progressively becoming more popular among today's youth as the era of social media continues to alter our sense of priorities and sets up a falsified reality. Technology has enabled us to communicate over continents and beyond the Planet Earth. Technology has also given us tools to edit and manipulate our messages. Careful analysis of social media accounts proves that any of these sites allow us to create a false reality, a version of ourselves as we want to be seen, a false self to increase the feeling of self-worth, reflected by the number of likes and followers.

How is this for a serious hit to social media? I found a certain Robert Sorokanich on the internet post this video and write this: "Ultimately, Facebook is a narcissistic playground where the best, the funniest, the most charming aspects of our lives are publicized and the…boring stuff, the beige that is most of our daily grind almost never gets posted."[14]

Sadly, that is one of the least disturbing things that experts have to say about social media. He quotes from various reports to argue that the development of long lasting meaningful relationships is diminishing due to social media. There's a lack of emotional connections being made; that people have been supplementing their real, physical life as a human being with something superficial and untrue to themselves.

The choice of the word "friend" by Facebook creators is an instant clue to the goals they had in mind for their millions of users. They wanted

Facebook account holders to see the people with whom they network as friends, and yet the connections don't really warrant that title.

After all, Merriam Webster defines a friend as, "A person who you like and enjoy being with."[15] One is hardly "with" an online friend, even when using online chat tools. Certainly, you are sharing information, thoughts, and ideas, but it is a radically desensitized approach to interaction and human communication. In fact, it is really the polar opposite of friendship.

Consider that studies now reveal that up to 75% of people using social networks experience disrupted sleep in the evening hours after using them. And even worse is that half of users surveyed pointed out that social media made their self-esteem diminish and their lives seem less vibrant or even interesting because of the seeming perfection of their "friends" lives. And here, as Shakespeare said, is the "rub". Why? Because, psychologists tell us that a friend is worthy of that title when they are committed to your happiness, refuse to ask you to compromise your principles, and is a good influence.

Since time immemorial, the wisemen have told us life is meant for living in the present, and more importantly in reality. Not everyone of the august gathering here needs to agree with me. However, most of us would be far happier without the artifice of social media, and if you find that it has been harming your self-esteem, drop out and just get out there and live life – there are plenty of friends to be found offline.

Notes

1. www. facebook.com, 2017.
2. www.statista.com, 2017.
3. Baran, Stanley J, *Introduction to Mass Communication: Media Literacy a nd Culture,* Boston: McGraw Hill, 2002.
4. "Social Media in India – 2013",http://www.iamai.in/media/details/1371
5. Iksander, Elizabeth, "Connecting the National and the Virtual: Can Facebook Activism Remain Relevant After Egypt's January 25 Uprising?," *International Journal of Communication,* 5: 2011, p. 1230.
6. Storck Madeline, *The Role of Social Media in Political Mobilisation: A Case Study of the January 2011 Egyptian Uprising*, St Andrews: University of St Andrews, Scotland West, Johnny, Karama, London: Heron Books, 2011.
7. Khamis & Vaughn 2011 as quoted in Storck Madeline (2011).
8. Rosaldo, Renato, "The Cultural Impact of the Printed Word, A Review Article," *Comparative Studies in Society and History,* 23:1981, 508 as quoted in Storck Madeline 2011.

9. Evgeny Morozov, *The Net Delusion*, London: Penguin Books, 2011.
10. Albrecht Hofheinz, "Nextopia? Beyond Revolution 2.0," *International Journal of Communication*, 5: 1417, 2011.
11. Nicholas D. Kristof, "Tear Down This Cyberwall!" *The New York Times,* 17 June 2009. Accessed on 24 March 2017.
12. Anonymous Cairo activist, quoted in Nadine Kassem Chebib & Rabia Minatullah Sohail, "The Reasons Social Media Contributed to the 2011 Egyptian Revolution," *International Journal of Business Research and Management,* 3: 139, 2011.
13. Mayfield, Antony, "What is social media? an e-book by from iCrossing", www.icrossing.com/...pdf.../hat%20is%20Social%20Media_iCrossing_ebook.pd, 2008, accessed on 28 March 2017.
14. Sorokanich, Robert, "What's on your mind?"https://www.youtube.com/watch?v=QxVZYiJKl1Y&feature=youtu.be, 2017
15. https://www.merriam-webster.com/

References

1. Newson, Alex, Deryck Houghton, and Justin Patten, eds., *Blogging and Other Social Media: Exploiting the Technology and Protecting the Enterprise*, England: Gower Publishing Limited, 2008.
2. Baran, Stanley J., *Introduction to Mass Communication: Media Literacy and Culture*, Boston: McGraw Hill, 2002.
3. Dewing, Michael, *Social Media: An introduction, Social Affairs Division*, Publication No. 2010-03-E, Ottawa: Library of Parliament, 2012.
4. Morozov, Evgeny, *The Net Delusion*, London: Penguin Books, 2011.
5. Melkote, Srinivas Raj and Steeves, H Leslie, *Communication for Development: Theory and practice for empowerment and social justice*, New Delhi: Sage, 2015.
6. OECD, Participative web and user-created content: Web 2.0, Wikis and Social Networking, Paris: Orgainzation for Economic Cooperation and Development, 2007.Storck Madeline (2011). The Role of Social Media in Political Mobilisation: A Case Study of the January 2011 Egyptian Uprising, St Andrews: University of St Andrews, Scotland West, Johnny (2011). Karama! London: Heron Books.

Websites

1. https://newsroom.fb.com/#_=_ (accessed on 28 March 2017)
2. http://ancacid.yolasite.com/resources/05.101%20-%20ISI%20-%20e-F%C3%B3lio%20A%20-%20Enunciado%20-%20Texto%20-%206446504-Lazarsfeld-Theory.pdf (accessed on 28 March 2017)
3. http://www.iamai.in/media/details/1371 (accessed on 28 March 2017)
4. "The False Self on Social Media", http://www.todaypictures.com/social-media-false-self/ (accessed on 24 March 2017); www.statista.com, 2017.

Video

1. https://youtu.be/QxVZYiJKl1Y

Corporate Kaleidoscope

Chapter - 4

Smart Cities and India's Model for Sustainable Urbanism

— *Mihir Bholey*

Introduction

Urbanization can be looked at from two very distinct perspectives; one being planning and the other being process. There has been conscious human efforts to design and build cities based on the best available technical knowhow. On the other hand, there have been naturally evolving social-cultural-economic, political and ecological processes which have laid the foundation of urbanization. Babylon, Ur, Erech, Mohenjo-daro, some of the earliest cities were specimens of the existing Neolithic technological competence. While the process of urbanization is safely believed to be some seven to eight thousand year old, the steep rise in urbanization has been experienced in the last hundred years alone. At the dawn of twientieth century there were only sixteen cities whose population exceeded one million mark. However, by the turn of the millennium (year 2000) the number of such cities increaded to 417. Not only that, the most rapid rate of urbanization is being experienced in socities which are transforming from small agrarian to big industrial economies (Hou et al. 2015). As per the UN World Cities Report 2016 more than half (54 per cent) of world population lives in cities because they create wealth, employment opportunity and drive human progress through industrialization and other processes. Policymakers recognize that the world is totally unprepared to handle the challenges of urbanization. Making urban human settlements environmentally sustainable, resilient, socially inclusive, safe, violence-free and economically productive is a big challenge (UN World Cities Report 2016). These factors give credibility to the rationale of creating smart cities.

India is among one of world's few oldest civilizations where planned urbanization existed even in the early phase of their history. Extended thoroughfares with north-south alignment, straight configuration of the house walls, drainage network, water chutes, manholes to clean slush, great bath, citadel etc. which marked the cities of Indus valley civilization were surely the models of smart cities way back in 3300 BC. Now in the 21st century India is once again exploring ways and means to rejuvenate its overstretched urban set up with smart interventions. The idea finds expression in one of India's most ambititous flagship policies of building 100 smart cities applying smart interventions in terms of technology and design in the existing cities. Decades of hiatus between policy and urban development is being reevaluated. There is an obvious correlation between urban dysfunction over the years and the policy bias. Policymakers in India for a long time have had a rural bias for their own justified reasons. The two most imminent were the concern for India's huge rural population and its dependence on agrarian economy which provided rural population the means of economic sustenance.

In the initial years of independence, close to 82 percent of India's population was rural. This was a kind of moral justification to follow the spirit *Gram Swaraj* – the Gandhian model of self-reliant villages based on equitable and non-violent order. It worked as a guiding principle for the policymakers for successive years and to an extent reflected in the policies of rural development in a rather subtle manner. However, despite Gandhi's socio-economic vision for rural sustainability and the need to strengthen and empower the village community, urban India keeps growing. Though it ranks among the least urbanized countries where urbanization increased at the rate of 13 percentage points only in fifty years between 1951-2001. Nevertheless, it has the second largest urban population in the world (Rai & Singh 2010). India not only experienced exponential growth in terms of size, demography and economic development but also attracted huge rural migration. In fact, it went through the same cycle of development wherein the share of agriculture to GDP often declines and industrial and service sectors dominate the scene. While the concentration of capital, skill and other resources in cities precipitated economic growth, the lack of corresponding investment in infrastructure and planning made the Indian cities suffer from urban decay.

Of late, the model of globalization-led economic development has also transformed the cities into the growth engines of economy. India is no exception. Contribution of Indian cities to GDP is estimated to be 58 per cent. It's expected to become 70 per cent by 2030. With nearly 377 million Indians comprising 31.14 per cent of the country's population now living in urban areas (as per 2011 census), the urban population in India is growing at the rate of 2.76 per cent per annum. If it continues growing at the same rate, by 2031 the urban population will touch 600 million mark (40%) and 850 million by 2051 which will be 50 per cent of its total population. Surely, this demography will throw major challenges before the policymakers, urban planners, architects, engineers, designers and the rest.

Urban Challenges: Global and Indian

Rising population particularly in the developing countries is the foremost challenge facing urbanization. It creates a widening hiatus between the urban requirements and supply of resources. It manifests in widespread urban poverty, unbridled growth of slums, environmental degradation, social insecurity and so on. The 2030 Agenda for Sustainable Development, and its Goal No. 11 seeks to make cities and human settlements inclusive, safe, resilient and sustainable. The diagram below depicts the various urban challenges posed by the ever rising global urban population.

Diagram 1: Emerging Global Urban Challenges Due to Increased Urban Population

At the macro level India's urban challenges are also quite similar to the overall global challenges. India's urban demography is changing at a fast pace which is contributing to the urban infrastructure deficit. Paul (2010) identifies weaknesses at three fronts namely: (1) infrastructure, (2) finance and (3) governance responsible for the urban problems.

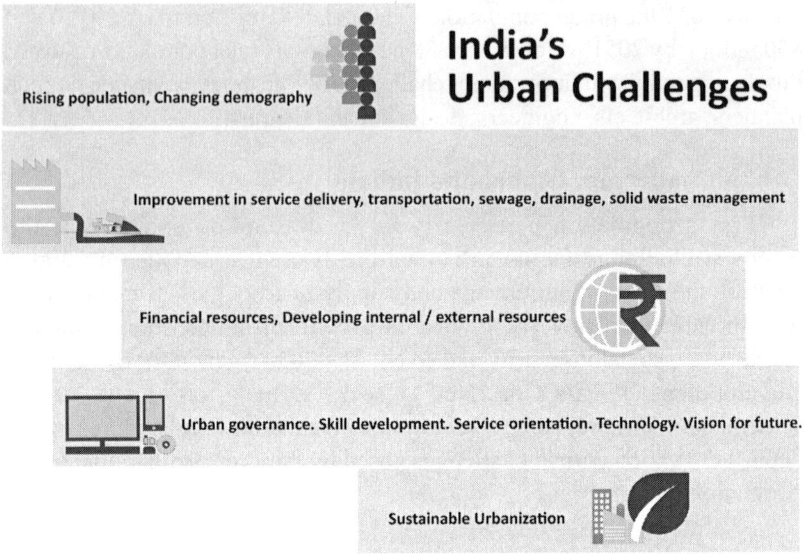

Diagram 2: India's Urban Challenges: A Graphic Model

The country faces the challenge of providing its 377 million urban population (and growing) safe water, sanitation, housing, healthcare, energy, services of waste management etc. as the basic requirement. However, from the smart city perspective these services need to be augmented with smart interventions in the form of ICT infrastructure, technology and design as well. Like everywhere else, cities in India too have evolved. It's visible in its demography, system, design, infrastructure, management and so on. Marshall (2012) looks at urban evolution as "a continuous process that applies as much today as in the past. That is, evolutionary urbanism is not some rudimentary historic process that was supplanted by modern town planning." The challenges these evolution pose are humongous.

The World Bank Report titled Leveraging Urbanization in India (2015), highlights that due to messy urbanization 65.5 million people live in urban slums and 13.7 percent urban population lived below poverty line. This poses a great challenge for urban inclusion. Ahluwalia and Mohanty (2014) blame it on the master planning and zoning regulations in Indian cities which has over the years neglected the need and aspiration of the low income group population for space. This is ironical because despite the apparent pro-poor policies of the successive governments, there is a stark deficit of proper housing for the urban which has resulted in the mushrooming of slums across all Indian cities particularly in the big ones. Bholey (2016) writes:

The question inevitably arises - where is the gap, whether at the policy or at implementation level? A democratic constitution that India has, nurtures the ideal of social inclusion in words and spirit. Good governance and satisfactory service delivery are some of the basic expectations of the people from the government. However, converting spirit into action is often better said than done.

The PWC report (2015) on making smart and sustainable cities points out one of the biggest challenges for smart city which will redefine its very concept and approach. It refers to the Sustainable Development Goal (SDG) of the United Nations which will soon replace the Millennium Development Goal (MDG). The SDG has a focus on sustainable cities and communities. It recognizes the fact that globally cities occupy only 3 percent of earth's land but they're responsible for 60-80 percent of energy consumption and 75 percent of carbon emission. Besides, they're putting tremendous pressure on fresh water supplies, sewage, living environment, and public health. It sees a possibility of bringing efficiency gains, technological innovation and at the same time reduce energy consumption. (Sustainable Development Goals, UNO). So while India will be setting its own agenda and putting its own plans for smart cities into action, the SDG will shift the goal post. This will emerge as the new challenge for smart cities in India. However, striking a balance between the old and the new and the varied degree of socio-cultural diversity is another big challenge for urbanization in India. Shaw (2012) rightly points out:

Urban built environment in India has been a product of the assimilation and hybridization of centuries of cultural contact with diverse influences... characteristics of Indian urbanism in such a varied context and stretching across several millennia that mark this civilization is too huge a task....

Indian cities differ from each other in terms of their social-cultural-economic and religious significance. That has made them evolve differently. For example, while Mumbai has remained India's commercial capital, Bengaluru has evolved as the IT capital. Both are metropolitan cities, yet both the cities demand different kinds of interventions to make them function properly. There're cities as old as Varanasi (or Banaras) and as new as Lavasa; one of the emerging smart cities in India. While the earlier is a perfect example of organic growth, the latter is probably the finest specimen of a city designed on drawing board and implemented on land.

Urban Challenge: Sanitation

For the densely populated Indian cities, sanitation is a big challenge. Most of the cities are still fced with basic problems of solid waste management, sewage and toilets. It's further complicated by large scale urban migration and the daily floating population coming to big and small cties. Planning Commission Approach to the 12th Plan titled 'The Challenges of Urbanization in India' underscored the dispersed nature of urbanization in India. It pointed out the 'distributed nature of urban India having a diverse range of large and small cities which are unevenly spread across the nation. India may continue with this distributed model of urbanization because as the report writes: 'this suits its federal structure and helps to ensure that migration flows aren't unbalanced toward any particular city or cities.' The report estimates that the demand for key services including water, transportation, sewage treatment, low income housing among other will increase five- to seven-fold in cities of every size and type in the years to come. There's also a huge deficit between the per capita expenditure on urban infrastructure estimated to be $17 to the required $100.

The Govt. of India Ministry of Urban Development 'Handbook of Urban Development' (2016) data reveals that the level of urbanization in India as a whole has increased from 25.7 per cent in 1991 to 27.82 per cent in 200 and to 31.14 per cent in 2011. The data in the report further reveals the skewed ratio between India's urban sanitation demand and supply. Swachh Bharat Mission, (a clean India drive) launched by the govt. in 2014 has to achieve the target by 2019. It has to take care of individual household toilets, community toilets, public toilets, municipal solid waste management etc which is a daunting task. The urban sanitation problem in India is compounded due to the socio-economic factors and the infrastructure deficit. Besides that, the culture of general hygine and cleanlinees is something often ignored by a large number of people and thus make all the sanitation effort by the government ineffective. The behavioural and attitudinal issues are being addressed by the awareness campaigns run by the government. The following tables (1&2) depicting the baithing and drainage and toilet facility give us some idea about the infrastructure deficit.

Table 1: Baithing and Drainage Facilities in 2011 (The Handbook of Urban Statistic 2016)

S.No.	States/UTs	2001		2011	
		Percentage of HHs having bathroom facility within premises	Percentage of HHs having Drainage facility	Percentage of HHs having bathing facility within the premises	Percentage of HHs having drainage facility
1	Andaman & Nicobar Islands	78.18	74.13	93.87	86.04
2	Andhra Pradesh	78.48	82.29	92.61	88.26
3	Arunachal Pradesh	53.93	63.26	80.65	66.21
4	Assam	52.98	52.62	84.54	56.35
5	Bihar	43.13	68.61	68.63	71.39
6	Chandigarh	78.38	89.89	89.72	96
7	Chhattisgarh	51.88	62.96	67.36	68.9
8	Dadra & Nagar Haveli	69.01	52.18	89.99	62.7
9	Daman & Diu	86.96	50.87	84.17	77.24
10	Goa	77.21	69.03	94.91	77.96
11	Gujarat	80.62	78.29	90.45	82.64
12	Haryana	75.41	88.41	92.63	92.25
13	Himachal Pradesh	74.93	86.08	92.8	93.56
14	Jammu & Kashmir	77.74	81.84	91.38	83.12
15	Jharkhand	54.55	72.36	69.8	70.8
16	Karnataka	79.15	80.97	96.39	87.6
17	Kerala	78.91	30.89	92.87	54.55
18	Lakshadweep	84.78	0	97.64	25.93
19	Madhya Pradesh	63.21	75.93	85.35	82.34
20	Maharashtra	81.6	87.58	95.36	91.15
21	Manipur	16.35	57.14	65.74	70.4
22	Meghalaya	69.81	76.66	79.9	80.34
23	Mizoram	64.8	63	89.72	79.48
24	Nagaland	58.29	72.24	94.38	76.52
25	NCT of Delhi	71.72	91.04	91.28	96.04
26	Odisha	48.94	57.49	64.33	59.04
27	Puducherry	70.94	68.07	91.98	82.58
28	Punjab	82.76	89.77	94.82	90.9
29	Rajasthan	71.4	80.19	89.18	86.04
30	Sikkim	83.38	94.19	91.99	92.12
31	Tamil Nadu	66.42	70.02	85.17	74.94
32	Tripura	43.37	53.06	63.96	53.45
33	Uttar Pradesh	63.76	92.38	84.61	93.36
34	Uttarakhand	77.87	88.24	93.1	92.9
35	West Bengal	58.56	67.14	70.66	66.83
	INDIA	**70.40**	**77.87**	**86.98**	**81.77**

HHs: Households

Source: Census of India-2001 & 2011

Table 2: Urban Latrine Facilities in 2011 (The Handbook of Urban Statistic 2016)

S. No.	State / UT	Water Closet	Pit Latrine	Other Latrine	Total HHs with Latrines	No Latrine
1	Andaman & Nicobar Island	86.80	0.20	0.10	87.10	12.90
2	Andhra Pradesh	79.40	4.10	2.60	86.10	13.90
3	Arunachal Pradesh	74.90	13.90	0.70	89.50	10.50
4	Assam	71.00	21.00	1.70	93.70	6.30
5	Bihar	63.40	4.60	1.00	69.00	31.00
6	Chandigarh	87.00	0.50	0.10	87.60	12.40
7	Chhattisgarh	58.70	1.10	0.40	60.20	39.80
8	Dadra & Nagar Haveli	80.30	0.70	0.30	81.30	18.70
9	Daman & Diu	84.20	1.10	0.10	85.40	14.60
10	Goa	80.60	3.50	1.10	85.20	14.70
11	Gujarat	85.20	2.10	0.40	87.70	12.30
12	Haryana	80.50	7.70	1.70	89.90	10.10
13	Himachal Pradesh	87.00	0.80	1.30	89.10	10.90
14	Jammu & Kashmir	68.50	4.30	14.70	87.50	12.50
15	Jharkhand	64.70	1.80	0.60	67.10	32.80
16	Karnataka	71.60	12.00	1.40	85.00	15.10
17	Kerala	75.30	21.90	0.30	97.50	2.60
18	Lakshadweep	97.20	0.50	0.00	97.70	2.30
19	Madhya Pradesh	71.50	1.70	1.00	74.20	25.80
20	Maharashtra	67.30	2.40	1.60	71.30	28.70
21	Manipur	63.70	23.30	8.80	95.80	4.20
22	Meghalaya	82.90	12.30	0.60	95.80	4.30
23	Mizoram	80.90	17.20	0.50	98.60	1.50
24	Nagaland	79.10	15.00	0.50	94.60	5.40
25	NCT of Delhi	86.00	1.70	2.10	89.80	10.20
26	Odisha	58.80	4.20	1.80	64.80	35.20
27	Puducherry	81.10	0.60	0.30	82.00	18.00
28	Punjab	85.60	6.80	1.00	93.40	6.60
29	Rajasthan	73.70	5.40	2.90	82.00	18.00
30	Sikkim	91.80	3.30	0.10	95.20	4.80
31	Tamil Nadu	66.50	6.80	1.80	75.10	24.90
32	Tripura	50.00	47.00	0.90	97.90	2.10
33	Uttar Pradesh	77.20	2.90	3.00	83.10	16.90
34	Uttarakhand	85.90	6.50	1.10	93.50	6.40
35	West Bengal	61.60	22.50	0.90	85.00	15.00
	INDIA	**72.60**	**7.10**	**1.70**	**81.40**	**18.60**

HHs: Households

Note: * Water Closet-Flush/Pour Flush Latrine connected to Piped Sewer/Septic Tank/Others

† Other Latrines include night soil disposed into open drains and service latrines.

Source: Census of India-2001

Solid Waste Management

There is a direct correlation between the rising urban demography and solid waste creation which makes municipal solid waste (MSW) management a humangous task. This is among one of the priority areas under the smart city mission. Uncollected piles of solid waste is not only an environmental and health hazard but against the spirit of smart city too. Solid waste management for smart cities is both a challenge and an opportunity because it requires new alternatives and models to handle it. Smart cities globally are experimenting with new concepts. Central Public Health and Environmental Engineering Organisation's (CPHEEO) Manual of Municipal Solid Waste Management (2016) indicates that during 2014-15, 1,43,449 tonnes per day (TPD) of MSW was generated in India with an average waste of 0.11 kilogram (kg)/capita/day. Of the total 1,17,644 TPD approximately, 80 percent was collected. Only 32,871 TPD (22%) was processed or treated. Besides, it also points out that segregation at source, collection, transportation, treatment, and scientific disposal of waste remains grossly inadequate which contributed to the urban mess.

Solid Waste to Circular Economy: A Smart Approach

Smart city Songdo has its own method of SWM. Benedikt (2016) writes: "To make the city more sustainable, innovative waste management was developed: every flat in the city has a pneumatic trash pipe. Once residents of Songdo throw their domestic trash in this pipe, it will be supplied to a central waste processing centre by the underground system and recycled there." No doubt, the nature of technological intervention will determine the effectiveness of smart city. However, technological interventions should be an outcome of the conceptual models. The Circular Economy model for example may help redefine waste and design the system of its management in such a manner where nothing goes wasted rather comes back with new utility. The concept may be converted into interesting and effective model of sustainable development in India. Circular economy talks of shift of the whole consumption pattern from the 'cradle to grave' to a circular model. Ellen MacArthur Foundation's report on circular economy (2013) refers to the 'Linear to Circular' model wherein recycalability remains at the core of production itself. 'Take-make-dispose' (Ellen MacArthur Foundation, 2013) model of production and consumption is responsible for the large scale creation of waste. Therefore, solid waste management should also address the problem at the source which will help in finding smart solution. The model of circular economy is based on some simple principles. 'Design out waste' is one of them. The principle states:

Waste does not exist when the biological and technical components (or 'nutrients') of a product are designed by intention to fit within a biological or technical materials cycle, designed for disassembly and refurbishment. The biological nutrients are non-toxic and can be simply composted. Technical nutrients—polymers, alloys, and other man-made materials are designed to be used again with minimal energy and highest quality retention. (Towards the Circular Economy, 2013)

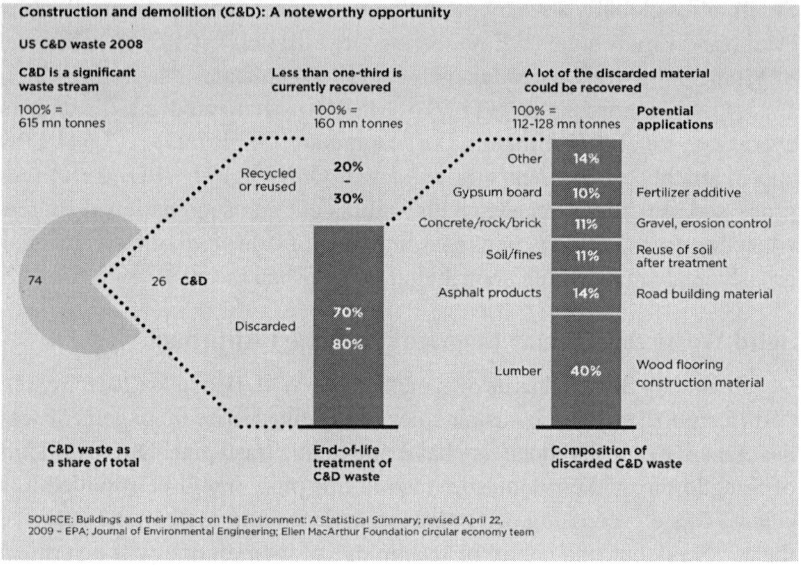

Source: Towards the Circular Economy, 2013.

Diagram 3: Circular Economy.

The rates of recovery for most of the materials after their first use is very high as compared to their first use. This adds up to the creation of solid waste of different kind in the cities. It's estimated approximately 65 billion tonnes raw materials were consumed by the global economy in 2010. It's likely to grow to about 82 billion tonnes in 2020. Europe alone generated 2.7 billion tonnes of solid waste in 2010, out of which only 40 percent of that was reused, recycled, or composted and digested.

The circular economy thus offers two models to manage the biological and mechanical wastes which may be a useful wholistic model for the solid waste management for smart cities. The conceptual diagram 2 of cicular economy explains the possibility of reprocessing the waste for useful applications. For the consumption driven modern lifestyle the model of circular economy is worth considering. The model can very well integrate with the *Swachch Bharat Mission* meant for improving sanitation in India and through that to the Smart City Mission itself.

Urban Transportation

Creating efficient, environment friendly, safe and affordable urban mobility system is integral to smart city vision. Host of policy nitiatves in recent years such as National Urban Transport Policy 2014, Atal Mission for Rejuvenation and Urban Transformation (AMRUT), Automotive Mission Plan (AMP2026), Make in India Scheme, Skill India programme and FAME (Faster Adoption and Manufacturing of Electric/Hybrid) India Scheme are expected to transform India's urban transport system into an efficient system over the next decade. The above policies will have to be aligned with the smart city mission. The varied modes of urban transport in India include man, animal to power driven vehicle options; all plying on the same road at the same time. Last mile connectivity which is rather poor at ths point of time will have to be loked into under the smart city mission.

India Transport Report – Moving India to 2032 (2014), estimates that from 10,375 bpkm (billion passanger kilometer) in 2011-12, it's likely to grow at the rate of 15 percent per annum to reach 168,875 bpkm by 2031-32. The aforesaid report also says that the population in the million plus cities has been increasing. As per the 2011 census, 468 urban class-1 agglomeration constitute 70 percent of urbn population. As a result, the pressure on the existing public transport system is increasing. However, there has not been commensurating rise in the public transport system rather a decline. 1991 onwards there has been a sixfold increase in the registered vehicles and the number has gone up from 21 million to 142 million. Number of twowheelers has gone up from 14 million to 102 million during the same period whereas the number of public buses has declined to 1.1 percent of the total registered vehicles from 11.1 percent in 1951. It's a clear indication of the inadequacy of public transport system and rising dependence on personal mobility options including twowheelers and cars. Its environmental fallout and impact on traffic condition are obvious.

Smart Mobility

The factors stated above thus necessitate designing mobility options. Masdar, the smart city in UAE which aims at attaining zero carbon emmison, has designed Personal Rapid Transit (PRT) system which uses sustainably produced electricity to shuttle within the city. The PRT system works on a magnetic system which is embedded into its concrete track. There is an overhead antenna that runs the length of the undercroft to provide wireless link between the PRTs and its computer system. This ensures zero carbon emission which is the USP of Masdar smart city. Besides, it also provides cars and buses run by electricity and biodiesel.

Acharya and Morichi (2013) explain the existing urban transport system of megacities as: "a combined result of dynamic interaction of institutions; the society's evolving need in mobility brought about by their changing physical, social, economic, and political environments; and the advancement in technology." The idea of smart city is an idea of change in which the socio-economic, spatial environment will be shaped by the technological interventions in order to make the cities sustainable. Smart sustainable cities will require sustainable urban transportation system too. In a comprehensive sense sustainable transportation system refers to the behavioral and socioeconomic aspects alongside new concepts viz. systems approach which analyzes the relationship between the part and the whole. Systems approach will help examine transportation in the context of economic, environmental and social systems and their interactive effects on development (TRB 1997).

Smart city creates its own eco-system driven by ICT, design, technology, innovation and so on which deal with various aspects of modern urban life including smart mobility. Benevolo, *et al.* (2016) describe Smart City as: "a complex, long-term vision of a better urban area, aiming at reducing its environmental footprint and at creating better quality of life for citizens." They have tried to analyze the interconnectedness between smart mobility and smart city. Their concept of smart mobility includes environmental and economic aspect of mobility on the one hand and application of technology and people's behaviour on the other. Thus, smart mobility has to strike a balance between citizens' opinions about liveability in cities and quality of local public transport services as well. Giffinger *et al.* (2007) who define smart city as "a city well performing in a forward-looking way in economy, people, governance, mobility, environment, and living, built on the smart combination of activities of self-decisive, independent and aware citizens" also underscore the improved options of mobility as a key feature of smart city.

Hence, smart mobility turns out to be not just a new nomenclature in the smart city taxonomy, but an essential aspect of the whole concept itself. Robuste (2010) believes: "Urban mobility (UM) is undergoing a change of concept (mutation) and needs a re-engineering and systems approach to interact with city planning and ICT." Here the application of design's systems thnking approach which helps analyze the relationships between the larger set and its sub-sets may be immensely useful. Design intervention at this level may help in developing a sustainable model of mobility based on the synergetic relationship between part and the whole which is smart city and mobility. The concept of urban mobility itself has acquired new meaning. Table 3 clearly explains the difference between the old and the new. The new concepts may help in designing smart and sustainable mobility solutions.

Table 3: Concepts of Sustainable Mobility Options; old and new

Old concepts	New concepts
Functionalism	Sustainability
Diffuse city (urban sprawl)	Compact city
Specialised land uses	Multifunctional city
Direct costs of operation	Ecological accounting
Commuting	Cloud-shaped mobility
Required (household-based) mobility	Daily mobility
Transport policy	Mobility policy and right to accessibility
Long distance	Proximity
Longitudinal use of streets	Cross-street use

Source: Noy, P., *Mobility is one of the most important problems of the country*, Public Transport Promotion Association, Barcelona (in Catalan), 2001.

Urban Policies in India

Smart city Mission in a way is a response to the decades of neglect that Indian cities had to face. The imperative of taking a quantum jump is due to the fact that the policies of urban development have been rather inadequate and not n sync with time. The first five year plan (1951-56) was mainly concerned with housing, rehabilitation of refugees in Delhi, Mumbai, Kolkata, Ahmedabad and cities of Haryana and Punjab states. Although Chandigarh as a modern planned city designed by Le Courbusier was set up during this period, nonetheless, the model was not replicated elsewhere. The plan looked at slum clearance 'a national problme' and 'disgrace to country'.

The 2nd Five Year Plan (1956–61) recognized "rise in land values, speculative buying of lands in the proximity of growing towns, high rentals and the development of slum areas" as common syndrome affecting most of the cities. The emphasis of the Plan was thus on regional planning and preparation of master plans. Besides, there was also some stress on constructing housing for low income groups. As a result, the first Town and Country Planning legislation was enacted and institutions to prepare master plan were set up in many states. Further, the Slums Areas (Improvement and Clearance) Act was passed in 1956. As per the Act a slums meant: "any area(where) buildings…(a) are in any respect unfit for human habitation, or (b) are by reason of dilapidation, over-crowding, faulty arrangement and design of such buildings, narrowness or faulty arrangement of streets, lack of ventilation, light or sanitation, or any combination of these factors, are detrimental, to safety, health or morals" (GoI, Slum Act). The Master Plan based urban development began during the 3rd Plan Period (1961-66). Urban Development Authorities viz. Delhi Development Authority (DDA), Mumbai Metropolitan Regional Development Authority (MMRDA), Madras Metropolitan Development Authority (MMDA), were set up during this period. The master plans were meant to ensure systematic development of cities driven by stringent spatial segregation between areas for housing, business and industries. However, the plans remained oblivious of the common mixed-land use was pattern in India. Despite all such efforts land prices kept increasing and consequently slums kept increasing.

The 4th Plan Period (1969–74) aimed at balanced urban growth and decongesting big cities like Delhi, Kolkata, Bombay and Madras by diverting populations to smaller urban centres. It emphasized the need to set up small towns having their own model for economic sustainability. The Plan recommended: (i) the optimum use of land (ii) availability of land for the weaker sections (iii) preventing concentration of land ownership, its rising value and speculative pricing and finally (iv) allowing use of land as resource for financing city's development plans. HUDCO the institution for financing urbn jousting was set up during the same period.

The subsequent Plans also mainly focused on creating the institutional set ups of various kind to tackle the issues of urbanization. However, what was missing was the approach to first accept it as an opportunity of growth and then to prepare a roadmap or blueprint for future development. Most of the policy initiatives were largely remedial rather than being futuristic.

The first significant endeavor to augment the capabilities of urban governments came through the constitutional amendment of 1992 which allowed state governments to decentralize several responsibilities to municipal bodies. It included among other land-use, economic development, water, roads and poverty alleviation etc. (*The Evolution of National Urban Policies A Global Overview*, 2014).

The first major urban programme for urban rejuvenation Jawaharlal Nehru National Urban Renewal Mission (JNNURM) was launched in 2005. It had wide scope. Through this programme it was expected to get investment of USD 24 billion for 67 cities over a period of seven years. It was later extended by another two years. To upgrade the slums and provide basic amenities Rajiv Awas Yojana (RAY) was launched in 2013 for a period of 10 years. Both the programmes however are hindered by local capacity constraints and lack clarity as to how the support will be distributed between cities and towns (Chaplin 2011; Kundu 2014).

In the the era of market economy Indian government is now trying to bring lots of reforms in its economic policies. They influence both urbanization and urban policies. Cities are being regarded as growth engines of economy. So the economic and administrative autonomy of cities will be essential to improve their performance. The growth disparity among Indian cities is a reflection of ill-conceived, shortsighted policies of urban development. However, the emerging new middle class nurtures global aspirations and want to live in global cities. Emergence of Bangalore, Gurgaon are cases in point. The aspirations to enjoy status of "global city" are now influencing India's urban planning policies (Dupont 2011).

Smart City Mission

India's present smart city mission has evolved from the earlier visions for urban future. While technology and design, at spatial, product, communication and systems level, will drive the smart city misson, but the issues it has to address will remain one of sustainable urban development. The Planning Commission Steering Committee Report (2012) on India's urban future dealing with sustainable urban development envisioned a slum free city having "less than 10 percent urban poor, 100 percent access to water and sanitation, more than 50 percent share of public transport and 75 percent of new commercial buildings to be energy efficient."

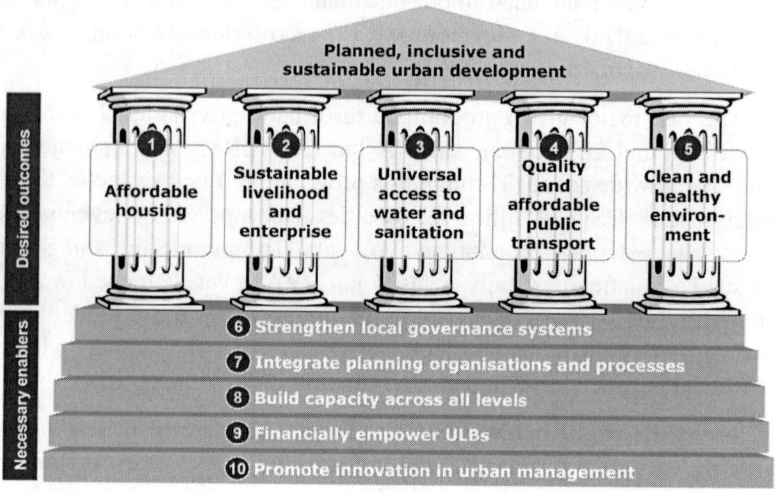

Source: Report of the Steering Committee on Urbanization. Planning Commission (2012-17) http://planningcommission.nic.in/aboutus/committee/strgrp12/strrep_urban0401.pdf

Diagram 4: Constituents of Urban Future

The challenges for smart city largely remain the same. According to The Smart City Mission Strategy of the Government of India (2017): "The strategic components of area-based development in the Smart Cities Mission are city improvement (retrofitting), city renewal (redevelopment) and city extension (greenfield development) plus a Pan-city initiative in which Smart Solutions are applied covering larger parts of the city." The focus of India's Smart Cities Mission remains city improvement (retrofitting), city renewal (redevelopment) and city extension (Greenfield development). These cities are meant to rejuvenate the ailing urban system, improve infrastructure, quality of life and achieve sustainable and inclusive development. Incremental addition of technology, design and IT-led smart features are envisaged to transform them into modern world-class cities eventually. Indian cities which are home to approximately 38 million people, are big, dense and overburdened and yet expected to become smart, efficient and sustainable. The rising population and urban migration are putting tremendous pressure on India's megacities, over 7000 towns and close to 1500 urban agglomeration. They desperately need improved infrastructure and basic amenities such as water, sanitation, sewage, road, transportation among other. Environmental sustainability and urban resilience are among the equally important concerns.

Smart City Models

The concept of smart cities arises both curiosity and expectations. This technology driven urban design where systems are run and regulated by apt and efficient application of technology are creating new models of smart urbanism. Songdo in South Korea and Masdar in the UAE; the two new smart cities are the cases in point which have been built afresh. However, smart interventions are also being made in pre-existing cities like Amsterdam which aims at reducing CO_2 emission to the level of 40 per cent by 2025. Apart from this, it also seeks to promote economic growth making smart application of ICT and changing its citizens' behaviour towards more sustainable lifestyle. It's planning to convert its ports into smart ports, introduce smart shipping traffic to prevent traffic jams on waterways, green energy playground for the families so that kids could be incentivized to play more. London Smart City vision includes use of smart grid technology for better use of energy and water. It plans to use data and technology to develop new markets for London's waste that brings efficiencies and scale to the segregation and utilization of waste as a resource. Its smart intervention also aims at using 3D visualization to minimize unnecessary digging of the road by different agencies. However, India's own conceptual framework for smart cities needs to look up to the contemporary global benchmark and also consider the exclusive socio-economic priorities of its own cities based on the data of India's urban challenges. Unlike the newly developed models of smart city like Songo, Masdar, PlanIT Valley (Portugal) and other, India's majoar challenge lies in making smart interventions in urban retrofitting. At present Lavasa is probably the only (private) city which has semblance of smart city and the one which is modelled on the principle of new (sustainablc) urbanism in India.

Sustainable Urbanism and Smart City

Rising urban population, depleting resources and environmental concerns have brought the issue of sustainable urbanism for serious discussion. Following the 'Brundtland report' (World Commission on Environment and Development 1987) sustainable urbanism has become central to urban policies and has influenced theories and practices of urbanism in different parts of the world (Roggema 2016). Broad principles of sustainable urbanism according to the Freiburg Charter (Daseking et al. 2012) entails three main aspects namely: spatial development, content and process. Farr (2007) defines it as "walkable and transit-served urbanism integrated with high performance buildings and high-performance infrastructure". However, a rather broad definition of sustainable urbanism by Sharifi (2016) explains the concept as: "the application of sustainability and resilient principles to the design, planning, and administration/operation of cities". In practical sense, nevertheless, cities have their own priorities vis a vis urban sustainability. For example, for Bogota it's transport, for Melbourne it's energy and for Mexico City it's air quality which figure importantly in terms of the priority of urban sustainability.

Cities not only have to be environmentally sustainable but socially and economically as well. Urban sustainability means evolving a harmonious eco-system of sustainable mobility devices, energy, water, housing, landscape etc. However, this eco-system has to be in harmony with the needs of people and their impact on resources. Sustainable urbanism is at the core of smart cities everywhere including India. It cannot overlook the concept of sustainable development which means "development which meets the needs of the present without compromising the ability of future generations to meet their own needs" (*World Commission on Environment and Development* 1987: 43). Thus, the whole approach of smartness ultimately depends on the fact that how sensibly the optimal use of resources have been made.

Smart city in ndia and elsewhere are expected to create sustainable and efficient urban clusters which can offer better quality of life to the city dwellers. Sustainable urbanism in itself is a holistic approach towards sustainability and urban design whch includes all the processes that shape the form and function of the built environment in its full complexity – infrastructures, land developments, built landscapes, social networks, systems of governance and economics and facilities (Ejigu & Haas 2011). It includes creating walkable mixed use urban environments that allow and encourage walking and bicycling; designing public transit and transport systems etc. The agenda of sustainable urbanism has many things in common with the concept of smart city. Like smart city, sustainable urbanism also deals with integrating various means of transportation, efficient land use, building sustainable neighborhoods, housing, walkable neighborhoods, universal accessibility, linking human life to nature, waste treatment, smart buildings and energy systems among other. However, the reason they are not used synonymously is because while sustainable urbanism remains the objective, smart city indicates the required intervention of technology, design and systems innovation.

From the urban planning perspective (including that of smart cities) sustainable urbanism has to be a normative planning model setting broader guidelines while sustainability or sustainable development have to remain as a governance objective (Rapoport 2014). Policymakers have to look at urban planning from the perspective of sustainable urbanism both for the existing and new cities. Lehmann (2016) observes that:

> ...urban developments are rarely purely the result of design considerations; rather they are shaped by economic forces, the evolution of policies, and a range of invisible forces such as land-use regulations, codes for floor space ratios and economic power structures.

Smart cities will not be exempt from these factors. Indian cities may be different from each other in terms of their size, original or proposed design, natural resources and landscape but they require something in common which include. Cities require efficient integration of transport, energy; integrated land-use, water and waste planning; re-engineering infrastructure, retrofitting the existing city and gentle densification; balancing compact city development at denser transport nodes with new public green spaces (Lehmann 2016). Use of ICT, electronic sensors, fiber optics, mobile telephony, network engineering, realtime monitoring and data collection and dissemination which drive the smart cities will have to be effectively used to provide answer to India's urban challenges. Sustainable urbanism, which smart cities will be expected to achieve will eventually include balancing environmental, economic and social objectives; all quite crucial from the Indian perspective where the nature of society and cities both are so heterogenous.

Design and Technology Intervention

From design perspective, smart city is a meta-system of sub-systems. It has social, cultural, economic, spatial dimensions. It incorporates people, various operating systems and infrastructure. IBM identifies them as an interaction of planning and management, infrastructure and people. Like other public policies, the efficacy of urban policies also lie in improving service delivery by creating better synergy between them. Planning and management uses longstanding visions developed through comprehesive data analysis. It's used in management of daily affairs of the city for its safety and security and ease of doing business. Infrastructure include basic urban services viz. roads, mass transit and mobility systems, energy, efficient housing, water and sanitation, robust IT set up among other. The infrastructure and its management are directed towards people so that their livelihood, education, healthcare and other essential needs are provided seamlessly. Intervention of technology, design and innovation at various levels are key to the very concept of smart city. Despite enormous scope of intervention from the product to systems level, neither the role of design has been clearly articulated in the smart city mission, nor the design community itself has envisioned its own agenda and creative solutions for India's upcoming smart cities. So far design intervention in cities has not moved beyond the architectural and spatial domains, whereas smart cities would require integration of urban systems, technology and innovation. In other words, design intervention in smart cities will require integration of people, infrastructure and planning as the diagram 4 expalins.

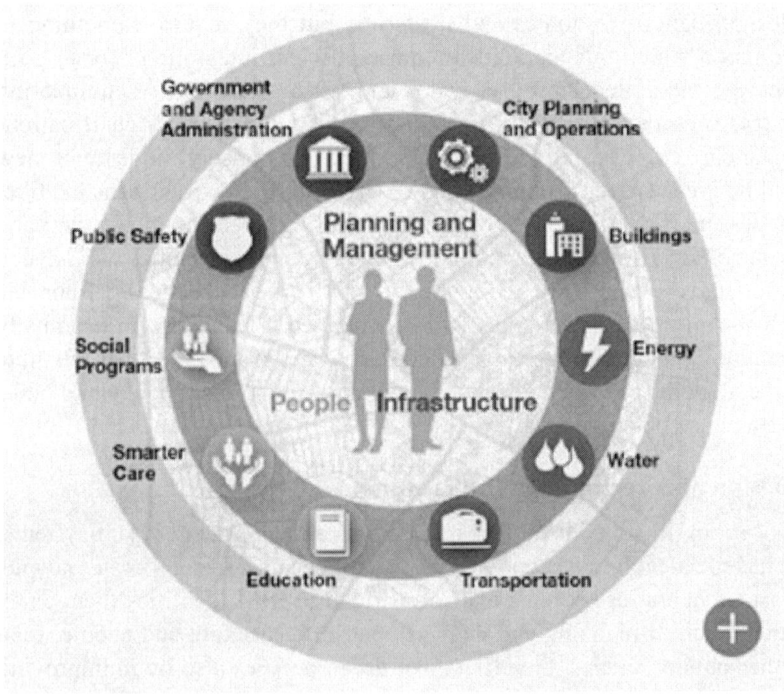

Source: IBM, Smarter Cities, New cognitive approaches to long-standing challenges.

Diagram 5: Key Elements of Smart City

Conclusion

In India smart cities are expected to transform urban systems to their highest level of efficiency through technology, design, innovation and policy reforms so that with optimum utilization of resources sustainable urbanization could be achieved. The premise on which the concept of smart cities rests indicates that in the light of the rising challenges of urbanization systems governing the cities need revolution rather than evolution. For example, communication in Indian cities both in terms of transport of people and data need radical improvement. Urban development and ecological imbalance are big concerns. Delhi, which is the fifth most populous city in the world having an estimated population of 17.8 million (2014), is also one of world's most polluted cities for example. The Air Quality Index (AQI) of Delhi remains in the range of 300 which is considered very unhealthy and hazardous. Vehicular pollution is the largest contributor to this mess followed by industrial pollution. As per the data of Delhi Government 847 million motor vehicles (of all types) were registered in Delhi till March 2015. As such, the city requires urgent smart interventions to improve the public transport system so that problems like air pollution, congestion, road rage etc. can be reduced to the limit of human tolerance.

The rsing urbanization poses both enormous challenges and opportunities in India and elsewhere. Smart city is a timely response to that. However, it can't ignore the concurrently emerging paradigms of sustainable urbanism. In fact, achieving sustainable urbanism has to be the ultimate objective of smart city. Critics of the idea of smart city believe that cities have always been smart and their intelligence resides in the people (Greenfield 2013), therefore, people will innovate new methods to cope with the inevitable changes. Nevertheless, contemporary actual and conceptual models of smart cities give new insights too which goes beyond Greenfields's proposition. The smart city models whether Masdar, Songdo or any other are trying to redefine urban living from multiple perspectives viz. resilience, business, growth of citizens or services within an urban environment and trying to find their solutions in emerging technologies. Although, some of our major urban problems such as depleting natural resources, pollution, environmental degradation and ecological hazards etc are caused by unsustainable technological processes.

However, it's interesting to see that to innovate smart sustainable urban processes it's technology once again which is being put to use. Today urban transformation is happening at several level; social, cultural, economic, spatial, architectural, ecological, technological and so on. So the idea of smart city is not just that of a planned city, rather a city that can break off the urban entropy and remain prepared to plan itself so as to manage the transformation smoothly. Smart cities inspired by the ideals of sustainable urbanism, may make intelligent use of technology to solve complex problems with greater ease and efficiency. But it must holistically reconceptualize the vision to create a fruitful long lasting synergy between man, environment and the emerging frontiers of technology. India's urban challenges are far more complex. The urban development plan for smart cities doesn't entail creation of new smart cities at this stage but to redesign and reinvent twenty existing cities. Thus, India's model for smart city can not be one driven by technology alone, but one which can quickly and effectively respond to the emerging socio-cultural-economic-technological-spatial needs and reinvent itself. After all smartness also means brainy ingenuity.

Reference

1. Acharya, Surya Raj., Morichi, Shigeru. (eds.), *Evolving Concepts in Urban Transport*, Springer, XII, 2013. Retrieved on 15 April 2017 from file:///C:/Users/Bhole_000/Desktop/9783642297427-c1.pdf
2. Ahluwalia, I.J., Mohanty, P.K., "Planning and Market for Urban Development in India", in Ahluwalia, I.J., & Mohanty, P.K. (eds.) *Urbanisation in India, Challenges, Opportunities and way Forward*, Delhi: Sage Publications, 2014, p. 69.
3. Batra, Lalit., *A Review of Urbanisation and Urban Policy in Post-Independent India* (Working Paper), Delhi: Centre for the Study of Law and Governance, Jawaharlal Nehru University, New Delhi, 2009, retrieved on 21 April 2017, http://www.jnu.ac.in/CSLG/workingPaper/12A%20Review%20of%20Urban%20%28Lalit%20Batra%29.pdf
4. Benevolo, C. , Dameri, R. P. and D'Auria, B., *Smart Mobility in Smart City: Action Taxonomy, ICT Intensity and Public Benefits*, Springer International Publishing, 2016, https://doi.org/DOI 10.1007/978-3-319-23784-8_2
5. Benedikt, Olesya, "The Valuable Citizens of Smart Cities: The Case of Songdo City", *Graduate Journal of Social* Science, April 2016, Vol. 12, Issue 2, pp. 17–36. Retrived on 10 April 2017 from http://gjss.org/sites/default/files/issues/chapters/papers/GJSS%20Vol%2012-2%201%20Benedikt_0.pdf
6. Bholey, Mihir., "India's Urban Challenges and Smart Cities: A Contemporary Study", *Scholedge International Journal of Business Policy & Governance,* Vol. 03, Issue 03, 2016, p. 21, http://www.thescholedge.org/journals/
7. Chaplin, S., "Indian cities, sanitation and the state: the politics of the failure to provide", *Environment and Urbanization*, Vol. 23, No. 1, 2011, pp. 57-70.
8. Daseking W, Köhler B, Kemnitz G, "The Freiburg charter", Stadtplanungsamt, Freiburg, 2012.

9. Dupont, V., "The dream of Delhi as a global city", *International Journal of Urban and Regional Research*, Vol. 35, No. 3, 2011, pp. 533–554.
10. Ejigu, Alazar., Haas, Tigran., "Contextual Modernism and Sustainable Urbanism as New Housing Strategies - A way for better understanding the phenomena of concentrated poverty", Presented at the Enhr Conference 2011, Toulouse, 2011. Retrieved on 24 April 2017 from http://www.enhr.net/documents/2011%20France/WS10/Haas%20and%20Ejigu-V3-WS10.pdf
11. Farr D, *Sustainable urbanism: urban design with nature,* Wiley, New York, 2007.
12. Giffinger, R. Fertner, C., Kramar, H., Kalasek, R., Pichler-Milanovicì, N., Meijers, E., *Smart Cities: Ranking of European Medium-Sized Cities,* Centre of Regional Science (SRF), Vienna University of Technology
13. GoI (Undated) Slum Act, 2007, http://www.indianrailways.gov.in/RPF/Files/law/BareActs/slumareas1956act.htm
14. Greengfield, A., This is Part I of The city is here for you to use: 'Against the smart city'. New York Do, 2013.
15. Hou, Jeffrey. et al. 'Thick City, Now Urbanism.' *Now Urbanism: The Future of City is Here* edited by Hou, Jeffrey. et al. Routledge, 2015, p. 3.
16. Deb, Sandip (Ed.), *India Transport Report – Moving India to 2032*, Delhi: Routledge, 2014. Retrived on 11 April 2017, http://planningcommission.nic.in/reports/genrep/NTDPC_Vol_01.pdf
17. Kundu, A., 'India's sluggish urbanization and its exclusionary development', in McGranahan, G. and G. Martine, eds. Urban Growth in Emerging Economies, London: Routledge, 2014.
18. Lehmann, Steffen., "Sustainable urbanism: towards a framework for quality and optimal density?", Springer Open, 2:8, 2016, https://doi.org/DOI 10.1186/s40984-016-0021-3
19. Marshall, Stephen., 'Sustainable Urbanism in Evolution', in Tigran Haas (ed.) Sustainable Urbanism and Beyond. New York: Rizzoli International Publication, 2012, p. 59.
20. Ministry of Urban Development, Government of India, Smart Cities Mission (Government Report), 2017. Retrieved on 21 April 2017 from http://smartcities.gov.in/content/innerpage/strategy.php
21. Paul, Samuel., 'Urban Infrastructure and Governance' in Ramesh, et.al. (eds.) Urban Growth and Governance in India an Overview, London: Routledge, 2010, pp. 3.
22. PWC, "Making cities smart and sustainable", retrieved on 21 February 2017 from https://www.pwc.in/assets/pdfs/publications/2015/making-cities-smart-and sustainable.pdf, 2015.
23. Rai, Nishith., Singh, A.K., New Dimensions of Urban Management in India, New Delhi: Serials Publications, 2010, p. 164.
24. Rapoport, E. R., "Mobilizing Sustainable Urbanism: International Consultants and the Assembling of a Planning Model", University College London, London, September 2014. Retrieved on 21 April 2017 from http://discovery.ucl.ac.uk/1449528/1/Rapoport_Mobilizing%20Sustainable%20urbanism%20final.pdf

25. Roggema, Rob., The future of sustainable urbanism: A redefinition. City Territ Archit, 3:22, 2016, Springer Open. Retrieved on 28 September 2017 from https://cityterritoryarchitecture.springeropen.com/track/pdf/10.1186/s40410-016-0052-y?site=cityterritoryarchitecture.springeropen.com

26. Robusté, Francesc., "The Future of Transport in Urban Areas. European Parliament", Retrieved on 15 April 2017 from http://www.europarl.europa.eu/RegData/etudes/note/join/2009/431580/IPOL-TRAN_NT(2009)431580_EN.pdf, 2010.

27. Sharifi A., "From garden city to eco-urbanism: The quest for sustainable neighborhood development", Sustain Cities Soc 20:1–16, 2016, doi:10.1016/j.scs.2015.09.002

28. Shaw, Annapurna., Indian Cities, New Delhi: Oxford University Press, 2012, pp. 1-2.

39. "Swachh Bharat Mission Municipal Solid Waste Management Manual Part I: An Overview" Central Public Health and Environmental Engineering Organisation (CPHEEO) Ministry Of Urban Development, 2016. Retrived on 11 April 2017, http://moud.gov.in/pdf/57f1e55834489Book03.pdf

30. Govt. of India, The Handbook of Urban Statistics 2016. Ministry of Urban Development. Retrived on 10 April 2017, http://www.indiaenvironmentportal.org.in/files/file/handbook%20of%20urban%20statistics%202016.pdf

31. The Planning Commission: Approach to the 12th Plan, 'The Challenges of Urbanization in India,' retrived on 30 March 2017 from http://12thplan.gov.in/12fyp_docs/17.pdf

32. Planning Commission, Govt. of India, "Report of the Steering Committee on Urbanisation (Twelfth Five Year Plan 2012-2017)", 2012, retrieved on 24 April 2017 from http://planningcommission.nic.in/aboutus/committee/strgrp12/strrep_urban0401.pdf

33. The World Bank, Leveraging Urbanization in India, 2015, retrieved on 21 February 2017 from http://www.worldbank.org/en/country/india/brief/leveraging-urbanization-india

34. Ellen MacArthur Foundation, "Towards the Circular Economy", 2013, retrived on 10 April 2017, https://www.ellenmacarthurfoundation.org/assets/downloads/publications/Ellen-MacArthur-Foundation-Towards-the-Circular-Economy-vol.1.pdf.

35. TRB, Toward a sustainable future; addressing the long-term effects of motor vehicle transportation on climate and ecology, Washington, DC: National Academy Press, 1997.

36. Turo, Ivan., "The Evolution of National Urban Policies A Global Overview", UN Habitat, 2014, retrieved on 21 April 2017 from http://www.citiesalliance.org/sites/citiesalliance.org/files/National%20Urban%20Policies.pdf

37. UNO, "Sustainable Development Goals: 17 Goals to Transform our World", 2016, retrieved on 19 February 2017 from http://www.un.org/sustainabledevelopment/cities/

38. *World Cities Report 2016*, "Urbanization and Development: Emerging Futures 2016", Kenya: United Nations Human Settlements Programme (UN-Habitat), http://wcr.unhabitat.org/wp-content/uploads/sites/16/2016/05/WCR-%20Full-Report-2016.pdf, accessed October 3, 2016.
39. World Commission on Environment and Development, *Our Common Future*, Oxford: Oxford University Press, 1987.

Chapter - 5

Plain Language for Professional Prudence

— Harmik Vaishnav

> Any fool can make things bigger, more complex, and more violent. It takes a touch of genius-and a lot of courage-to move in the opposite direction. – ALBERT EINSTEIN

Introduction

Language is considered as the most potent weapon of a lawyer, manager and leader after his/ her domain knowledge or maybe with the respective domain knowledge. It is the language that is useful when he/she wants to manifest erudition, practice rhetoric or deliver a speech, insert obscurity in the minds of opponents, drive home a point, negotiate the terms, make a bargain or appeal to the stakeholders. There is a little he/she can do with the prevalent law, procedures, products and markets or precedents already set but he/she can employ language skills. Language is certainly the most important weapon or tool, depending on the manner it is used and the motive. It is the language that puts the points effectively, narrates impeccably, gives a smooth flow to the incidents or ideas and arguments, sharpens the manifestation of logic and negotiation skills and displays the technical qualities of products.

The contemporary trend of Globalization in the field of business, technology, international relations, and cross-cultural interaction experiences the use of language more and more, especially the English Language. The language in the contemporary world, like internet, has become a medium to bring the people from various cultures and geographical areas to a level of common understanding, empathy and intellect. When language skill is very important for a professional dealing with people and situations, there are challenges about what type of language to be used. Lawyers use the legalese and traditional language, leaders also employ sonorous rhetorical language and managers too use jargon based language. This language may not appeal to the reader or listener. When we are in the world of "user-friendly" things, we need to employ the language that is also user-friendly. A lawyer will not always write for a lawyer or a leader's rhetoric may not be for the philosophers and poets and the manager does not always write to fellow managers. The end user of the language must be able to understand it. "He that will write in any tongue must follow this counsel of Aristotle, to speak as the common people do, to think as wise men do; so should every man understand him, and the judgement of wise men allows him.[1] If a lay person can understand the document with one reading, language has done its job well by hitting the bull's eye.

When we talk about various other mediums of communication, plain language is already quite popular. In the field of business, advertising is one of the key mediums of communication and reaching to the customers. Advertisements, from clips in newspaper to TV ads, are created using catchy captions and plain language. Even these catchy captions are in clear plain language so that the reader or listener remembers it and understands instantly. Business negotiation or business meetings become successful because of the use of plain language in verbal communication. Facts and plain ideas in negotiation can be put forth only in plain language. And general instructions, sharing of knowledge and ideas and feedback in meetings are all in plain language. Imagine a negotiation table or a meeting room where pompous and verbose language is used. There will never be any business; agreement is far-fetched with such talk. It would look like a dramatic enactment of a Greek Classic but certainly business doing firms.

The challenge and pertinence of using plain language is more so with the written document where the drafter has enough time to deliberate upon, construct and re-construct sentences. Moreover, there is always the influence of the tradition in drafting. Traditional drafting style is more comfortable, it may not be always easy or clear, but since one has grown with it, it comes naturally. The phrases and jargons are already in the mind ready to be put on paper.

Discussion

English is the most widely used language of communication but the concept of Plain Language is applicable to any language of the world. We will limit the scope of discussion on plain language here with the examples of English. It is a foregone conclusion that the language of drafting official and legal documents is not for common man to understand or write. This is more pertinent in the countries where English is used as a second language and yet the only language of the courts; like India. This language used in courts, board-rooms etc. is construed not as English but a hybrid form of elite English that not even the English educated people can understand. This language is again embellished with myriad of Latin legal maxims, management and technical jargons, financial verbosity and philosophical loquaciousness. The language is also structured with long intertwining sentences and clauses for which a single reading is not enough to understand even with your good knowledge of English language.

The expertise of any professional is the respective domain knowledge and technical nitty-gritty, the procedural aspects and study of various cases. He/she employs this education and experience accompanied with language for his clients and public at large. A professional has to understand the complicated aspects of his/her domain and transform it into simplified version for lay person. "Be short, be simple, be human."[2] This is possible only if he/she uses understandable-plain language and shuns the temptation of being pedantic. There has been a lot of demand and talk of necessity about the use of plain language for communication, especially drafting. Experts and users from parliaments to court rooms, from board-rooms to company showrooms insist on use of plain language which is free from the traditional and jargon based language hitherto in vogue among the elite experts of various professions.

What is Plain Language? There may be different definitions and views about plain language and there are innumerable examples showing what a plain language is. Oxford Advance Dictionary defines plain language as 'simply and clearly expressed without using technical language'. "Plain language writing is just the practice of writing English [or any language] in a clear and simple style."[3] The definition of plain language itself is plain and simple. Many experts have defined it in different words with the same connotation like Dr Robert Eagleson, "Clear, straightforward expression, using only as many words as are necessary. It is language that avoids obscurity, inflated vocabulary and convoluted construction. It is not baby talk, nor is it a simplified version of... language" and Richard Wydick defining as, "Language that is clear, concise and correct".

Plain language does not mean colloquial or baby-talk. The characteristics of plain language are:

- clarity and brevity
- precision,
- apt use of words,
- no superfluous words or jargons,
- familiar, concrete words
- reasonable length of sentence- 18 to 20 words per sentence in average
- one thought per sentence
- avoidance of doublets and pomposity
- use of verbs instead of nouns
- use of verbs to describe activities and process
- use of active voice instead of passive
- to produce full legal, official and professional effect
- avoid abuse of language found in traditional precedents
- to avoid confusion of thought and expression found in some traditional precedents
- make documents shorter and save time and money for professional
- logical order of document
- sensible use of punctuation

Source: https://writerswrite.co.za/what-is-plain-language.

However, this list is general and not exhaustive. It may vary from context to context. Let us take the comparison of active and passive voice. The active is more direct and driving home the point. The passive is less direct and the syntax can be confusing. "The passive voice can obscure who is to do something, causing the drafter to overlook important matters."[4] "On occasions the passive is convenient-for example, where the doer of an act is intentionally left unstated."[5] It depends on the discretion of the drafter or speaker and only use of active or passive voice or use of nouns over verbs is not the hallmark of plain language. Plain language is about clarity and precision. The nature of plain language has above mentioned characteristics but not limited to them only. It is also a wrong assumption that only a communicator with limited knowledge of language and vocabulary uses plain language, on the contrary, one needs better language and richer vocabulary to apply the discretion of its use. The same wisdom applies in any field; a person with tremendous knowledge only can make things simpler. The purpose of any language is to enable the sender to deliver the message clearly and to the point and the receiver to understand fully the intended meaning. "Plain language is not artificially complicated, but is clear and effective for its intended audience. While it shuns the antiquated and inflated words and phrases, which can readily be either omitted altogether or replaced with a more useful substitute. It does not seek to rid documents of terms which express important distinctions. Nonetheless, plain language documents offer non-expert readers some assistance in coping with these technical terms. To a far larger extent, plain language is concerned with matters of sentence and paragraph structure, with organization and design, where so many of the hindrances to clear expression originate."[6]

Many experts from various fields ranging from law, technology and science, management and education still ponder and argue about the use of plain language in their documents, reports etc. They have also shown their reluctance in its use. It is perhaps a psychological lacuna that one shows the expertise and scholarship just by using technical jargons, verbosity and freely quoting legends from respective fields. The question comes, is scholarship or expertise in using jargons or understanding the technicality behind them? Is expertise in technical verbosity or translating your technical know-how to non-technical people in simple manner? To put it with examples, a lawyer's expertise is not in use of technical language but understanding the law and the procedure, the manager's expertise is not in management jargons but the concepts behind them and putting the concepts into day to day management and the technocrat's expertise is in making gadgets which can be easily operated and user-manuals which can be easily understood. "If investors are promised information and they don't get it in a form they can understand, they are being cheated."[7]

When the contemporary world has defied geographical detachment and cultural barriers for the sake of business, science and inter-mingling of people, language has to bring them to a level intellectually and emotionally rather than separating them. The modern world uses language to communicate faster and effectively. There is no ownership or even rigidity in use of spellings and grammatical syntax is receding. Plain language first of all gives clarity and precision to the technical person before drafting or preparing a document. Step by step clear drafting of points will enable the writer to ensure that nothing has been missed technically and clarity restored in his/her mind. "The results are substantive; not merely cosmetic: improving the quality of writing actually improves the quality of thoughts."[8] A long document drafted in plain language saves lot of time and hassles for the writer and reader. The receiver or reader will have minimum queries and doubts because he/she can understand with one reading and will trust instantly. Imagine a lawyer or manager sending a long document to his/her client which is verbose. The client will keep coming for queries and there will always be doubt lurking in the client's mind. But if the document is simple and clear, a client who has not studied law or who is just a purchase officer without technical knowledge will be easily understand and accept. "A 2009 survey in Ireland showed that 89% of the people surveyed would prefer banks to use plain English, and 20% say they would switch financial institutions if they provided their information in a more user-friendly manner."[9] Time is saved in to and fro of queries.

Drafting in plain language also saves stationery. A document that normally takes 5 pages can be ready in 3 pages thus giving one more dimension of saving. The twin effect of saving- time and stationery will help any organization to invest their energy to more productive resources rather than drafting long documents, answering to innumerable and repetitive queries and printing too many documents. Though it may seem magical that how use of plain language can save time, cost but as the maxim goes, small drops fill the ocean, and it is true and tested. "The Victorian Attorney-General's Department said it had saved over $400,000 a year in staff time after rewriting and redesigning just one court form."[10] After the UK government adopted a plain English policy for government forms in 1982, various government departments rewrote, redesigned and eliminated many thousands of forms. They estimated that they saved millions of pounds as a direct result and that in 1984-85 alone they saved 4 million. USA also has a Plain Language Act. The law requires that federal agencies use "clear Government communication that the public can understand and use." A 2006 comparative study of plain language court forms concluded that "plain language court forms and instructions are better understood, easier to use, and more economical".[11] The European Union too moved towards the use of Plain Language. In Germany there is a dictionary of Plain Language and France the Constitutional Council ensured clarity and intelligibility of their law through the use of Plain Language. If a lawyer or manager can save up to 20% of his/her time and stationery, it will be substantial saving for the entire firm. This can be saved through reduced time in drafting, reduction in queries and less time in explanation and negotiation. The saved time can be used productively elsewhere.

The innumerable advantages of plain language are beyond debate as it is the need of contemporary times and the layman. The government machineries, banks and industries have started practising it. The use of plain language is also quite simple. But many a times for a seasoned drafter who has the experience of drafting in traditional language, it seems daunting and simplification makes him/her uneasy. The drafter feels as if clutch has been removed from his driving equation.

Plain language use deals with a few fundamentals of written communication. a drafter has to keep them in mind while producing a document and while proof-reading. First of all one has to be clear about the audience. The audience may be a non-technical person or having education of some other domain. Plain language is also equally effective if you are addressing audience with technical knowledge. One need not focus on the verbosity but the technical aspect of the communication even while dealing with people from the same domain. A judge may appreciate and comprehend a plea in plain language from a lawyer or same may be with CEO's document addressed to the board. The target of plain language is not to cater to the non-technical audience but everyone. Plain language focuses on clarity not technicality. "It does require that every effort be made to make them intelligible to the widest possible audience."[12] The drafter also then has to be clear about the purpose of the document. Is it meant for advertising? Is it to get a response? Is it meant to comply? Is it for further discussion?, etc. The flow of the language, use of words and the syntax of the sentences may vary from purpose to purpose. The drafter must also heed the tone and formality that the document shows. In verbal communication the tone comes naturally but when drafting official or legal documents the tone has to be taken care of consciously. Again, the audience and the purpose have connection with the tone of the document. Precision in language and inserting the right tone will enable the reader to understand quickly and clearly. Let us see the examples below:

Traditional/ Verbose Language	Plain Language
There are four different proposals I want you to review before our next meeting.	Please review these four proposals before our next meeting.
It is the responsibility of our Production Department to see that it meets the requirements of our Sales Division.	Our Production Department must meet our Sales Division's requirements.[13]

Clarity is perhaps the soul of plain language. The purpose of communication is to clarify or satisfy. One sends message to clarify information, ideas etc. or satisfy urges, curiosity and anxiety. In both the cases, plain language meets the requirement. The traditional drafting, especially legal drafting, believes that the more the complicated the case or the law, the more complicated the draft. Should it not be the other way round? If there is more complication, the explanation ought to be simpler. Clarity is first born in the mind of the communicator. One has to take certain precautions for imbibing clarity. Clarity of concept, purpose, words to be used and sentences to be put and even the structure of the entire document to be considered. Simple words and smaller sentences will help the drafter to give clarity to the reader. The best practices for clarity is to re-read and check what sense the sentence or paragraph makes. It would also be a good idea to ask a person with non-technical background to read or a person with limited knowledge of the language to read and see what sense it makes. If a lay person can read and understand in single reading, it is good use of plain language.

Let us see the following examples:

Traditional/ Verbose Language	Plain Language
The Senate, having tried William Jefferson Clinton, President of the United States, upon two articles of impeachment exhibited against him by the House of Representative, and two-thirds of the Senators present not having found him guilty of the charges contained therein: it is therefore, ordered and adjudged that the said William Jefferson Clinton be, and he is hereby, acquitted of the charges in this said article.	After a trial on two articles of impeachment against the President William Jefferson Clinton, fewer that two-thirds of the Senators present have found him guilty. Therefore, it is ordered that he is acquitted.
The Trustees may distribute funds Provided that it has a surplus of funds and provided that the beneficiaries are over 21 and further provided that no loans to beneficiaries are outstanding.	The Trustees may distribute funds if: 1. it has a surplus of funds; or 2. the beneficiaries are over 21; or no loans to beneficiaries are outstanding.[14]

The clarity of sentence construction is very important when it comes to language. There should not be multiple clauses in a sentence, unnecessary use of phrases, repetition and superfluous words must be curtailed. A good exercise is to break long complex sentence with multiple clauses into smaller sentences. Smaller sentences are easier to comprehend and step by step understanding takes place in the mind. When we talk about language, punctuation plays an important role. In plain language the use of punctuation is minimal. A long sentence with commas and colons must be avoided. Plain language shuns the use of verbosity and pomposity of vocabulary and mixture of tenses and clauses and many punctuation marks. A paragraph with many punctuation marks does not show the language skills of the writer, it shows the opposite.

Traditional/ Verbose Language	Plain Language
High-quality learning environments are a necessary precondition for facilitation and enhancement of the ongoing learning process.	Children need good schools if they are to learn properly.[15]
This temporary injunction remains in effect against both parties until the final decree of divorce or order of legal separation is entered, the complaint is dismissed, the parties reach agreement, or until the court modifies or dissolves this injunction. This injunction shall not preclude either party from applying to the court for further temporary orders, an extended injunction or modification or revocation of this temporary injunction.	You must follow this order until the court changes or ends it, your case is finalized or dismissed, or you and your spouse make an agreement. Either spouse may ask the court to change or cancel this order, or to issue new orders.[16]
Citigroup today announced a series of repositioning actions that will further reduce expenses and improve efficiency across the company while maintaining Citi's unique capabilities to serve clients, especially in the emerging markets. These actions will result in increased business efficiency, streamlined operations and an optimized consumer footprint across geographies.	Citigroup today announced lay-offs. This will save cost.[17]
We must strive to warrant that simplicity is rigor-ously sustained so as to facilitate comprehension.	Keep it simple.

One has to be conscious of what to avoid while using plain language. Plain Language is for everyone, we all want to communicate in a manner that is clear and avoids confusion. Professionals who resort to plain language can explain their subject in better way and can concentrate on the knowledge rather than using verbose language which may impress the opposite person but not make him/her understand. Plain language is also quite considerate as you don't waste time in forming sentences with grandeur, you solve problems easily. A very important aspect of Plain Language is its inherent trait of being open and honest. Since it avoids circumlocution and verbosity, it tends to be transparent and sincere be it expressing feelings, ideas or solving problems.

As we saw some the salient features of plain language, let us also examine what to avoid while using plain language:

- wordiness and redundancy
- overuse of the modal verb 'shall'
- obscure language
- unusual word order
- superfluous words and adjectives
- foreign words and phrases
- unduly long sense-bites
- legalese and technical jargons
- use of noun phrases instead of verbs
- overuse of passive
- overuse of capitals.[18]

Source: https://ohscommittee.wordpress.com/plain-language/

Conclusion

Plain language is good and clear, unambiguous and never muddled or confused. There are no pitfalls of written language, misuse of vocabulary, mixed metaphors and pedantic sentence constructions. It is common-sense skill for any professional who wish to express fluently and clearly. It is professional prudence to use plain language for legal, official and business communication and documentation.

A document has several functions like carrying out legal, official or business purpose, communicating, informing and persuading. These documents create private laws and binding for the parties and govern their relationship for a particular time and purpose. In such cases it is prudence to use plain language. Plain facilitates instant clarity, ease of drafting and interpretation, time and cost saving. A document in plain language can be amended or scaled easily without much discussion or confusion. A manager can easily amend or scale the terms of agreement etc. if it is drafted in plain language without the active help of a lawyer. If the business of professionals is to give ease and comfort to their clients and stakeholders, the business of plain language is to give the same to the professionals while doing business. Plain language is a user-friendly tool where you do not require an engineer to put the pieces together. Brevity with simple words and structure with clarity and precision is the key. "Structure and precision play a more important role in written language. The importance of precision and conciseness can never be overemphasized. As Dr. Seuss puts it:

There's so much to be read
You never can cram all those thoughts in your head
So the writer who breeds
More words that he needs
Is making a chore for the reader who reads.
That's why my belief is
The briefer the brief is
The greater the sigh of the reader's relief is.[19]

The people of the contemporary world have defied the geographical remoteness and even overcome cultural barriers for which technology and language are responsible. People want learning, alliance, attachment and have empathy overlooking cultural and linguistic blockades. Like use of technology for communication, language plays an important role in levelling them intellectually and emotionally. When there has to be interface among various people and professionals, understandable and comprehensive language is mandatory. The role of plain language, be it any language, comes into being and will expand as the world opens up more and people mingle more and more.

Notes

1. Toxophilus Ascham Roger, To All Gentlemen and Yeomen of England, https://www.archerylibrary.com/books/toxophilus/yeomen.html, 1545.
2. Ernest Gowers, *The Complete Plain Words,* London: Penguin Books, 1987, p. 19.
3. Michele Asprey, Plain Language for Lawyers, Universal Law Publishing Co., New Delhi, 2011, p. 12.
4. Peter Butt, Richard Castle, *Modern Legal Drafting,* New Delhi: Cambridge University Press, 2006, p. 153.
5. ibid, p. 154.
6. Discussion paper 1, "Legislation, Legal Rights and Plain English", Law Reform Commission, Melbourne, 1986, p. 3.
7. M Mercer, "Plain Language Symposium: A Success by Any Measure", *Simply Plain,* vol. 2, no. 2, October-December 2007, p. 2.
8. G Gopen, J. Swan, "The Science of Scientific Writing", *American Scientist,* Nov-Dec 1990.
9. Research Commissioned by the National Adult Literacy Agency and the EBS Building Society. See J. Walshe, "Jargon Buster debunks bank-speak", www.pressreader.com, 20 February 2009.
10. International Literacy Year Secretariat, "Reader Friendly Campaign Materials", Canberra, 1990.
11. Maria Mindlin,"Is Plain Language better? A Comparative Readability Study of Plain Language Court Forms", *Scribes Journal of Legal Writing,* Vol. 10, 2005-2006. Retrieved 28 November 2011, www.transcend.net/library/html/PLStudy.html
12. "Plain English and the Law", Victorian Law Reform Commission Report No 9, 1987, p. 45.
13. Meenakshi Raman, Prakash Singh, *Business Communication,* New Delhi: Oxford University Press, 2006, p. 243.
14. Asprey, n. 3, p. 98.
15. Plain English Campaign,"Before and after", 24 July 2012. Retrieved 17 March 2013.
16. Maria Mindlin, *Readability,* Transcend Translations, 2010.
17. Derek Thompson, "Citigroup Eliminates 11,000 Jobs in History's Most Corporate-Jargony Paragraph Ever", *The Atlantic,* The Atlantic Monthly Group, 5 December 2012. Retrieved 17 March 2013.
18. Peter Butt, Richard Castle, *Modern Legal Drafting,* New Delhi: Cambridge University Press, 2006, pp. 127-128.
19. Rajesh Vishwanathan, *Business Communication,* Mumbai: Himalaya Publishing House, 2010, p. 329.

Chapter - 6

Millennial Generation HR Concerns

— *Neeta Sinha, Supriya Pal*

The resonance between the generational thought and the organizational thought is the most critical question that leads to an efficient and effective future workforce. Studies conducted on human capital theory reveal that the productivity in labor market is the result of various kinds of educational sources which needs to be imparted to the stakeholders, employer and employee (Becker 1975, Mincer 1974). It is a known fact that the employees who are clear with the priorities and commitments prove to be the most efficient workers. With the clear definition of role expectation from the employee and job specification of the profile the compatibility between the employee and organization can be observed to be very strong. The incompatibility between the two can lead to occupational role stress that is the major concern of the organization.

As per National Chamber Foundation (NCF) study, 2012, millennial generation has received an upbringing that is more nurtured, protected and have close relation with their parents. They expect and try to impart the same orientation in their future personal life. From the book *No Man's Land: Men's Changing Commitment to Family and Work* one man says to sociologist Kathleen Gerson "I want to make a lot of money and spend time with my daughter but obviously I can't have best of both the world". Unfortunately for most male executives there is little social support available to enhance men's equal contribution in domestic life. Men make use of various employer policies to accommodate their work role to their family obligation to a far greater extent than is generally realized," reports psychologist Joseph H. Pleck in Jane C. Hood's *Men, Work and Family*, a useful collection of cutting-edge empirical research on men's shifting priorities on the job and on the domestic front. The definition of success is changing from achieving more money to achieving quality and healthy lifestyle.

Millennials also known as Generation Y, echo boomers, facebook generation, generation next, net generation and so characterizes the human population of Generation X. There are no exact dates for when this begins or finishes; Demographers and specialists normally mark the mid 1980s as beginning birth years and the mid-1990s to mid 2000s as closure years. For this research we are targeting the year range from 1980 to 1995.

Table: Generational Cut-offs

Generation	Timeline
Alpha Kids	Born between 2010 to 2025
Generation Z	Born between 1995 to 2010
Generation Y	Born between 1980 to 1995
Generation X	Born between 1965 to 1980
Baby Boomers	Born between 1945 and 1965

Source: M. J. Parul Saxena, 2012.

Authors William Strauss and Neil Howe are generally credited with naming the Millennials. They began the term in 1987, around the time kids conceived in 1982 were entering preschool. "In my life I play a role where I catch all balls of life and I have to balance all of them 24×7". This statement seems to come from a typical working mother who is balancing various roles of her life like being a professional, mother, wife, mentor, home maker, driver, chef, technician so on and so forth. But in today's era surprisingly male also echo the similar thought. It might be surprising to many but that is the truth of the millennial male. In the Indian society where the patriarchal ideology dominates we tend to ignore the fact that a male particularly from millennial generation is willingly contributing equally in professional and domestic spheres of life. Millennial males have the courage to break the so called societal barriers and to accept the feminine profile so that their female partners can contribute equally in all segments. Today's male can be a work at home father who doesn't chase the status symbols and gives priority to raise his children for healthy life style and bright future. He is a professional who doesn't believe in slogging late office hours just to be noticed by the seniors and get his promotion chances high. He believes in efficient working who will deliver quality performance within defined time set and can switch to another role. He is a confident person who wants to reflect his unconventional thoughts of lifestyle into implementation. He is no longer expecting a stay at home life partner but a challenging one who want to face corporate world and be financially and socially independent.

In various dimensions of life the horizon of choice adopted by Gen Y can be overwhelming. The decision taken by them in terms of career, residence, organization profiles, wages, compensation and salary, future or additional education, life partners, and life style can be bewildering. Many times this dilemma to choose from the range or to take tough calls of life can lead to sense of isolation, confusion or in terms of corporate language burnout. Again the fact that these preferences of Gen Y will influence the future dynamics of management and it should be considered by the thinkers and policy makers. It will literary create a scenario where it is the way done by them will be the way it is done. The collective population will also find and ensure that the Gen Y population will be a significant voice in business and the world beyond that.

With the change in the scenario the management is adopting new approach of managing the emerging youth. We can reconnect with the latest vocabulary where semantics showcase is an important indicator of how our values are changing. The term "workforce" that conveys a sense of rigidity and power based hierarchy that is not appealing with the majority of Gen Y working population. With such change in the mindset of new and potential employees, the need to tap the human capital is the need of the future. Today in many dimensions most corporations are not compatible as it was made to understand in school, colleges or in various social groups. Most of the corporate policies which are still in action were designed by the boomer generation. Majority of the organizational policies have evolved over a period of time (for example: development of horizontal organizational structure, process thinking etc) though many policies still have their fundamentals from mid 1990s. Various dynamics of organization like hierarchical structure, rigid-individual oriented job designs, unilateral employment relationships and cascading decision making process does not collaborate with the requirement of millennial male who is in dual career couple status. There is a compatibility issue between the need of the millennial male with the existing organizational cultural aspects and policies.

In terms of occupation, the choice is based on individual life experiences and each individual brings his own set of expectation for the profile when he/she is recruited to any organization. The expectation can be split into two:

(a) achievement expectation about what to accomplish in performing his job, which in case of professionals can be imbibed by formal or professional training (E. Gold, et al. 2010)

(b) Organizational expectations about his/her job and profile that as a member of organization is sculpted by organization at the time of recruitment and selection (Wanous 1973).

The net generation with high quotient of awareness about their rights and duties always develops a high expectation towards the employers. They emphasize towards a balance in their personal and professional goals with the inclusion of organizational support. With the rise in recruitment of gen Y, the ratio of the availability of this generation and the socialization factors increases manifolds. The interaction has somewhat lead to an increase in high expectation towards employer's inducement in work life balance policies.

Any individual who enters into the professional world has more of an individualistic approach rather than an organizational approach. They begin the path of the career with an ideology of self enhancement and growth rather than developing the organization as each employer or management would aspire or expect. Though millennial males have more of ambitious attitude, they actively and proactively seek for the career opportunities. Career advancement was always a strong motivational driver for millennial males.

In the ever changing world, millennial are very particular about the training and development given by the organization. According to Struges et al. (2002), millennial emphasize on training and development heavily as it makes them grow on continuous basis and makes them desirable in the labour market. As per Rawlins et al (2008), millennial are found to be less interested in financial rewards. They are more interested in enhancing their personal fulfillment in job and be more socially responsible. They expect to face challenging and difficult learning platforms where they can yield effective value addition and ultimately advancement in career path.

As per the study conducted in "Massachusetts Institute of Technology", they were able to prove that employees get motivated by meaningful work rather than financial reward. The concept of autonomy and mastery of skills always gives huge career satisfaction as compared to other motivators. As millennial believe in unbounded career they are always willing to expand the horizon of their KSA (knowledge, skill and attitude). They tend to believe in the popular thoughts "Love your job rather than the organization". They do tend to have less inclination towards job security. As per Blau and Boal (1987), categorization of employees, millennial fall in *lone wolves* category, as they are confident about their individual skills set for their survival rather than the organizational support. They tend to create their own platform to showcase their talent rather than to wait for organization to provide a readymade platform with various milestone to match as a reference.

Table 2: Blau and Boal's Employee Model

	Low Job Involvement	**High Job Involvement**
High Affective Commitment	Corporate Citizens	Institutional Starts
Low Affective Commitment	Apathetics	Lone Wolves

Source: Hafer & Martin (2006)

In Indian work culture, employers and employees often treat the existence of work dynamics and personal life as two different spheres of existence. Till now the thought prevails that a competent worker/employee will handle the work life balance issues on their own without any external support and organization cannot handle incompetent workers. The employees tend to face the imbalance from work and family when the demand from both domains becomes huge and difficult to satisfy. Though a lot of research work has been done in this aspect but the conflict between dual career couples from a male perspective need to be understood in depth.

Organizational culture on a general understanding is the overall expectation, experience, logic, history, philosophy and values that act as a binding factor and co creates the self image, internal work dynamics in collaboration to external world and ultimately builds the future expectation. Human resource department is always expected to be in the process of evolution wherein the ongoing process of learning, unlearning, inventing and re inventing keeps the change constant. The construction of value adding human resource practices and competencies need to be complementing the strategic portfolio of the organization. With the increase in the diversity of the Indian population, the organization can also witness the rise of new segment of employees. Amongst them we can see the rise of dual career couples, which somewhere is a profitable factor as there is more integration of intellectual female employees which was neglected before few decades.

The main concern over the emerging scenario can be the dilemma faced by the Indian male partner of the dual career couples. With the strongly existing set up of patriarchal mindset in the society and the rigid organization policies, some policies of HRD needs to be re invented. Levner (2000) wrote of the "three-career family"—with family life represented as the third career. The management needs to analyze the scenario and determine the rational way to absorb the new current dynamics of the upcoming cohort and strategize the intended goals and achievement as required by the organization.

If we analyze the outlook of society or rather the organization for our study we need to understand the main perspectives which are the moderating factor in the religious perspective; we can observe various similarities across the religious mythologies.

As per the Hindu mythology Mahabharata, in chapter 146 where there is a conversation between Lord Shiva and Goddess Parvati about the duties of women. Goddess Parvati replies that the life of a woman revolves around her husband as her god, her friend and as her highest refuge. Woman's duty is to impart physical and emotional nourishment, satisfy all requirements of her husband and her children.

As per the Christian mythology, the position of female is considered to be relative with her husband. While both male and female are made in the image of the God, the woman share His divine image through the man because she was created out of him and as His glory.

As per the Muslim mythology, all through the history of Quran, different Islamic officials and lawmakers continually reinterpret the females as a result of the dominating ideology and in the historical context of time. In the recent scenario, many scholars are re visiting the original work of history, re examining the acknowledged classical adaptation on females and rethinking on the lady's part in Quran.

If we focus on the legal or judiciary background we can have the following analysis. Significant conditions of history (e.g., the British rule in India, the development under Gandhi's administration for freedom from the British rule, a development that included ladies from rich background) and mainstream powers (e.g., education of western qualities, particularly those relating to equity, present day science, and innovation) have registered the traditional position of females. Maybe the pivotal changes in the legitimate status of ladies have been made, for example, equity guaranteed by the Constitution for the rights to abortion and divorce, and property rights. So, with respect to their position in old India or, then again that of their partners in numerous modern social orders, contemporary Indian ladies have made progress in enhancing their legitimate status from the near recent past. In any case, it shows up that, while huge numbers of these progressions mirror a social climate that empowers and maintains sexual orientation fairness, there is as yet a reasonable crevice between the proposed objectives and genuine achievements. For instance, in 1981, just 25 percent of ladies were educated, as opposed to almost 47percent of men. Even though there are many mandatory and informative initiatives from the government the rural females were not allowed to get educated (Kishwar and Vanita 1985). For the urban females the requirement of the education was to enhance their portfolio for the marriage prospects for their husband and in laws (Kishwar 1985: 1-47). In like manner, numerous changes in the law really helped the ladies and put them on a strong foothold. For instance, different laws now give property rights to ladies, entitling them to an equivalent share in the joint family property. In any case such a privilege has little significance for most of the ladies on the grounds that their family may have little property to exchange or the legacy is still denied, as is the situation with many females in the country (Sharma 1980).

The new generation cannot prioritize between family and work. For the individual's who take family on the top priority don't either consider work at the second position. For them life comes together as a whole package. The individuals who are concerned about their family, their children and their issues are considered to be more focused, more efficient and more result oriented. The employees who are involved into taking care of the family members are developing attributes like patience, empathy, creativity, adaptability and resilience which is very much required in high speed, horizontal networked global economy. The companies who are winning the "Best Employer" awards are the companies who believe in providing flexible work environment. In 2008 a national study conducted in US showed that such organization have employees who are more engaged in their work, are more satisfied, more loyal, show less level of stress and have high level of mental health. A study conducted in 2012 showed that deep flexible practices actually lower the operating cost and increase adaptability in global service economy. In Norway, there is a policy that the males are given three months of automatic paternity leave. In case the employee doesn't avail the leaves there are eyebrows up in the organization. So in corporate culture of Norway it is considered to be a character of defect, if a male employee is not willing to be a fully engaged father.

Men who have achieved success as traditionally defined- such as high package, position, exposure; overall a complete package of a provider to the family – they will feel that something is missing in their personal life competency. As per the survey conducted by sociologist Robert S. Weiss on 80 executives, when defining themselves against the valuation of their ambition they seemed to be more in content with ground reality – like being called good husband, father, and provider. But majority of them were reporting stress and irritability, most had close social circle, they would rather categorize their days work. Even if the 80s father contributed in sharing the household responsibility and childcare they would consider their children a commitment, an investment or an obligation. But with the given change in economic scenario and female's desire and ambition to stay in work force have given rise to dual income couples. This has brought the millennial male to face their children in a novel way. Willingly or unwillingly they are trying to find new way or meaningfulness on their relation with their child. Concurrently there is an increase of competition, job insecurity and scrutiny of performance which had left the man to find new ways to regulate their life outside of work.

Joseph H Pleck, a psychologist, reports in the book of Jane C Hoods *Men, Work and Family*, a collection of reports of changing priorities of men from professional to domestic front. He notes that due to lack of enough corporate support, males may find new ways to suffice the so called domestic requirement. For example, the male may take sick leave or a mini extended vacation in order to attend their child birth or other such requirements. Almost all the family committed man will try to bypass the work life balance policies which were framed by top management especially for females. The males will openly declare that they require flexibility in order to manage their personal commitments.

It is also being observed that many committed male partners have quit the jobs altogether. Instead they have started their own business or opted flexible work options. The males who want to enrich their sense of purpose to their life are considered to be the male with lot of sense of self esteem. The male who are vocal about the policies; which are the result of ageism and the mediocre work prove to be having much clear sense of choice and priorities. They prove to be better managers, more committed workers, better human beings and more creative as team players. The involved father or husband can understand and respect the presence of female in the workplace which gives rise to a holistic egalitarian work culture. As they are emotionally more flexible they tend to make a better future which is envisaged right now.

Amongst all the characteristics of the millennial professionals, one of the most evident traits is their focus on work and the urge to keep on enhancing their skill and also to have a quick access to growth path in their career ladder. They don't mind in shifting their loyalty to different organization if their expectation is not satisfied. As an employee, millennial crave for adaptive and flexible approach at workplace, they want interactive and detailed feedback system which encourages skill enhancement, they want to feel on a continuous basis that their work is being analyzed. They appreciate criticism if it is in a constructive way. Majority of the successful companies have understood the basic requirement to retain millennial. They need to focus on the organizational culture, approach and attitude in recruitment and retaining process to make the organization more appealing to generation Y.

With the increase in the competition and comparisons, the organization is looking for the evolution which has catered the need of the employees beyond the salary and infrastructure. They have gone beyond the conventional way of grooming and retaining employees. With the reference of 3 H theory, the organization has approached the employees with the philanthropic attitude. They play an important strategic role in the professional lives of their employees. They focus on the micro requirements of the employees leading to the understanding the macro view of organization, making important changes in the organization policies and decisions. They strive maximum to dilute various boundaries of diversities and appreciate all the changes in their workforce. Many organization work towards increasing the parameters of the diversity and convert them into their strengths.

Intense competition across globe can lead to various necessary evolutions in the management policies and practices. However there is strong evidence in research that the policies and practices are influenced by *culture bound factors* like society and organization and *culture free variables* like size, life cycle, age and nature of the organization. The influence of the factors vary region wise and uniformity across nation is found to be weak. There were plenty of proposals which attempted to create a framework with national setting (Brewster 1995, Budhwar 1999, Schuler et al. 1993, Sparrow and Hiltrop 1997). Even though after the presence of such a framework the mutual consensus for the related contingent factors and organizational variables which strongly affect HRM policies and practices, cross national model were not implemented.

With the evolution of Human resource management from Welfare Officer to Human Capital Facilitator, the HRM has shifted its orientation from being a supporting function to being a strategic partner. The HRM is now not only responsible to attract and retain the best talent in the market but it has increased its horizon by looking after the socio-psychological requirements of the employees.

These developments, however don't influence the work environment specifically, be that as it may it affects the path in which we work. The working environment today, is not quite recently the physical infrastructure and the amenities provided by the organization; it is more about how cheerful are the employees working at the organization, and what sort of chances are accessible for them, which can encourage both their personal and professional life dimensions.

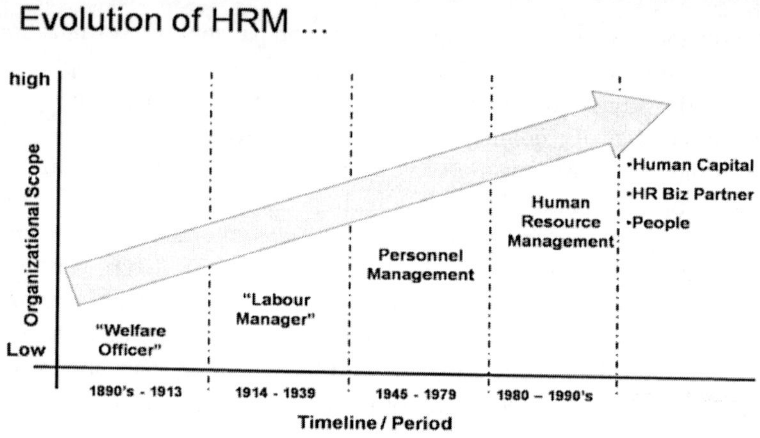

Source: hrdictionary.files.wordpress.com, 2012.

With this amendment in the viewpoint towards the latest strategic partner, the part that the Human Resource Professionals had played so far has additionally experienced considerable changes. Presently they are assuming a more vital part towards the advancement of the association by having an unmistakable comprehension of the full scale perspective of the association and consequently having the capacity to take an interest and contribute towards the real strategies and choices. They are assuming the part of progress operators and are adequately supporting the workers to accomplish their objectives. Truth to be told their part has turned out to be extremely adaptable since the working environment decent variety has additionally turned out to be so common. They are the champion of work esteems, morals and convictions and enable the association to keep up its way of life, which is the foundation of each association.

The latest workplace practices which have been creating difference in the professional and personal life of employees across the globe are as follows:

1. Ever Increasing Importance of Time Rather than Money at the Workplace

The new generation is now susceptible in calculating the maximum returns from all the activities around them. They are smart enough to understand with the ever increasing pace of competition and conflict the skill enhancement process should never face stagnation. They many times fail to substitute the monetary or financial assets as their motivational anchor in their professional life. They are very serious about their overall growth and they will just not accept any hurdle in the pace. With the raised ratio of the expectations of an employee and employee hold from each other in today's age as compared to the previous generation, the work dynamics has also changed their horizon. As a business manager they expect elite and efficiency; and as an employee they expect more extensive social networking for themselves and their wards. The later do not just expect money related help however additionally respect their organization to give chances to build up their abilities, enable them to end up noticeably more stable actually, give them sufficient chances to development, so they can exceed expectations in life, develop and raise their societal position, furnish them with an environment which widens their group of society.

2. Culture of Trust

With the growing distractions at work, it usually becomes very difficult for the management to retain an effective and committed workforce. It has been observed that the conflict arising in majority cases are based on the issues like trust. With the increase in diversities of ideas, mindset and generation, the climate of trust becomes very mandatory. A culture of trust wherein all the dynamics are considered is displayed as to be matured and thoughtful.

In a recent report, Steingerdur Ólafsdottir investigated an Iceland programming counseling organization that had been acknowledged by workers as being exceptionally focusing on adjusting work, group, family, and self-improvement needs within this association, Ólafsdottir recognized a few things that managers and top management did to make this culture more effective:

- They made themselves accessible to the employees

- They allow their employees to be vocal whenever they experienced difficulties
- They exhibited trust among their workers
- They gave their representatives constructive criticism on their work

3. Open Door Policy

One of the essential elements of an effective workplace is to provide a platform wherein the employees feel the freedom to discuss about their issues. They can look forward to create a solution through the discussion with the management. With the existence of more dispersed and diverse workforce, the task to create an open door policy for communication becomes essential and important. Again with the help of technology and virtual existence of organization, the communication gap tends to cease and also the flexibility in transfer of ideas and discussion increases.

In today's era there is a plethora of means of communication which is considered to be effective in various situations. With the existence of concepts like work at home and virtual organization, the physical interaction amongst the manager and employees becomes difficult. But then again there are young mangers of generation Y who are becoming more flexible and capable of utilizing all the available sources of communication.

4. Get Rid of Generalized Policy

The generation Y is the most impatient, multi talented, optimistic, immediate, confident and unapologetic workforce of management. They on many occasions don't feel the compatibility with the existing policies running across the management. Many of the so called work life balance policies like casual Fridays, managing the diversity doesn't touch the nub of their problems in work life balancing. Flexibility in the workplace is the wave of the future. There are several time-honored benefits to this growing trend. Rather if employees are given independence in choosing how to deliver results and strike better work-life balance, it could end up being an extraordinary device to support reliability towards the business. Many organization works on the concept of rigid rules and regulation which was a beneficial tool for many segments of workforce.

The below mentioned table showcase the difference between the reality and expectation of generation Y towards the policies.

Dynamics of Organization	How Millennial would Like to Work	How Most of the Organization Actually Work
Fundamental design	Collaborative and loose like a spider web; connected across all designations	Pyramidal structure hierarchy
Source of authority	Based on field expertise and trust irrespective of tenure and designation	Designation
Source of Dispersion of Information	Any latest and updated trustworthy networking technology	Established networking channels
Pace and frequency of feedback		Hierarchy and tenure based dispersion of information
	Throughout the process and without editing the critical details	Once or twice in a year
Communication	Lateral co ordination with all the team members throughout the process	As per the rules
Career Path	On the basis of learning curve, challenges faced and contribution to the growth of the team	Subjective
Priority	A perfect balance of personal and professional	Work
Networking within your organization	Inclusive of all social and personal circle, mentors and colleagues	Only your job connects you with your company

Source: Supriya Pal, "Identifying the relationship between Work Life Balance, Organizational Policy and Organizational Stress of Millennial Male Employees in Private sector of Gujarat- An Empirical Study", PhD thesis, 2017, unpublished.

5. Matching the Profile and Skill set Available in Market

Adequate and updated skill set is the utmost desired asset of an individual and for the organization. It is no wonder that the dominating reason for the increasing level of job dissatisfaction is unemployment and underemployment. Many organizations try the traditional matching skill approach but the expected return out of the logic is not always released. There is a shift in the organization's orientation towards employees from "work first" concept to "learn first". However the employers are facing lack of qualified and required candidates. Many constraints arises like inability to pay competitive pay, flexible and attractive work amenities, poor working conditions, rigid corporate rules and regulation, ineffective HR framework and blurred career opportunities. As a result, there are much evident dearth in terms of competitive high performers, promoting talent and training process.

6. Shadowing in the Entry Phase of the Career

As we understand in Hershey- Blanchard situational leadership theory (SLT) wherein the management needs to show directing leadership wherein there is a one way interaction from the leader to follower as in the initial phase there is less competence and high in commitment. This stands true in entry phase of the employees wherein the theoretically fresh amateur students enter into the professional fields as young professionals with low competence and high level of commitment. In the initial phase they need a leader/mentor who can display directing style of leadership. In directing type of leadership, there is low supporting and high directive behavior which is considered ideal as in this phase they need to be directed towards their goals and their path to achieve that with the required instructions. The leaders will showcase one way communicating approach which will not encourage the feedback. This particular process is known as shadowing. Job shadowing involves working or rather helping him or her to learn new aspects related to the job, organization, certain behaviors or competencies. Organizations have been using this as an effective tool for learning

7. Spiritual Health in the Workplace

American Psychological Association has stated that a spiritually healthy place of work promotes good health and well being for the employees and enhances organizational performance and productivity. The workplace practices that are generally considered as important are broadly classified into five types, as stated ahead:

- Measures on increasing employee engagement or involvement,
- Striking a correct work-life balance for them,
- Promoting the growth and development of the employee,
- Ensuring the employee has a sound mental and physical health and the work surroundings are safe, and
- The employee is motivated enough by various "recognition programs" over and above the hygiene factors. It is important to note that, organizations today are progressively focusing on both the physical and mental health of their employees.

Various wellness programs for employees are being run by their work organization. They are no longer viewed as an extravagance but a "must have" in every organization. As the importance of these initiatives continues to grow, organizations are not only focusing on fitness centers as a means to get their employees healthier but also lay value to short programs encouraging small recreation and entertainment breaks for the employees; promote and spread awareness about spirituality health of the employees that they can do at their desks; focus on meditation, mindfulness, and non-traditional "well-being" interventions. In order to measure the efficacy of such programs, organizations need to measure these three things:

- How much they are able to save on the health care expenses,
- The percentage by which the rate of absenteeism goes down and
- By what percentage does the output increase, after running such programs?

Till some decades back, organizations were more focused on the "ROI" and any expense on employees was seen as a cost to the company however in the modern era, any such form of spending on the employees is seen as a "VOI" (Value on Investment) which measures the soft aspects or the intangible benefits, unlike ROI that is seen as a measure of the hard or tangible benefits.

8. Increased Utilization of Intangible Way of Positive Reinforcement

Last two to three decades have witnessed a lot of changes in workplace. Loyalty is no longer prevalent. Competition has become intense, organizations have changed, and they are reducing their costs to become more productive, resort to frequent layoffs to become leaner. All this slowly ended the trend of decades of service with the same organization. During the downturn of the economy high unemployment was witnessed. As the upswing returns, the skilled employees stand to get the benefit. With the limited talent pool, they are demanding more, and are increasingly having a say in how the work is assigned to them, how should they be assessed and rewarded for their performance. Today, it's the employee, who is defining the workplace and not the employer; their liking, and inclinations are being accounted for in designing the workplace of the future. Employee engagement is given due importance and the rewards and recognition programs are helping the employer in the same. It reinforces positive behavior which assists the firms in the achievement of its goals. A motivated workforce certainly will impact the bottom line positively. The importance of non monetary rewards has increased multifold, rewards need not be expensive and in cash. A pat on the back, a certificate, a trophy, or a hall full of the audience cheering you on your achievements, all works wonders.

9. Utilizing the Social Media and Networking for Socialization

Social Networking has become a vital part of everyone's life today.

There are hundreds of millions of personal users on sites like Twitter, Facebook, LinkedIn; it has also become an important means of doing business with growing number of firms that sell their things through these mediums. It's noteworthy that across the world, HR professionals are occupied in developing policies for the usage of these websites at the work place. HR professionals and their organizations are increasingly using social networking sites to scan candidates before they are invited for an interview and this trend up picked up first in the United States, followed by rest of the world. According to a SHRM survey in November 2009, only 3 per cent of the organizations included this practice into their recruitment process by the end of 2008. It also stated that 86percent of HR professionals felt that they would not prefer hiring a candidate whose social networking profile showed indicated "unprofessional behavior". The social networking media and the increased prevalence of blogosphere are helping the prospective candidates to learn more about employers before they attend an interview. Chat boards, are available both to consumers and job seekers which serve to clarify a lot of information about the organizations. There is a new trend to hire "social media managers" to help organizations in find their way more effectively through the internet way.

10. Increasing the Usage of Technology in Daily Activities

In an economy which is progressively more global in nature, technological advancement is the central driving force for the same. Usage of technology is increasingly eliminating the geographic barriers. For an HR professional, recruitment process has gained the advantage with alternatives like video interviews and video conferences which provides the hiring experts the choice to track the prospective job candidates from any part of the world. Usage of Internet to obtain education, to learn more for professional development and various distance learning programs have also become very rampant mostly for firms which have multiple domestic and/or international locations. Special budget allocation is kept towards the development of search engine optimization (SEO), so that pertinent information is readily available when a job seeker conducts an online search.

"Digital divide" is a phrase referring to the gap between the 'heavily wired urban' and the 'wireless rural' regions that are deficient in high-speed Internet access. A gap is also been observed at the workplace between tech-minded workers and their less technologically literate co-workers. Generation Y is the first generation to grow up with computer/internet access readily available at all times. In comparison to them the other generations like Boomers, who have been in the workforce since long have recently learned the basics of the online world. Employers are encouraging workers of all ages to embrace technology on the job.

11. Bridging the Barrier between All the Generation (Generation Y, Generation X and Baby Boomers)

The key to have an effective workforce is to have the capacity to viably address and analyze the uniqueness in qualities and desires of each generation. The organization should at the same time take care not to burden the elder generation, even unintentionally, or take heavy retention issues.

Here are a Few Researched Techniques to Do that:

- Send your manager to work station so they can figure out how to perceive generational contrasts and compatibility factors. It's crucial that mangers adapt the change instead of attempting to change the staff.
- Encourage training between various matured and experienced employees to support more cross-generational collaboration. Generation Y employees should figure out how to look for the experience and insight offered by senior workers. Generation X and Baby Boomer workers should figure out how to be interested in the new viewpoints offered by Generation Y workers.
- Offer distinctive working choices like working from home and working offsite. Concentrate on the outcomes workers deliver as opposed to on how they complete it. This will give employees some adaptability on how they need to function and put everyone, paying little attention to where they are investing the majority of their energy working, on a similar scale to quantify achievement. Working from home can likewise urge Boomers nearing retirement to remain on staff longer since the alternative enables them to 'equip down' their workloads.
- Oblige diverse learning styles. Baby boomers may support more customary and conventional way of preparing strategies like Power Point presentations and handbooks, while generation Y may float towards more intuitive, innovation based types of learning.
- Keep workers occupied. Give focused and customized training that can keep all employees committed to the organization's progress. Fuel the exclusive standards of aspiring Millennials

with extraordinary assignments that are outside of their sets of expectations. Consider putting them on a team to tackle an issue or building up a network that can create camaraderie for the organization.

- Open up the workplace. Millennial by and large don't function effectively under rigid administration structure. They lean toward open collaboration that enables employees to share data for everyone.
- Adopt effective meeting policy. Specialists say Millennials and Gen Xers loathe the custom of standard gatherings, particularly when there's nothing to examine. Constrain gatherings to when there's a genuine need.
- Make customized rewards and recognition programs. Indeed, even basic signals like a gesture of congratulations or positive email congrats can help support profitability with Gen Xers. Boomers may look for status so may react best to an all inclusive update that reports that they are meeting or surpassing their objectives. Millennial may look for approval and endorsement that will enhance their skill set and career. To this end, Millennials may likewise favor more regular feedback sessions.
- Satisfy individual employee needs. Each cohort will be in various phases of life and may require that adaptability and flexibility from the organization to give them the opportunity to deal with their crisis. Be that as it may, keep up equality so each generation doesn't feel alienated. Boomers who are considering retirement, for instance, might need to cut the quantity of hours they work in return for lessened pay. Gen Xers who need to leave work ahead of schedule to go to a parent/teacher meeting can agree to compensate the work at another schedule. Millennial might want to pursue another degree part time and extend the same educational opportunities to other employees.
- Give all employees a voice. Irrespective of age and hierarchy, give all employees a platform in which they can display thoughts, concerns and grievances. Management ought to encourage open correspondence all through the workplace and put aside time to give fair feedback.

Summary

With all the recent trends emerging at the workplace, employers globally have realized the importance of attracting and retaining employees, and also understood that practices and offerings that were effective in the labor market till some years ago may no longer be equally effective, in the current times. Hence Employers have to be:

1. More receptive to the needs of employees, in a diverse pool of people working together, which is a big challenge since as diverse the group, more varied the needs.
2. Create a workplace with alternative work practices like flexible working hours, work from home, parental leave, and focus on performance rather than work hours.
3. Be more supportive and understand and help their employees strike a better balance between their personal and professional lives.
4. Strike backward integration with the educational institutes and expand and develop education programs using new technologies so that a right pipeline is created which has the right managerial and technical skills for the future.
5. Need to be ready with their contingency plans and the disaster management policies well chalked out ,since working in a globally connected world with the aid of technology , the threat of data loss or theft, is always there .Employees have to be well trained on IT security and data protection policies ,in order to reduce the risk.
6. Provide the right sources and channels of information to the employees, allowing them the access to various blogs, online resources and professionals from the industry, so that employees are constantly updated on the happenings and developments in the Industry and across the globe.
7. Train and inform employees about the significance of intellectual property and on the type of information which should be shared and what should be protected.

Bibliography

1. M.H. Becker, L. A. Maiman, "Sociobehavioral determinants of compliance with health and medical care recommendations", *Medical Care*, 1975, pp. 10-24.
2. G.J. Blau, K.B. Boal, "Conceptualizing how job involvement and organizational commitment affect turnover and absenteeism", *Academy of Management Review*, 1987, pp. 288-300.
3. C. Brewster, "Towards a 'European' model of human resource management", *Journal of International Business Studies*, 1995, pp. 1-21.

4. K. Gerson, *No Man's Land: Men's Changing Commitments to Family and Work*, Basic Books, 1994.
5. E. Gold, et al., "Mindfulness-based stress reduction (MBSR) for primary school teachers", *Journal of Child and Family Studies*, vol. 19, no. 2, 2010, pp. 184-189.
6. J.C. Hood, *Men, Work, and Family*, Sage Publications, 1993.
7. N. Khatri, P. Budhwar, C. T. Fern, *Employee Turnover: Bad Attitude or Poor Management*, Singapore: Nanyang Technological University, 1999.
8. M. Kishwar, "Gandhi on women", *Economic and Political Weekly*, 1985, pp. 1691-1702.
9. Madhu Kishwar, Vanita Ruth, "Can Police Reform Husbands?", *Manushi*, no. 31, 1985.
10. L. Levner, "The Three-career Family", in P. Papp (ed.), *Couples on the Fault Line: New Directions for Therapists*, 2000, pp. 29-47.
11. J. Mincer, "Schooling, Experience, and Earnings", *Human Behavior & Social Institutions*, no. 2, 1974.
12. J. Rawlins, et al., "The Elderly in Trinidad: Health, social and economic status and issues of loneliness", *West Indian Medical Journal*, vol. 57, no. 6, 2008, pp. 589595.
13. R.S. Schuler, P. J. Dowling, H. De Cieri, "An integrative framework of strategic international human resource management", *Journal of management*, vol. 19, no. 2, 1993, pp. 419-459.
14. U. Sharma, *Women, work and property in North-West India*, London: Tavistock Publications, 1980.
15. P.R. Sparrow, J.M. Hiltrop, "Redefining the field of European human resource management: A battle between national mindsets and forces of business transition?", *Human Resource Management (1986-1998)*, vol. 36, no. 2, 1997, p. 201.
16. J. Sturges, et al., "A longitudinal study of the relationship between career management and organizational commitment among graduates in the first ten years at work", *Journal of Organizational Behavior*, vol. 23, no. 6, 2002, pp. 731-748.
17. J.P. Wanous, "Effects of a realistic job preview on job acceptance, job attitudes, and job survival", *Journal of applied psychology*, vol. 58, no. 3, 1973, p. 327.

Economic Veracity

Chapter - 7

Post Demonetization Portfolio Basket: An Outlook to Financial Planning and Portfolio Management for a Retail Investor

— *Swati Gupta*

Introduction

Financial planning is a sequential process of creating and developing a roadmap for one's financial security and wellbeing. It is a blue print of where one can invest based on one's personal goals, available finances, risk appetite and return expectations. The output of the Financial Plan would be achieving one's life goals keeping in consideration the macro and micro economic factors working on the investment avenues, the tenure, the risk and the real return from the portfolio.

An individual can gain the following through wise financial planning- Long term financial goals need security from the point of view of investing in insurance, saving tax by investing in tax savers, increasing networth, encouraging guilt-free spending, creation of wealth and improving the standard of living.[1]

Hence, right at the start one needs to chart out his life goals. The question is when to start, and the answer is no time is the right time and any time is the right time. As soon as that is sorted, one needs to sit and work on making his financial plan.

Process of Financial Planning

To make the most of financial planning, one should preferably start early. It is not only how much one invests but also when does he do so. So even if a person starts with less funds, instead of waiting for the time that he can afford to save more for investment, he should start right away with whatever less amount he has. Due to the multiplier effect, the funds will grow much faster. Once the life goals are in place, the next step is to identify one's current financial status, followed by prioritising goals in terms of timeline and quantifying them, identifying the gap of where the investor stands today and where he wants to reach, prepare the Financial Plan based on risk and return appetite and his goals timeline and finally implement his plan to be reviewed periodically.

Basis for Financial Planning

The basis for financial planning remains the same in any economic situation, hence the steps written below are generic in nature and can be applied at all times by a new investor. One needs to understand that macro-economic factors such as inflation, interest rates, tax slabs and policy changes affect the financial environment and would be inherent in each of the basis for financial planning. The basis for Financial Planning has been explained through an example of an early investor, Myra.

(a) ***Personal Goals***

Myra, a 30-year-old IT professional working in one of the top IT companies in India, drawing a salary of Rs 75,000 (CTC) per month, single, only child to affluent parents, living in her own 2 bedroom flat Pune, has never invested. She had never thought of investing until a colleague of hers introduced her to Mutual Funds and ULIPs mainly for tax saving purpose, one year post her joining work and her first year of filing tax returns. She diligently invested in tax saving mutual funds for few years after that, but that was it. Her objective then was just to invest only that much amount to save tax based on her tax slab. With no liability and a good salary with her own home, Myra thought all was smooth in life and there was no need to invest. Then in an accident, she lost her parents, and inherited their property and her father's philanthropic initiative that he had built from the money he had earned. She didn't quite understand if the property was an asset or a liability since most of the asset was in shares and real estate, and of course the orphanage. It was her father's dream to build another orphanage and an old age home, but that remained a dream. Being her father's dearest Myra felt a need to fulfill his dreams. That was when a new Myra was born- Her goals had changed, from being the carefree girl with no worries and responsibilities, she moved to being someone who pursued a dream.

Myra determined to uphold her father's interest in the share market and the real estate market, started passively, initially and then actively involving herself in investing. She always remembered her father's words on never to keep the money idle, investing it and making it grow. She did the same and whatever gains she made from investing, she sent it to the orphanage that her father had set up. She started saving money and investing it wisely to make it grow, and then came the day when she had enough funds to fulfil her father's dream of another orphanage. With the same enthusiasm, she went on to setting the Old age home her father had thought of. All in a period of 8 years. By then goals kept improvising and she kept moving, making changes, investing, re investing and growing according to them. The start point of any investment is setting of personal goals and then aligning your income, savings to the goals. The first set of goals provide an outline to what kind of investment pattern and timing should one have to achieve those set of goals. Once a time line is planned, the investment process gets a lot streamlined, making it structured and controlled.

(b) ***Risk Appetite***

In Myra's case, her risk appetite was between medium and high, since her cash inflows from salary was consistent and risk less; her spending planned and only from her salary and since she had her own house. The funds that she played around for investment was the one that she had inherited and also the existing assets in the form of shares and real estate left by her parents. Hence the risk that she took was between medium and high, balancing between various investment avenues having different risk and return profiles. As an investor one needs to carefully analyse his current financial status and should keep some of his assets risk free and out of investment. There should be an amount that he can decide for investment and should create a portfolio with a risk-return portfolio based on his current profile and his appetite for risk and subsequently return.

(c) ***Return Expectation***

The return expectation and the risk appetite of an investor is closely related. If the return expectation is high then subsequently the risk to be taken would also be high. According to Investopedia, the principle of risk return trade-off is that expected return increases with an increase in risk. Low risk is associated with low returns, whereas high risk is associated with high returns.

Money can give higher profits only if an investor is willing to accept higher probability of making losses, in other words taking higher risk will lead to making higher profits, popularly termed as the risk and return trade-off.[2]

The Linkage: Personal Goals, Investment Space and the Economy

Once the investor charts out his Personal Goals, Risk Appetite, Return Expectation and maps all off them to a timeline, his next step would be to select the right investment avenues basis the amount of funds he wants to invest.

There are several investment options or avenues through which an investor can invest his money and hence create capital and increase his wealth. Any investment has a certain amount of risk associated with it so though there is risk of losing one's hard earned money in investments due to wrong decisions of investment avenues and timing of investment, if the investment planning is done wisely and timely, the potential to increase wealth is higher than if one does not invest. Long-term investments are one of the best ways to earn good returns with relatively lesser risk of losing money.[3]

There are many options through which you can invest and increase your wealth. Though there is risk of losing your hard earned money in investments, but if done wisely, the potential to gain money is higher than if you never invest. Long-term investments are best way to earn good returns with minimum risk of losing your money.

The Indian Financial Market offers a number of Products for investment. From the humble Fixed deposit to varied levels of risk bearing financial products such as Mutual Funds, Debt Funds, Equity, Derivatives, Hybrid Funds. Investment opportunities in the traditional Real Estate Market, Jewellery have never lost their charm either. So, while there are ample avenues for an investor to explore, he should do so with caution and careful planning.

The investor not only needs to do a personal financial and goal profiling, he should also understand the Financial Markets, the economy and the factors that impact the economy currently and in future, and thus his investments and their risk return profile. Inflation rates, Interest rates, drives such as Demonetization, implementation of policies such as GST, changes in monetary policies, change in Government, International policy changes- all affect the economy, industries in it, every corporate entity and every individual, investor or not. But if you are an investor, it affects you more than your non- investor counterpart since you are associated with more entities than he is. For instance, if you are an investor in shares, then you are associated to a number of companies where you have invested, which is not the case with a non-investor.

So, while knowing yourself is important before taking a step into investing, knowing the market and the economy is equally important. An active investor who analyses the market and the factors affecting the economy does better in creating wealth out of his investments.

Demonetization 2016 and the Investment Space

Every year, events take place that affect the investment pattern and quantum of the investors across the Financial Markets. One of the significant events that will mark the year 2016 will be demonetization and its impact. For investors in the Indian financial market, the period post November 2016 was a mixed bag of emotions and opportunities to explore.

The Indian economy saw one of the biggest reforms in the month of November 2016, when Prime Minister Shri Narendra Modi announced the Demonetization drive ceasing Rs 500 and Rs. 1000 notes as a part of legal tender in India, in order to curb black money and corruption in the country.

The Indian capital market saw a sharp correction in November 2016 after demonetization coupled with the results of the US presidential elections. While the long-term effects of demonetization are expected to be promising, the short-term effects were negative mainly on account of reduced spending. The sectors that were cash dependent were hit the most. The real estate and the Jewellery segment were the ones that were affected the most since both the sectors were cash driven as was the unorganised sector according to Angel Broking in a research report[4].

Corporate earnings are likely to show negative impact of demonetization in the financial year 2017. However, from FY 2018, with a likely increase in consumption and ease in liquidity, the companies are expected to show better results.

Post Demonetization: What can be a Part of an Investor's Portfolio and Why?

(a) *Equity/Equity Mutual Funds*

The equities market began on a promising note in 2016 and ended in a disappointing note (Refer Table 1).

Table 1 - Performance of Equities in 2016

Nifty	3.22%
BSE 200	3.95%
Large Cap Funds	4.50%
Multi Cap Funds	5.00%
Small Cap Funds	6.40%

Source: Zaidi, Babar, 10 smart money moves to improve your finances in 2017, *Economic Times*, 02 January 2017.

With the Nifty moving over by 18% from the 7738 mark as on 31st March 2016 to 9173 on 30th March 2017, analysts see it moving towards the 10000 mark in the next 12 months or so. While indices such as Metal, PSU Banks, Small cap, Media, Realty, Energy Mid cap, Banking, Auto, Infra and FMCG did well, indices such as Pharma and IT gave negative returns mainly on account of strong Dollar and Regulatory impediments (Refer Table 2).

Table 2 - Nifty Indices

Index Name	GY 17% Change
NIFTY METAL	61%
NIFTY PSU BANK	42%
NIFTY SMALLCAP 100	41%
NIFTY PSE	40%
NIFTY MEDIA	36%
NIFTY REALITY	35%
NIFTY ENERGY	35%
NIFTY MIDCAP 100	34%
NIFTY BANK	33%
NIFTY AUTO	22%
NIFTY INFRA	21%
NIFTY FMCG	20%
NIFTY 50	18%
BSE SENSEX	17%
NIFTY IT	-5%
NIFTY PHARMA	-5%

Source: Kshitij Anand, "Forget Sensex or Nifty, these top ten sectors likely to sizzle hot in FY18", *Money Control.*

Citing that there is ample liquidity with local and FIIs, VK Sharma, Head, Private Client Group, HDFC Securities told Moneycontrol.com that they expect a 20% Earnings CAGR in the next 3 years as compared to the earnings growth in the last 4 years.[5] The equity market is expected to remain resilient in the FY 2018 despite the fact that the valuations are trading higher than the long-term averages. The impact of Demonetization and GST would be experienced in the FY 2018. These reforms will lead to a shift from an informal to a formal economy with the backdrop of transparent system, and efficient utilization of resources.[6]

The markets are expected to remain flat in the first two quarters and improve from the 3rd quarter, so it would be a good time to accumulate and invest in stocks at a low price. It is also advisable to start investing in SIP.[7] For Mutual Fund Investors in the equity market, SIP is a good way as irrespective of the market noise, the money gets invested on a predetermined date, so the principle of rupee cost averaging and risk diversification comes into picture. The market rally has been positive coupled with the GST Rollout, stable government, good monsoons, indices touching new highs, the equity markets are expected to give better returns.[8]

According to the Association of Mutual Funds in India (AMFI) data the monthly inflow though SIPs in April 2017 was Rs 4,269 crores as compared to Rs 980 crores per month in 2012, which is a growth of around 435%. The SIPs allow retail investors make regular small amount investments that go into equities instead of making lump sum investments at various points in time which may or may not be the right time due to market anomalies. Post-demonetisation, investing through SIPs appeals more to the risk-averse households across India, than holding cash in hand and not investing or investing in assets like gold and real estate.[9]

After demonetization, investors who do not want to take a risk in a complete equity-oriented fund, could opt for balanced funds as such funds give an exposure of debt and equity in the 50:50 ratio which hence gives safety under volatile condition alongside will help growing their investment amount.[10]

Keeping this in perspective, an investor should certainly have part of his portfolio in the equity market. With a positive expectation on the performance of the equity markets, an investor can look into investing in the upcoming IPOs, in the secondary market and in Equity Mutual Funds through the mode of SIPs.

(b) *Debt/ Bonds/Debt Mutual Funds*

As compared to the equity market, investors in the debt market saw better performance in the year 2016 The performance of the Debt market is shown in Table 3, while the effect of demonetisation on the yields and the Returns from the Debt Categories between the day of announcement of Demonetization to a week from then, are depicted in Chart 1 and Chart 2.

Table 3 - Performance of Debt in 2016

Fixed Deposits	8-8.50%
Long Term Debt Funds	15.6%
Medium Term Debt Funds	11.8%
Short Term Debt Funds	9.8%
PPF	8-8.75%

Source: Babar Zaidi, "10 smart money moves to improve your finances in 2017", *Economic Times*, 02 January 2017.

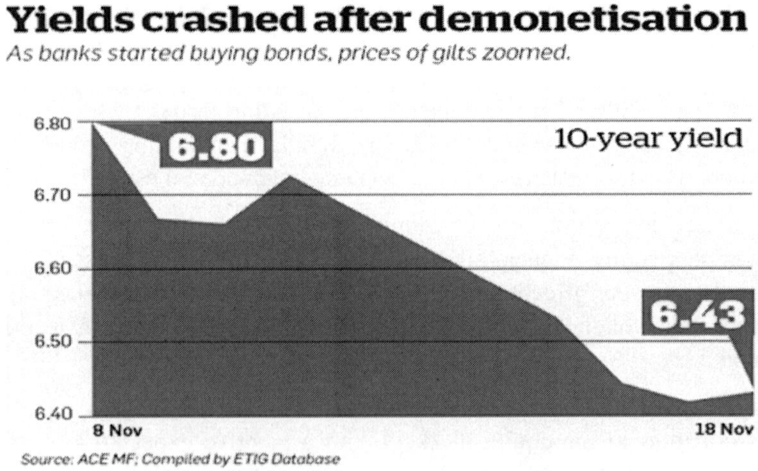

Chart 1- Yields Crashed after Demonetisation

Debt funds shot up as bonds rallied

Returns from debt fund categories between 8 and 17 November.

Category	Sub-category	Average return (%)
Gilt	Long Term	2.79
Gilt	Medium Term	1.88
Gilt	Short Term	1.15
Income	Long Term	1.88
Income	Medium Term	1.42
Income	Short Term	1.08
Income	Ultra Short Term Plan	0.51
Liquid		0.16

Source: Narendra Nathan, "What should debt fund investors do post demonetisation?", *Economic Times*, 21 November 2016.

Chart 2 - Debt Funds Shot up as Bonds Rallied

The post demonetization situation is such that with an increase in the bond prices in a falling interest market, Debt Funds are expected to gain. Investors who are currently invested in debt funds are advised to remain invested.[11] Debt investors are being advised to take some accrual based duration funds. Experts are advising investors not to get into liquid funds and take some accrual based duration funds.

Experts are of the view that the downward trend of yield may continue in the short term, so aggressive fixed income investors could invest in dynamic bond funds, income funds and gilt funds, which will benefit from falling rates as Bond prices and yields move in opposite direction.[12] The outlook for investing in Debt Funds in 2017 is that short term funds earning from accruals will do well and the interest rates on the small savings are expected to reduce further.[13]

One could also look at investing in short term Debt funds which usually deliver upto 7-8% returns a year. The benefit of the same vis a vis an investment in Fixed Deposit is that the income from Mutual funds is treated as capital gains and is taxed at a lower rate if held for a minimum of three years. Also, it is a lot more flexible from the point of withdrawing small amounts in between. According to Vidya Bala, Head of Mutual Fund Research, FUNDSINDIA, liquid funds have an advantage in terms of redemption facility, over traditional savings avenue, so people who have large bank balances should use them.[14] Debt Mutual Fund carry more flexibility and offer paperless investment and withdrawal at one day's notice.

Another attractive investment avenue post demonetization is the PPF (Public Provident Fund) and EPF (Employee Provident Fund). According to Suresh Sadagopan, Founder Ladder7 Financial Services, the PF interest rate is a market anomaly which is improbable to go away and unlike the bank deposit rates, will not be cut beyond a certain point.[15]

(c) *Real Estate*

The Real Estate Sector in India witnessed a series of radical and transformational reforms right from Demonetisation, Real Estate Regulator Bill (RERA), FDI relaxations, GST, Benami Transactions (Prohibition) Amendment Act to Change in Accounting standards IFRS, all the reforms coming one after the other in quick succession. The year 2017 will see the Indian real estate sector to be a lot more transparent, credible and attractive. Home/ Property ownership has always be an ambition and an investment objective hence with the implementation of these reforms the real estate industry is expected to have positive implications for the home buyers.[16]

The Real Estate Sector is one of the sectors that has been hit severely by Demonetization. The decline in demand post Demonetization has led to sellers reduce their property price, many have gone into a wait mode expecting the prices to rise after the impact of Demonetization reduces.[17] This maybe the right time to purchase properties from Distress sellers who are looking at offloading their real estate investment. Though according to Shilpi Johri, a Certified Financial Planner, Real estate requires a very high investment so one should assess his needs before buying [18]. In the year 2017 the real estate market will go through a phase of consolidation.

The industry is expected to see increased confidence of buyers and investors, better transparency and a positive outlook by foreign investors.[19]

Having said so, the current situation of the slackening demand for property has increased the rentals in major cities. The current trend is that people are postponing property purchases and are preferring to stay on rent instead and it is expected that this trend is likely to continue for some time.[20]

Table 4 - Performance of Real Estate in 2016

Mumbai	-0.42%
Delhi/NCR	-29.30%
Bengaluru	4.25%
Hyderabad	7.90%
Pune	9.70%

Source: Babar Zaidi, "10 smart money moves to improve your finances in 2017", *Economic Times*, 02 January 2017.

According to Anshuman Magazine, CBRE Chairman, India and South East India, the year 2016 was the year of landmark decisions for the Real Estate Industry in India as the sector saw efforts by the government to bring in transparency along with boosting consumer sentiments in the sector.

He mentioned that the outlook for the year 2017 is positive. He expects steady growth, stability and revival in the market which forms basis for the positive outlook of the sector.[21]

Demonetization is expected to help the economy in the long run, the implication that it had in the short term were harsh on the residential real estate market as the volume of transaction went down drastically. While the impact on the residential real estate segment was greater, the commercial real estate market may also see an impact in the terms of shortage of supply and increase in rents of properties. The general notion is that the transaction volume in the residential sector will remain restrained. With few new projects being launched, the current over supply of properties in the market will get mitigated. The experts expect that by the end of 2017, the market will start to look up. The author concluded that having said all this she believes that despite such small hurdles as was seen in 2016 in this market, there will be a positive impact of all reforms and the real estate market will come to the point of recovery soon.[22]

Based on the available literature on Investing in Real Estate in the current situation post demonetisation and reforms in the sector, an investor in Real Estate should time his investment in properties well so that he can maximise his returns in future.

(d) *Gold-Physical/Bonds and ETFs*

On the eve of Demonetization, after an initial gold buying rush the prices of precious metals went up to a 3-year high, after which the prices started moving downward. As per Prathamesh Mallya, senior research Analyst - commodities & currencies, Angel Broking Gold is likely to see demand from those who would want to invest in safe options. He added that in the long run, demand for gold will rebound and would benefit from the decision of the Government.[23]

Table 5 - Performance of Gold in 2016

Physical	9.20%
Gold ETFs	11.00%
Gold Funds	9.00%
Global Prices	7.5%

Source: Babar Zaidi, "10 smart money moves to improve your finances in 2017", *Economic Times*, 02 January 2017.

But the question is that is gold a dead investment or not? While gold as an investment may have had poor returns, the Indian Jewellery buyer does not think so. According to a World Gold Council report, the Indian purchases for the gold jewellery in the first quarter of 2017 was over a fifth of the total worlds jewellery demand with India's demand being 92.3 tonnes and Investment demand for gold in the form of bars and coins was 31.2 tonnes. In demand for gold, India trails only China (bought 176.5 tonnes of the precious metal in Q1 of 2017). Both India and China put together account for over half of the world's gold consumption.[24] An investor could view investing in Gold purely from the point of view of investing, but since the Gold market is not expected to do well in 2017, so a better investment strategy would be to invest in Gold Bonds and ETFs rather than in the physical form, as the ETFs would be giving better returns, is cheaper, safer and easier to sell.[25]

Epilogue

This paper highlights on what could be in a retail investors Investment portfolio in the era of demonetization. Please note this article is based on available literature and is generic in nature. Investors should make sound decision based on their personal research and advice of their Financial Consultant. The investors should chart out their life goals before making a sound Financial Plan by mapping their life goals to it. A financial plan would reach its objective with constant review and corrections based on the dynamic and ever changing macro- economic factors and change in personal goals and risk-return appetite. Demonetization has curbed mindless spending and has made a lot of investment avenues affordable. One needs to take advantage of the current subdued market conditions, review his current investment status and the possible investment avenues and take a leap towards financial growth through effective portfolio management. An investor would benefit by taking advise on where, when and how much to invest from an experienced Financial Planner. Start investing early and create a portfolio that helps maximise and optimise your returns.

Notes

1. Navneet Dubey, "Why do you need financial planning? Here are 7 things to know", *The Financial Express,* 19 March 2017.
2. Investopedia, "Risk Return Trade-off"
3. "How to Invest in India", *Times of India Business,* 21 July 2017.
4. Sanjeev Sinha, "10 top investment picks from Angel Broking post demonetization", *The Financial Express,* 08 December 2016.
5. Kshitij Anand, "Forget Sensex or Nifty, these top ten sectors likely to sizzle hot in FY18", Money Control.
6. *Ibid.*
7. Babar Zaidi, "10 smart money moves to improve your finances in 2017", *Economic Times,* 02 January 2017.
8. Diksha Ramesh, "Don't miss out on the SIP wave. Here are 5 top performing funds you can start SIPs", *Business Today,* 19 May 2017.
9. Amit Kapoor, "How mutual funds have won over risk-averse Indian household", *Economic Times,* 25 July 2017.
10. Navneet Dubey, "Market remains volatile: Is it right time to invest in equity mutual funds?", *Financial Express,* 10 January 2017.
11. Avneet Kaur, "How demonetisation offers an opportunity to invest in debt funds", *Business Today,* 26 November 2016.
12. Prashant Mahesh, "Demonetisation: Time to invest in long-term bonds", *Economic Times,* 14 November 2016.
13. Zaidi, Babar, 10 smart money moves to improve your finances in 2017, *Economic Times,* 02 January 2017.
14. *Ibid.*
15. Zaidi, no. 7.
16. India Infoline Business Service, 2017 Forecast: How the year 2017 would be for Indian Real Estate Sector, 28 December 2016.
17. Zaidi, no. 7.
18. *Ibid.*
19. Vanita Akauri, "Demonetisation: Strong foundation laid for real estate but price correction could be limited", 21 December 2016.
20. Babar Zaidi, "Steer clear of investing in property", *Economic Times,* 24 July 2017.
21. PTI, "Indian real estate sector to witness $7 billion investment in 2017: CBRE", *Business Standard,* 27 April 2017.

22. Surabhi Arora, "India Infoline Business Service, 2017 Forecast: How the year 2017 would be for Indian Real Estate Sector", 28 December 2016, Moneycontrol.com23. Kumar Shankar Roy, "What happens to gold after demonetization?", *Value Research,* 30 November 2016.
24. FE Online, "Falling gold returns fail to deter Indian buyer; Gold buying in India among the highest in the world", *Financial Express,* 18 July 2017.
25. Ramganesh Iyer, "Your investment options in 2017 post-demonetisation", moneycontrol.com

Chapter - 8

Decent Work and Employment Stability in Information Technology Industry: A Case Study of India

— *Nausheen Nizami*

Introduction

In the era of globalisation, stability and security of work has become a defining feature of decent work. Work needs to be stable and secure for the economic and mental well-being of an employee. Assurance of regular flow of income in the distant future is necessary for a worker to provide his labour peacefully and productively. Anticipation of sudden job loss either due to business downturns or company's down-sizing initiatives is detrimental for the well-being of an employee. Self-assessment of job-security is considered a better indicator because it involves element of probability. Moreover workers are in a position to better evaluate their own situations at the workplace. However perceived job insecurity is different than actual job loss, and that's why subjective judgement of this indicator has some potential disadvantages. Nevertheless, since the objective of this study is to examine decent work provision to IT employees, their own self-assessment on the indicators of decent work will throw light on the current work scenario in the industry.

Rodgers (1989) notes that there are several dimensions of precariousness. First, there is the degree of certainty of continuity work. Precarious jobs are those with a short time-horizon or for which the risk of job loss is high. Second, there is an aspect of control over work – work is more insecure the less the worker (individually or collectively) controls working conditions, wages, or the pace of work. Third, protection is of crucial importance: that is, to what extent are workers protected, either by law, or through collective organisation, or through customary practice – protected against, say discrimination, unfair dismissal or unacceptable working practices, but also in the sense of social protection, notably access to social security benefits (covering health, accidents, pensions, unemployment insurance and the like).

Rodgers has rightly addressed a crucial aspect of work that often goes unnoticed and unmeasured. Certainty of continuation in work is best known to an employee. It is self-known as it directly depends on the work atmosphere, employer-employee relationships, current state of the domestic and world economy, etc. The parameters of a productive employment are thus multiple and can be suitably measured through subjective assessment of the employee itself. An attempt has been made in this study to examine the extent of precariousness (read as decency) of work in Information Technology industry of India. (Nizami & Prasad 2013)

IT industry of India is significantly different from the labour market found in agriculture and manufacturing sectors. The primary distinction is that the business model of IT industry is based on 'human capital' or 'knowledge worker' where technical knowledge is embodied in the labour itself via academic qualification as well as training. As a result of it, the IT industry can neither be termed as labour-intensive, or capital-intensive, but rather the more appropriate terminology is 'human capital intensive'. Any industry characterised predominantly by human capital is bound to have distinct labour market features and issues. From the labour market perspective, there are several factors that distinguish IT segment from other old economy commodity sectors. Firstly, IT services offer employment opportunities for white-collar, educated labour-force in a relatively clean and standardised office environment. Moreover, these activities don't need much capital investments being human capital-intensive. The level of fixed capital per employee is comparatively low (Datar 2004).

Secondly, although the IT companies provide formal employment, yet the nature of work changes from being a lifelong one to contractual or self-employed one. As a result of it, insecurity and uncertainty still prevail despite it being a highly remunerative employment of formal sector. Thirdly, another peculiar feature in this industry is the apparent blurring of industry-worker classifications and an unclear demarcation of tasks. Despite different designations, the tasks often get overlapped among themselves as a result of no rule-bound job hierarchy. Fourthly, employability in this industry is secure only by sustained hard-work and growth of skills. So life-long learning is important to generate income regardless of the fate of the employer. The industry has been witnessing high attrition rates since a decade and jobs are often changed voluntarily rather than due to retrenchment. Fifth, although IT industry has a large potential to generate employment for the educated unemployed, yet still there is a demand-supply mismatch due to poor role and regulation of the Government.

This paper examines the diverse characteristics of nature of work and labour in IT industry and makes an assessment of decent work on the basis of indicators developed by ILO. The first section of the paper investigates the characteristics of labour in the labour market of IT industry. The second section outlines the research methodology to draw inferences based on employees' perspectives about the current status of stability and security of their employment. The last section discusses the implications of the findings for policy makers and employers.

Characteristics of Labour Market in IT Industry

From the labour market perspective, there are several factors that distinguish IT segment from other old economy commodity sectors.

Firstly, IT services offer employment opportunities for white-collar, educated labour-force in a relatively clean and standardised office environment. Moreover, these activities don't need much capital investments being human capital-intensive. The level of fixed capital per employee is comparatively low. (Datar 2004)

Secondly, although the IT companies provide formal employment, yet the nature of work changes from being a lifelong one to contractual or self-employed one. As a result of it, insecurity and uncertainty still prevail despite it being a highly remunerative employment of formal sector.

Thirdly, another peculiar feature in this industry is the apparent blurring of industry-worker classifications and an unclear demarcation of tasks. Despite different designations, the tasks often get overlapped among themselves as a result of no rule-bound job hierarchy.

Fourthly, employability in this industry is secure only by sustained hard-work and growth of skills. So life-long learning is important to generate income regardless of the fate of the employer. The industry has been witnessing high attrition rates since a decade and jobs are often changed voluntarily rather than due to retrenchment.

Fifth, although IT industry has a large potential to generate employment for the educated unemployed, yet still there is a demand-supply mismatch due to poor role and regulation of the Government.

Research Methodology

Sample data has been classified into various socio-demographic categories such as- gender, marital status, age-group, background, social class and academic-professional categories such as- maximum attained qualifications and size of the IT Company.

Sampling Design

Sampling design consists of the techniques and tools used for data collection and processing. Technique of data-collection: *Questionnaire method and Interviews*

Since IT employers were reluctant to provide the names and addresses of IT employees given the nature of the study, random sampling method could not be used to select the respondents. Hence snowball sampling, which is one of the methods of non-random sampling, has been used to select target respondents for this study. It is an informal method to reach the target population (IT employees) as this study is of exploratory nature. The method ensures that the responses are free of any influence/scrutiny from the employer's side. The technique of purposive and snowball sampling has been used to contact a sample of approximately 300 IT employees in the IT industry of India out of which 272 IT employees responded to the study. Some of the selection criteria adopted was:

- IT employees having work experience of 1+ years in the industry
- Focussed group selection of IT employees only, and doesn't consist employees of ITES/BPO
- IT employees working in IT departments of large-scale companies (Both MNCs and Indian companies) were also included

Tools of Data-collection

The study is based mainly on primary data collected through a well-designed questionnaire as well as by conducting telephonic interviews. The questionnaires were mailed to the respondents by email and were also circulated by hand. A web-link to the questionnaire was also created for easy and quick access to the IT employees. The electronic media devices like email and telephonic contacts were used to gather the information from the respondents. The secondary data sources used were – Papers and articles published in journals, government publications, other survey publications, books, internet, etc.

Techniques of Data-analysis

Inductive logic has guided the data-analysis of this report. Inferences have been drawn on decent work –related issues based on collected qualitative and quantitative data from questionnaire. Classification of data on socio-demographic dimensions and academic/professional details of the employees have been depicted with the help of figures, tables and charts. The entire data has also been coded and saved in the SPSS software files for quicker analysis.

(a) *Index Construction*

Indices have been created for measuring the extent and range of decent work provision with respect to stability and security of work in the IT industry. This index has been made by coding, normalising and aggregating the responses with the help of the standard formula developed by United Nation's Development Programme (UNDP) for the construction of HDI and other indices. The Range Equalisation method has the following formula: (Actual Value – Minimum Value) / (Maximum Value – Minimum value)

Normalisation of the values ensure that the final values are in the scale of 0 to 1, with 0 being an indicator of decent work and any value above 0 shows the extent of decent work deficit.

Socio-Demographic Characteristics of the Sample

A non-random and purposive sample of 272 IT employees has been collected on the basis of questionnaire. Let us note some of the basic socio-demographic characteristics of the sample:

- **Male-Female Ratio:**

The proportion of males and female IT employees as respondents has been unequal which bears resemblance to the male-female ratio in the IT industry. 25 % of the employees were found to be female, while remaining were male employees. Efforts were made to balance the gender ratio in the study but despite prolonged pursuits only 67 female employees responded to the questionnaire. Ironically the male female ratio in IT industry is also imbalanced and is approximately 1:4. Hence the imbalance reported in the sample should not hold repercussions to the conclusions of the study.

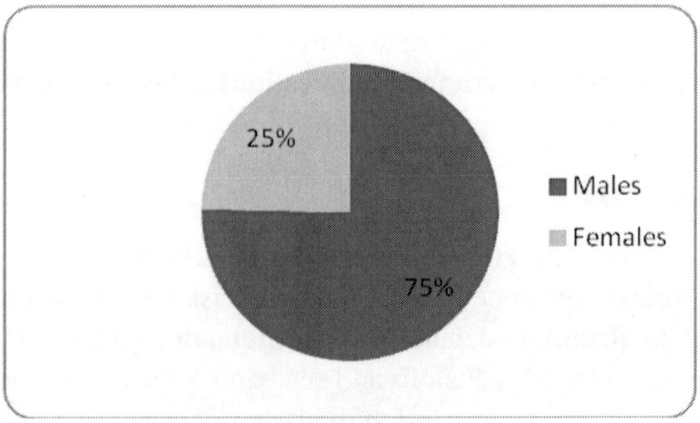

Chart – 1: Gender-ratio of the Sample.

- **Marital Status**

Marital status of an employee has an important bearing for a study on decent work because responses on few indicators like work-life balance, stability of work, etc. would be different from the married and unmarried sections of the society. As high as 62 % of the employees in the sample were found to be single/unmarried, out of which 29% were female. On the other hand, 38 % of the IT employees were found to be married.

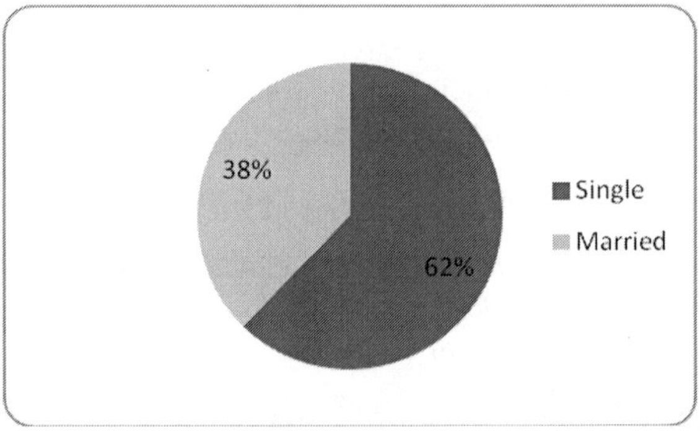

Chart – 2: Sample Distribution as per Marital Status.

- **Age-group**

A peculiar feature of India's IT Industry has been employment of a relatively younger age-group labour force. Industry-analysis on the grounds of decent work can be found to be different as the work experience of the employees increase. In this study, majority of the IT employees were found to be in the age-group of 20 to 30 years.

Particularly 39% of the employees were found to be below 25 years of age, from which 18% were females. Besides, another 39% of the sample fell in the age-group of 25-30 years. On the other hand, 16 % of the employees belonged to the age group of 30-35 years and 6% above the age of 35 years.

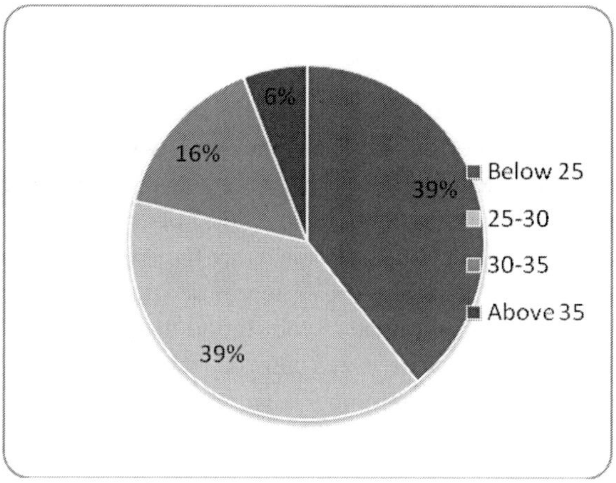

Chart – 3: Age-group-wise Sample Distribution

- **Background / Native Place**

The background/native place of a respondent shows his mobility for work. It also gives an insight that how globalisation is leading to a change in migration patterns and as IT Industry is expanding, more and more

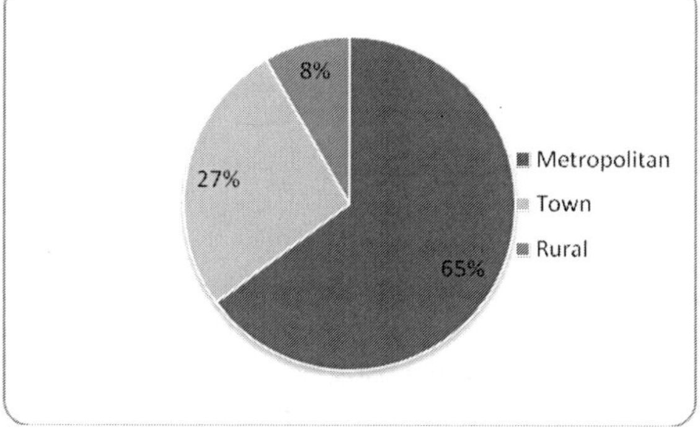

Chart – 4: Sample Distribution as per Background/ Native Place

workers with diverse backgrounds are becoming a part of it. There is a perception that generally professionals of urban backgrounds are found in IT industry. However in this study, although 65 % of the employees had a background of Metropolitan city/NCR region, yet 26.7 % had a background of township and 8.4% employees had a background of a rural area. This variation is evident given the fact that IT firms are now putting footholds in 2-tier and 3-tier cities too.

- **Social Class**

An initiative was taken in this study to assess the social class of IT employees and a staggering 96% response-rate was received for it. The prime objective was to ascertain how and whether the reserved category labour force is getting absorbed in the IT industry and what are their experiences of working in IT industry, whether they work in decent working conditions, how do they fare in the different decent work indicators, etc. As high as 79% of the respondents were found to be of General category and remaining 21% were of reserved category wherein 7% were SC, 4.6% were of ST category and remaining 9% were OBCs.

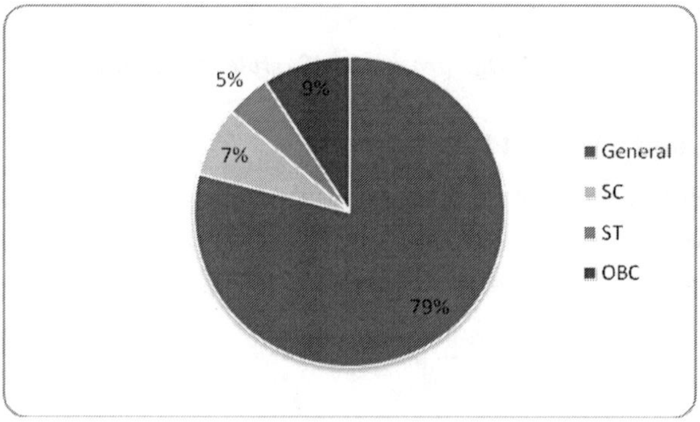

Chart 5 - Sample Distributions as per Social Class

Academic and Professional Details

- **Academic Background**

A characteristic feature of IT industry is predominance of technically skilled labour force. In this sample, 56% of IT employees were graduates and 43% of the employees were post-graduates. This is justifiable because majority of the employees get recruited in IT companies through campus placements or direct applications primarily because of their professional qualifications. The average age of an IT employee with an engineering background of entry in the workforce is 22 years. Pursuing higher education especially in research areas is typically difficult for employees already working in IT industry owing to their extremely busy schedules and reluctance to take career-breaks. That is why, employees pursuing research were found to be exceptionally low with 1% M.Phil and Ph.d degree holders.

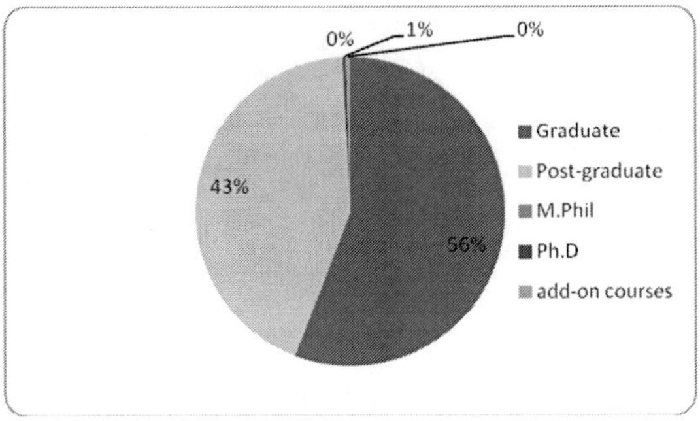

Chart 6 - Sample Distributions as per Academic Qualifications

• Company (Current Job-profiles)

The criteria for size of the firm was large if it employed more than 500 employees, medium if the size of employment was between 50 – 500 and small-scale if the size of employment was less than 50 employees. In the sample, 80% of the employees worked in a large-scale IT firm, 17% in medium-scale IT firms and only 2% in small-scale firms.

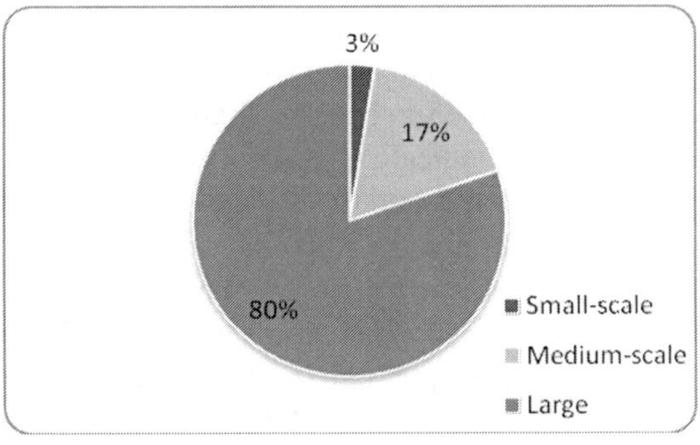

Chart – 7: Sample Distributions as Per Size of Company

• Type of Employment

The study examined whether the employees in IT industry have a contractual or regular employment in their companies. It was found that 91% of the employees had regular employment and only 9% had contractual employment. This is a positive sign and is expected from an organised industrial sector.

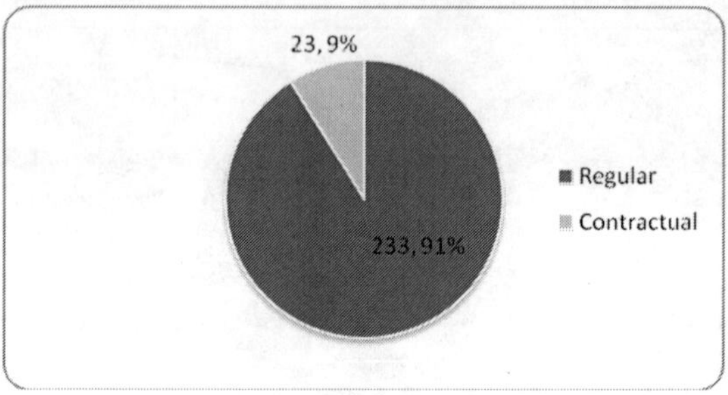

Chart – 8: Sample Distributions as per Type of Employment

Analysis and Discussion

Work needs to be stable and secure for the economic and mental well-being of an employee. In order to assess the stability and security of work, the following criterion was adopted in this study:

(a) Employment in IT industry is generally contractual in nature and the contracts are revised later by companies as per the performance appraisals. So, the first criterion for this indicator taken was *whether the employment was contractual or regular.* It is to be noted that this question was posed twice in this study so as to serve as measure of cross-verification and the results discussed hereby are likely to be slightly different from the ones mentioned in the indicator for adequate earnings and productive employment. It was found that 91% of the employees had regular employment and only 9% of them had contractual employment. This poses a satisfactory picture as far as stability of career in IT industry is concerned. This result also partially reconfirms the earlier result that majority of employees are satisfied with their employment in IT companies and are not at the immediate risk of retrenchment.

(b) ***Self-assessment of the ability*** *to retain one's current job in the next 12 months*. Stability and security of work was assessed by requesting employees to introspect their own situations and confidence about their jobs. This is generally considered a better indicator of job security in the context of decent work because the perception of employees will better examine their concern of job stability. This was considered as the second criterion because it reflects how secure an employee feels while working in the current company. It was found that 87% of the employees were confident that they would be able to keep their current job in the next one year and only 3% of the employees were sceptical of their job-retention. 9% of the employees were doubtful of holding their jobs for the next 12 months. Confidence to retain one's job can be linked to the regularity of employment in IT industry as assessed earlier.

(c) Another new indicator ***on-the-job search*** was taken as the third criterion for stability and security of employment because of the following reasons. If an employee is satisfied in the current working conditions and holds a permanent position in the company then there would be little inclination towards other jobs in the job market. However IT industry is a dynamic industry and quite vulnerable to global business downturns suffers from high attrition rates and lays-off a fraction of employees in the wake of pessimistic business environment or less work. Being laid-off from a company suddenly without a prior notice can tremendously affect the mental well-being and livelihood of an employee. It can bring in financial troubles for the employee's family and can account for deficit in decent working conditions. In order to mitigate the risk of sudden job-loss, an employee may engage in 'on-the-job' search. And so, the practise of 'on-the-job' search does have a partial correlation with lack of stability and security of current employment. In order to assess the same, a weight of 1 was given if the employee doesn't engage in 'on-the-job search' and of 2 if he does. It was found that only 28% of the employees engaged in on-the-job search while 72 % did not spend time looking for job prospects elsewhere. This result is again in tandem with the findings of regularity in employment. As majority of them were found to be having regular employment, they are likely to spend less time on on-the-job search.

Respondents were also asked what kind of benefits they derived from on-the-job search. 30% of the employees responded that on-the-job search safeguards their risk of retrenchment from the companies while 4% felt that it saved their travel cost and information costs. 16% felt that it maintained their self-respect and dignity by ensuring absence of the unemployment phase while 49% of the employees felt it was a good mechanism to search for a good/dream job.

These responses were coded, normalised and aggregated with appropriate weights in order to arrive at the Decent work Index -2 (DWI-2).

Table 1: Stability and Security of Work Index

Range for Index	Percentage of Employees
0.0 - 0.10	64
0.11 - 0.20	1
0.21 - 0.30	0
0.31 - 0.40	23
0.41 - 0.50	4
0.51 - 0.60	0
0.61 - 0.70	7
0.71 - 0.80	0
0.81 - 0.90	0
0.91 – 1.0	1
Total	**100**

Majority of employees (64%) found their work to be stable and secure which indicates good status of decent work among IT employees as far as work security is concerned. The extent of decent work deficit was found to be highest for 11% of the employees as they were in the range of 0.61-1. This result reconfirms the earlier results in two ways.

If the majority of IT employees have regular employment in their companies, there is a greater likelihood to feel a sense of security and stability in their career paths. 27% of the employees were found to be facing relatively high deficit in provision of stable and secure work as they were found in the range of 0.31 to 5. Overall, the results have been quite positive in respect of the fact that the recessionary wave globally is far from over.

Gender-wise classification of the results revealed that 67% of the employees in the decent work range of 0-0.1 were males and 51% were

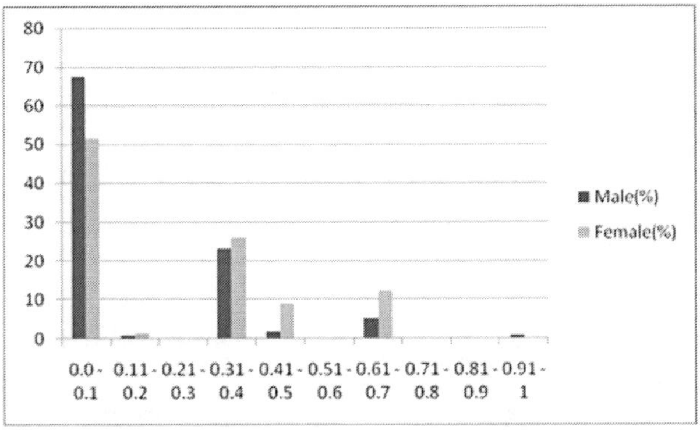

Chart – 9: Gender-wise Index

females. This implies that majority of employees of both the genders were found to be facing decently stable and secure work. On further observation it was found that in the range of 0.31 to 0.7, 30% of the employees were males and as high as 47% of the employees were females. This implies that female employees faced relatively unstable and insecure work in their companies. This result needs further examination to ascertain whether they faced any type of discrimination at their workplaces, which has been taken up in the later part of this study.

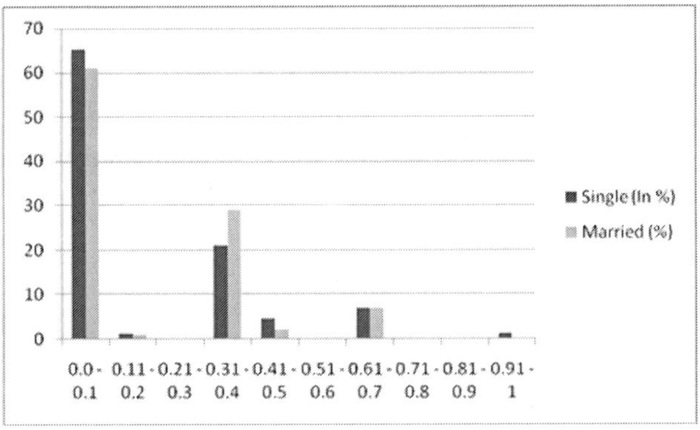

Chart - 10: Marital Status-wise Index

Classification of IT employees with respect to their marital status revealed that 65% of the employees were single and 61% were married in the range of 0 to 0.1. Thus majority of employees in both the categories experienced decently stable and secure work in their companies. However 31% of the married employees were found to having relatively high deficit in decent work as they were found in the range of 0.31 to 0.5. Further 7% employees, both single and married were also found in the range of 0.61-0.7 reflecting similar working conditions for both categories of employees.

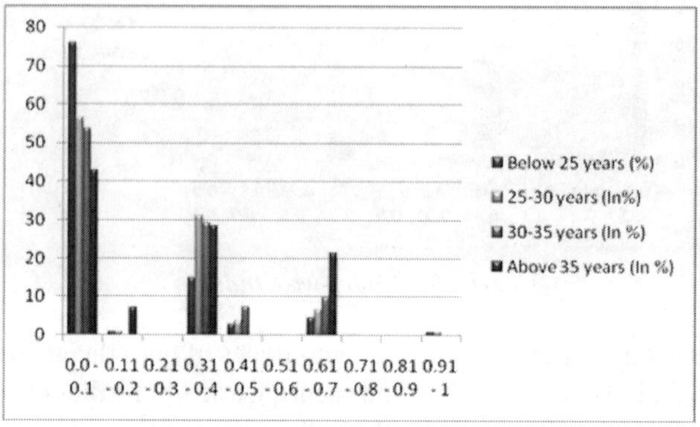

Chart – 11: Age-group-wise Index

Classification of the employees as per their age-groups revealed a positive picture for those in the age-group of 20 to 35 years as majority of them were found in the decent work range. However only 43% of the employees aged above 35 years were found in this range and 21% of these employees were found in the range of 0.61 to 0.7. This result is contradictory to the general perception of a layman that with age and experience, employment in any IT company becomes stable and secure. In fact, a closer look at the results reveal that employees below the age of 25 years experienced better, stable and secure work as compared to their senior employees. Nevertheless IT industry is a young industry with predominantly

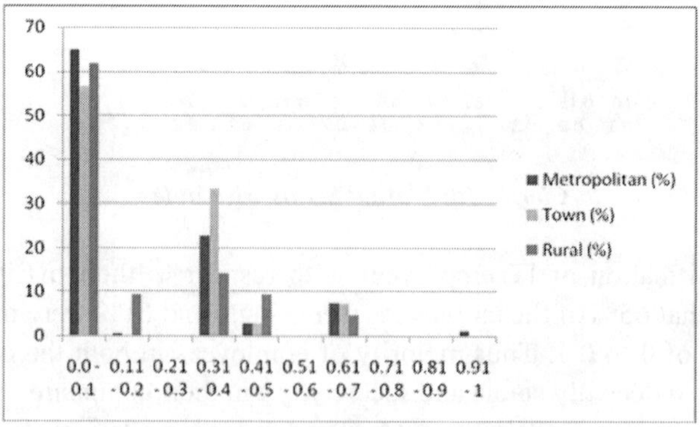

Chart - 12: Background-wise Index

younger age-group employees. A positive development is however provision of stable and secure work to these younger age-group employees.

Classification of employees as per their background revealed that 65% of the employees in the decent work range of 0-0.1 were from Metropolitan cities while 57% and 62% were from township and rural areas. Further examination reveals that 36% of the employees from township and 24% from rural areas were found in the range of 0.31 to 0.5. This implies that when compared with employees from Metropolitan cities, the results are slightly different for the ones from township and rural areas.

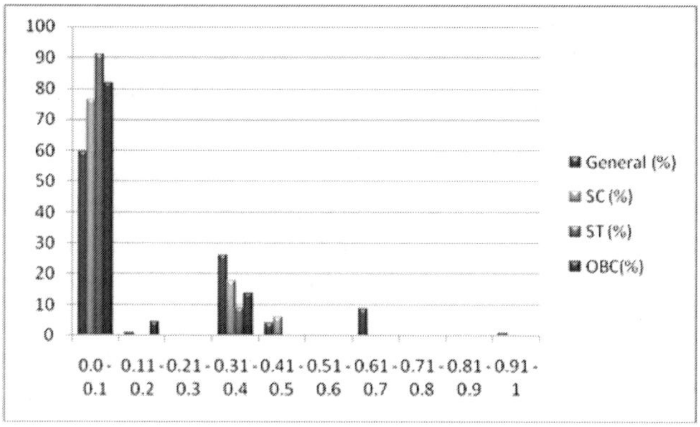

Chart - 13: Social Class-wise Index

Analysis of results on the basis of social class of IT employees revealed that 59% of the employees were of general category in the range of 0-0.1. However as high as 76%, 91% and 82% were respectively of SC, ST and

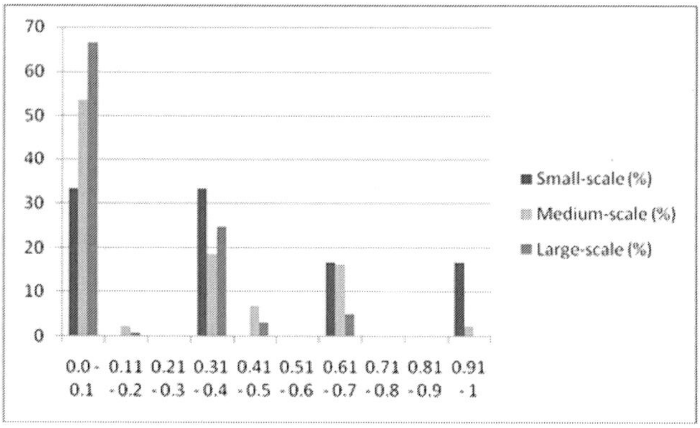

Chart – 14: Index Results as per Company Size

OBC category reflecting that there is no discrimination in IT employees from the ground of their social class.

Classification of results from the purview of size of an IT company revealed that work in large-scale companies was more stable and secure as compared to the medium and small-scale companies. This is so because in the range of 0-0.1, 66% of the employees were from large companies while 33% and 53% were from small and medium companies. A startling fact was that in the range of 0.6 to 1 which reflects high deficit of stable and secure work, 34% employees of the small companies were found and 18% and 5% employees were of medium and large IT companies. This implies that although small and medium companies provide productive employment, however they do not ensure stability and security of work to their employees.

Conclusion

Stability and security of work is an important indicator of decent work. By providing the same, it is possible that IT industry can also find a plausible solution to its high attrition problem. Retrenchment based on appraisals and tied to business cycles erodes the job-related security in the minds of IT employees and encourage them to search for better jobs on-the-job leading to their eventual exits and high attrition rates of the companies.

The main challenges faced by IT employers are tighter deadlines and employee retention. The essential linkage of a happy employee being a productive employee is by enabling the employees to connect easily with the company and organisation. Measures adopted by the companies to tackle high attrition rate have been enactment of employee-friendly and family-friendly employment policies, active policies for decent work, improved employer-employee relations and by giving salary hikes and promotions. In-depth questions about attrition rate gave the view that attrition was highest among males at the lower level, among females at the middle-level and again amongst male employees at the highest level. Retrenchment based on appraisals and tied to business cycles erodes the job-related security in the minds of IT employees and encourage them to search for better jobs on-the-job leading to their eventual exits and high attrition rates of the companies.

Employment security preserves and protects the long-run financial well-being of a worker. It is in the essence of the decent work agenda to enable employment opportunities in conditions of security. A positive result was seen in this context as majority of the IT employees found their employment as stable and secure. However more efforts are needed to enable stability and security to employees of IT industry with the objective of reducing the attrition rate.

References

1. M.K. Datar, "Human capital approach and Indian labour market: The case of Information Technology Industry", *Indian Journal of Labour Economics,* vol. 47, no. 4, 2004, pp. 825-832.
2. P. Vigneswara Ilavarasan, "Occupational Classification of the Software workforce: Case of India", *The Indian Journal of Labour Economics,* vol. 51, no.1, 2008, pp.105-114.
3. K.J. Joseph and K.N. Harilal, "Structure and Growth of India's IT exports: Implications of an export-oriented growth strategy", *Economic and Political Weekly,* vol. 35, no. 34, 2001, pp. 3263-70.
4. Priya C. Nair, "The B.Y.O.D Party", *Times Ascent*, 13 June 2012.
5. Priya C. Nair, "The Corporate summer camp", *Times Ascent*, 09 May 2012.
6. Akanksha Prasad, Indu Nandakumar, "Archair Labour law returns to Haunt IT", *The Economic Times*, 23 July 2012.

Strategic Discourse

Chapter - 9

Pandora of Paradoxes: Right Wing Upsurge in the Twenty-First Century

— Shilpa Parasrampuria

The liberal global order of the last few decades today faces a great challenge as new nationalist chants echo across continents. With the US now led by a President who rejects "globalism", a Europe in disarray and a China who does not have the wherewithal to formulate a coherent universal vision of world order, there is every chance that the international system will continue to exhibit enormous instability in an age of growing uncertainty.[1] From Sweden to Switzerland, from Belgium to Bulgaria, a tide of reactionary populism is sweeping across the European mainland, which demands nothing less than a restoration of a mythical golden age of sovereign nation-states defined by culture and racial homogeneity.[2]

In the 21st century, far right political parties have made major gains in divisive elections amidst strong nationalist overtones in Asia, Europe and North America. Fed by worldwide recessions and refugee crisis, nationalism and populism are newly ascendant political forces in the global landscape. The two fundamental ideas trending in many western countries are uplifting the poor working class in a globalized economy and constricting immigration from the Middle East. People have lost trust in institutions as politics is perceived to be governed by self-interest. The rise of the far right is due to the feeling of insecurity[3] compounded by Islamic fundamentalist terror that defies reason and logic. The economic pendulum swinging towards Asia has contributed to the growing Western insecurity. "This is not a unique phenomenon to the United States, and 2016 is not a short moment that will pass," says Yascha Mounk, who teaches political history at Harvard

University. "This is a real populist turn that is happening for the last 15-20 years." In recent years nationalist movements have shifted from vocal minorities to political parties.[4] The leadership change in Russia at the eve of the 21st century was perhaps a premonition of the right wing upsurge.

Russia: The Enigma

At the threshold of the 21st century, Russia had a new President, Vladimir Putin. Winston Churchill famously said of Russia, "it is a riddle wrapped in a mystery inside an enigma." Putin stormed into the corridors of power in Russia riding the wave of deep resentment. In the fall of 1999 bombs obliterated four apartment buildings in Moscow and other cities at night, hundreds died, it was Russia's 9/11. The country seethed with rage and fury. Prime Minister Putin swore revenge pointing at rebels in Chechnya where separatist movement was gaining ground. The new invasion of Chechnya was brutal, the man who waged a new national hero. Stoking nationalist sentiments helped Putin rise from relative obscurity to political prominence which ultimately culminated in presidency on 31 December 1999.[5]

Traditionally Russian nationalists have focused on perceived need to maintain a large and strong state, and have been less concerned with ethnic interests and racial purity. The backdrop of rise of Russian nationalism was a state that was more Russian in demographic terms then before 1991. When the Soviet Union broke up, the share of ethnic Russians rose from just above 50 percent in USSR to 81 percent in the Russian Federation. Russia now had a chance to develop into a 'nation-state' based on a high degree of common values and common identity. The Russian ethno nationalism was spurred by two issues, concern for Russians co-ethnics abroad, stranded in the other former Soviet Republics when the USSR collapsed; and, somewhat later, the influx of non-Russian migrants from the Caucasus and Central Asia into Russian cities. The enduring combination of nationalism and imperial consciousness in Russia has led to the creation of 'imperial nationalism.'[6] President Putin exploited both sentiments and whipped it into a frenzy.

In the initial years of Putin's presidency Russia strode forward. Russia is a petro state, and its economy is dependent on international oil prices. The eventual fall in global oil prices resulted in a sharp decline in the economy. The woes were further compounded when Western sanctions were slapped on the dwindling economy in 2014 following Russia's aggressive annexation of Crimea.[7] Yet surprisingly Putin's popularity remains unfazed. His strength lies in whipping nationalist sentiments and projecting a strong image that stands defiant in front of enemies. His excursions in Syria reveal that Russia is again a power broker in the Middle East wrenching control from reluctant US hands. Yuri Levada, a sociologist wrote about Russia's "wily man", who is neither fooled nor intimidated by the sprawling state but instead "not only tolerates deception, but is willing to be deceived and even requires self-deception for the sake of his own preservation."[8]

Massive corruption scandals and a decaying economy has not hampered Putin's popularity which rests on a surge of nationalist aspirations and nostalgia of the now disintegrated empire. Extensive regime consolidation has found only a few murmurs of protest. His defiant sojourns in Chechnya, Ukraine and Georgia are intended to compensate for the humiliation experienced during the long period of Soviet poverty, the failed aspirations of the 1990s, the enduring sense of inferiority and the collective trauma from the loss of the Soviet identity.[9]

With 66 percent of Russians believing that Western sanctions are meant to "weaken and humiliate" Russia, many have rallied around the flag and embraced Putin as "father protector" defending the country against foreign onslaught. The enemies of Cold War have returned to haunt Russia again. If the West succeeds in further weakening Putin economically, it may end up strengthening his position domestically.[10]

On 04 March 2012 Vladimir Putin secured a third non consecutive term as President of the Russian Federation securing 63.6 percent of the vote, beating his closest rival Gennady Zyugarnov who received 17.2 percent of the vote.[11]

In the uncertain political times of the 21st century with popularity plummeting for Theresa May and Angela Merkel, Putin is one leader who has the support of the whole nation. Massive centralization of the government structure, emasculation of the opponent or any voice of dissent and a dwindling economy, all combined have not been able to dislodge the Tsar from his seat of overwhelming authority. His popularity remains unfazed despite massive administrative corruption.[12] Vladimir Putin won the 2018 elections despite a diplomatic row with England following the Skripal poisoning incident in Salisbury. His rhetoric remains unapologetic while his nationalist fervor has many supporters. Putin registered a victory with a 76.7 percent of votes. He managed to get 70 percent of the votes in Moscow up from 47 percent vote share in 2012 elections.[13]

Europe Catches the Nationalist Fire

Russian centralism and the consequent popularity of a corrupt but strong regime reverberated throughout Europe. Right wing political parties hitherto sidelined, gained ground in Hungary, Poland, Italy, Germany, France and Austria. In Hungary the political victories of the national conservative party in 2010 and 2014, and the PiS ("Law and Justice") party in the 2015 presidential and parliamentary elections in Poland, raise the question of a more general nationalist turn in Central and Eastern Europe. The fundamental paradox is that populist nationalism sweeping the globe is not in every case anti-democratic since it often strives to mobilize majorities in order to win elections, it is nevertheless not a trivial development because it encourages conflict and polarization and tends to depict political opponents as "enemies of the people".[14]

Fidesz won the 2010 Hungarian election with 52.73 percent of votes, which gave the party a constitutional majority in parliament allowing it to change the constitution at will, carry out controversial constitutional court appointments and change electoral laws. In particular, the so-called "fourth amendment" to Hungary's Constitution – limited the independence of the judiciary, brought universities under governmental control and opened the door to public prosecutions and provoked criticism of the European Union. The Nationalist right wing politics often introduces social schemes to benefit the marginalized sections yet is singular in its tone. Fidesz government introduced a number of social measures aimed at improving the living standards of average citizens.

In Poland the PiS candidate Andraz Duda unexpectedly took 51.5 percent in the presidential election of 2015. He ushered in new reforms on media and counterterrorism laws, and controversial appointments at the Constitutional Court.[15]

Italy's Tilt towards Right Wing

The Five star Movement (M5S) in Italy is a glaring example of the rise of populist, anti-establishment and Euroskeptic movements gaining momentum across Europe, with two of its party members elected as mayor of Rome and Turin.[16] M5S's ragtag army of populists, euroskeptics, environmentalists, centrists, right-wingers and left-wingers—the party draws candidates and voters from the entire political spectrum. Formed only 8 years ago it won more than a quarter of the vote in the 2013 general elections, making it Italy's biggest opposition party and Europe's biggest elected anti-establishment party. The Five Star is an expression of the growing disenfranchisement with the established parties.[17] The spirit of the Italian rebellion echoed through the Brexit campaign in England.

Brexit Defies European Union

The success of the 'leave Campaign' put Davis Cameron out of job and Britain out of European Union. The economic and political turbulence that engulfed Britain found its striking manifestation in success of Brexit. On 23 June 2016, Britain voted narrowly to secede from the transnational formation of EU by 52-48 percent.[18] The leave campaign narrative was a deep nostalgia for empire, of past glories of colonialism, of the disdain of globalization that dwarfed the size of the colonial superpower, challenging not only the income of the people but also flooding the country with foreigners and increasingly refugees and a society coming to terms with stagnant incomes and a rising Asia.[19]

The neoliberal era witnessed a British disbelief at its structural decline. Experiences of downward mobility, alongside the persistence of class injuries, have produced a politics of national resentment. Englishness has been reasserted through a radicalizing, insular nationalism. The Leave Vote campaign reinstated the sovereign will of the people with the slogan "Let's take back control", to wrest power form the EU that was becoming more centralizing, interfering and anti-democratic.[20]

Britain could detach itself from a trading block that was in decline and would rejoin the capitalist world economy as a sovereign state. Global Britain evokes memories of its hegemony days where everything from ships to spoons was marked by *Made in Britain* stamp. It was the inability to come to terms with the realities of 21st century global capitalism whose epicenter has shifted decisively towards Asia. According to Nigel Farage – the figurehead of EU – the EU has done great harm to Britain by facilitating uncontrolled immigration: the unskilled labour market now had multiple employment options which resulted in a suppression of wages and lesser employment for the native white population. This phenomenon meant that living standards have failed and that life has become a lot tougher for many British citizens. To top the economic woe is the bigger national threat of security. "Taking back control of our borders" represented an important opportunity to limit the number of Muslims entering Britain."[21]

The unexpected turnaround of the Brexit result reverberated across the seas and shook the election ground of America, churned the battleground of the Republicans and Democrats with the new aggressive insular ideals that had gripped Europe and threw the victory of the iconoclast candidate Donald Trump.

America in the Throes of a Nationalist Upsurge

USA joined its British cousins in identifying more closely with a nationalist upsurge as effectively raked in by Donald Trump. Throwing political correctness to the winds Trump put together a winning electoral coalition that stressed the unity and common interest of all Americans across the full spectrum of policy, from immigration to diplomacy. Politics dipped in patriotism made an appeal in February, David Gelernter stated that the "havoc" that political correctness "has wrecked for 40 years (has been made) worse by the flat refusal of most serious Republicans to confront it." Indeed, he noted, "only Trump has the common sense to mention the elephant in the room. Naturally he is winning."[22]

Since the fight over the Gang of Eight Immigration Bill in 2013, patriotic and populist opposition to amnesty and to increases in low-skilled immigration has intensified. The low skilled immigration particularly from Mexico eats into the job bandwidth of the unskilled native population. The basic idea is that National conservatism, or "one America" conservatism, is idealistic without being native or utopian, Many Americans today believe that the U.S. Constitution is superior to international law, that immigrants – though welcome – should become part of a unified national community rather than join an ethnic enclave in a balkanized America, and that the American national identity was more important than any ethnic or transnational loyalty. According to a Harris survey of over 2,200 eligible voters, U.S. citizens prefer national self-government to "global rules".[23] Nationalism spews through the notion that the nation is bigger than its people.

The election of Donald J. Trump as 45th President of the United States was a major upset and came as a shock to many—perhaps even the billionaire himself. The election result proved all the pre election surveys wrong. Here was a man with no political or military experience; who had angered just about every minority group; whom a dozen women had accused of sexual assault—and yet millions of people had just elected him to the highest political office in the United States. Trump's success among white voters is particularly attributable to his tapping into concerns about immigration and a feeling among many voters that the U.S. should be a white, Christian country. While his opponent Hillary Clinton's speech failed to evoke enthusiasm, his rhetoric hit the right nationalist buttons. Allyson Shortle, assistant professor of political science at the University of Oklahoma said that by targeting Muslims and undocumented immigrants he addressed the growing insecurity amongst the white Americans. His slogan of "Make America Great Again," a broad-base populist slogan that supported a more isolationist, protectionist, "America First" posture toward the wider world resonated with the voters.[24]

Trump's comment that a wall should be erected on the border between USA and Mexico was approved by the Americans. Mexico was sending "its most unwanted people into the US, in many cases criminals, drug dealers, rapists," resonated with some of the supporters who feared that America was being overrun by immigrants. On November 1, the *Crusader,* the official newspaper of the Ku Klux Klan, threw its support behind Trump with a front page article headline "Make America Great Again." Part of what led to Trump's rise, says Jacqueline Gehring, associate professor of Political Science at Allegheny College, was a growing frustration among some people simply at having a black President. Sara Wallace Goodman, associate professor of Political Science at the University of California, Irvine, agrees that Obama's two-term presidency might have pushed voters towards Trump. "There is a feeling in the US that there has been an excess of liberalism," she says. "People want to take back what was rightfully theirs and for some that includes taking back the colour of the presidency."[25]

The echo of trump's victory reverberated in Europe and toasts were raised in Russia. Marine Le Pen, leader of France's far right National Front, told the BBC that Trump's win improved her chances of being elected French President. Trump, she said, has "made possible what had previously been presented as impossible." These rightist groups predate Trump politically and tie themselves more tightly to nationalism, but they are also happy to ride the coattails of his victory.[26]

When France Sneezes, Europe Catches Cold

The French election was a victory for liberal forces, for EU and some say for rationality. However it was also a historic victory for the far-right Marine Le Pen and her National Front Party. Le Pen was one of the two candidates who qualified for the second round, soundly beating the standard-bearers of both of France's traditional establishment parties – the center-right Republicans and center-left Socialists. The winner Emmanuel Macron (pro EU) won 23.9 percent vote share against Le Pen's 21.7 percent.[27] However, the slim margin of the victory demonstrated the strong right wing undercurrents in the election. Le Pen lost also because she fared somewhat poorly in the debates against Emmanuel Macron. Macron convinced the voters because of his strong economic sense.

The French election with its twin mandate of acknowledging the right wing rise and the triumph of European Union and liberal world order set a similar ball of confused political spectrum and discourse throughout Europe. Germany subsequently followed the momentum with Angela Merkel's victory but also gave in to a significant rise in the voter share for right wing politics.

Germany Defies the Brexit Verdict

In September 2017, Angela Merkel who is pro EU and pro immigration won a fourth term in office. Her decision in 2015 to allow 1 million refugees from the Middle East to enter Germany has not gone well with the average voter. The direct repercussion of immigration was the rise of the right-wing movement in Germany, not seen since the collapse of the Nazi party. Alternative for Germany (AfD), a far-right populist and Euroskeptic party missed the 5 percent threshold to even sit in the Bundestag during the 2013 elections, however, after the 2017 federal elections became the third largest party in Germany with 94 seats in the Bundestag.[28] The most important story was the collapse of support for the country's mainstream political parties, which lost more than 100 seats in the Bundestag. Cas Muddle, a professor at the University of Georgia blamed the "undemocratic liberalism" of mainstream politics for the loss of voter support. Professor Fritsche's research shows that when people feel a loss of control, they seek a stronger connection to group identity, and experience a desire to make their group more powerful. The AfD's message of border security and a return to national pride was perfectly placed to fulfill that need.[29] The AfD's loss was also due to infighting within the party and the lingering memory of Hitler's rhetoric in Germany.[30]

Internal Dissension in Spain

Catalonia a province in Spain represents one fifth of Spain's economy. The Catalan government had held a referendum to break away from Spain. The referendum was overwhelmingly in favour of secession garnering a vote share of 90 percent. However only 43 percent of the region's 5.3 million eligible voters had cast their vote.[31] A massive rally took place in downtown Barcelona on 8 October, 2017, to protest against the plans of Catalonia's regional government to secede. Spanish Prime Minister Mariano Rajoy negated the result of the referendum.[32] The government says the referendum contravenes the constitution, which states that Spain is indivisible.[33] Spain and Catalonia both were inspired by feelings of nationalism. The pro independence fervor is a backlash to the deep economic recession in Spain.[34]

Liberalism and Globalisation in Crisis

The fiery debate engulfing the comparatively liberal democracies of the West is between the liberals and the populists. The sordid play of events during World War II filled humanity with disgust. Leaders vowed for politics of greater integration and economic globalization. However contemporary politics born in the aftermath of the wars has also failed to fulfill the aspirations of the people. There is an economic stagnation among the mid and lower segments and a comparative indifference on the part of the elites to address the problem.

Mounk pegs social stagnation among lower and middle class whites as a main driver for nationalism's global rise. "You have a socially descending middle class that hasn't had real gains in the standard of living in 30 years," he said. "And at the same time, you seem to have real improvements in social status, if not necessarily economic status, for ethnic minorities. So they feel like our country is being taken away." Add to the economic cauldron of disgust is the inflow of greater number of refugees from Syria and the inexorably large population size of their families looking for jobs, social service protection and housing.[35]

Across Europe, although political parties themselves rarely capture more then a small minority of vote, their success has pushed mainstream parties to court far-right voters by mimicking elements of their platforms.[36] This was visible when French mayors banned Burkini France banning burkini, an all-encompassing swimsuit worn by Muslim women.[37] Center-right politicians have swung hard to the right on matters of immigration and Muslim integration in the Netherlands, France and even Germany itself, where Ms Merkel gave a speech in December calling for a ban on full-face veils for Muslim women. This movement too faces a backlash from leftists and liberals and a distinct polarization is emerging.[38]

It is felt that traditional institutions are ignoring the demands of the masses. A combination of economic and social problems seething for some decades are coming to the forefront. The populist movement bears a dangerous concoction for Hungary and Poland then other Western countries because democratic norms and institutions are weaker there. The real danger of populism is that it shifts from populism to authoritarianism as evident in Hungary, Turkey and Venezuela. Populism is rising because liberal democracy too has its shortcomings.[39]

Both Hillary Clinton and David Cameron failed to address the economic anxieties of the masses and their liberal rhetoric only seemed to make the problem bigger. Liberal leaders too have to make sound economic sense for them to cut a dent in electoral politics. Emmanuel Macron in France was able to ally the economic fears of the people and hence could wrest the election result from the strong hands of Marine Le Pen.

The economic rise of Asia particularly China, India and Singapore is shifting the economic power base from the West towards the East. American stands in danger to lose its superpower clout as the new strong economies are now confident and in no mood to tolerate the hegemony of the West. The global shift has inspired Asian ambitions to revive the national and cultural greatness that was eclipsed during the age of Western imperialism. A rising Asia is also witnessing a right wing nationalist upsurge.

Secular India: Going the Nationalist Way

In May 2014, the Bharatiya Janata Party won the Indian national election, the largest election in human history. The sweep by the right wing party in the largest and most diverse democracy in the world surprised many Indians. The recent success of the party in India's largest state Uttar Pradesh is setting the mood of the national elections of 2019. The key to BJP's landslide victory was India's current Prime Minister Narendra Modi who presented himself as the embodiment of anti-establishment sentiment and rode on the public's disgust with the long-standing centre-left Congress party, whose corruption and scandals include the 2008 2G-spectrum scam and the 2012 Indian coal allocation scam.

Many parallels can be drawn between Trump and Modi's flamboyant images, campaigns and politics. Shalabh Kumar, Trump's Indian-American acolyte, described the two as "kindred spirits; committed nationalists and willing to forego the niceties of the political elite sin both the countries to get things done on behalf of a population eager for more jobs and economic growth. Trump's exclusionary politics and claims that "a nation without borders is not a nation" resonates in India just as it does throughout the world, with striking similarities arising between the right-wing populist campaigns and politics of Modi, Trump, Brexit and France's Le Pen.[40]

India is one of the most liberal bastion of Asia and there was bound to be a liberal backlash with the Indian Media and Intelligentsia voicing serious concerns, but increasingly their voices are getting drowned as the right wing government is proving to be stronger then the opposition who is facing a disarray because of weak leadership. According to Ashish Nandy, the concept 'Nationalism is the refuge of scoundrels', which arose in the 17th century is very relevant today also. Amit Chaudhary is weary of nationalism which he says has intimate ties with violence.[41] However, right wing politics that had stayed in the fringes of Indian politics has made a comeback, and if BJP succeeds in swaying the economy, then populism is going to get firmly entrenched in the Indian soil. The populist ripples from the West and India affected the Asian landscape with strong economies like China and Japan too following suit. Turkey and Myanmar too drifted towards right wing.

Centralization in Turkey

President Recep Tayyip Erdogan's popularity is due to a nationalist uprising and a growing awareness of ethnic belonging. He enjoys almost unchecked power after surviving an attempted military coup in July 2016 and carrying out a vast clampdown on his opponents. The Turkish parliamentary system has changed to a presidential form with concentration of powers in the hands of the executive. The centralization of the governmental machinery is justified in the name of democracy. Erdogan and his party are whipping a nationalist frenzy to further their support and consolidate even more power.[42]

Myanmar Immigrants: A Security Threat for India

The fleeing Rohingya Muslim immigrants from Myanmar pose a security threat for India who is eager to deport them back. Rohingyas are a minority in Myanmar, where a military crackdown – likened to an ethnic cleansing by the United Nation – had driven thousands to Bangladesh and India.[43] Aung San Suu Kei, noble peace prize winner, an icon of human rights and democracy, stormed to power when her political party NLD won in a historic 2015 election. She became the state Counselor promising democracy and equality. She fought for ushering in democracy in her country, is now accused of being guilty of ethnic cleansing.[44] She claims it is a counter-terrorist operation to catch the militants who started the crisis when they attacked police outposts.[45] Muslim immigration is also a problem for Asia and Myanmar succeeded in doing what others aspire to do.

Strong Asian Economies Fall Prey to the Nationalist Rhetoric

When political leaders are in domestic disarray they often look for salvation by deftly turning public attention towards contentious foreign policy issues. The most appealing sentiment in both China and Japan is the sentiment whipped by leaders against each other. The anti-Chinese feeling in Japan centers on the territorial dispute between the two countries over the Sankaku/Diaoyu islands. Although robust trade between China and Japan have touched $350 billion, yet Japan is piqued at being overtaken by China which has emerged as the second largest economy displacing Japan who now has to contend with the third position. The present Chinese leadership has channeled domestic discontent into anti-Japanese sentiment. The visit of Japanese Prime Minister Shinzo Abe to India and the growing ties between the two countries was looked with disfavor by China.

China's GDP continues to falter leading to acute internal dissension and greater inequality. The richest 10 percent Chinese hold 45 percent of China's wealth with 83 billionaires listed as members of the National People's Conference amidst a declining economy. The political leadership in China is trying to deflect the concerns from the economy by raking nationalist sentiments, popular revulsion against Japan is apparent because of the atrocities conducted by Japan on China during World War II.[46]

The Chinese President Xi Jinping recently accomplished something which other leaders can only dream of: getting himself written into his party's constitution. The Chinese communist Party has voted to put Xi into the same pantheon as Communist Party legends Mao Zedong and Deng Xiaoping, paving the way for him to lead the country into the indefinite future. He will have new power to crackdown dissent at home and pursue aggressive policies in the South China Sea and with many of China's neighbours. More than 2,300 delegates voted unanimously to enshrine "Xi Jinping Thought on Socialism with Chinese Characteristics for a New Era" into the party's constitution.

Xi championed China's growing influence on the world stage, celebrating the country's increased control of the disputed South China Sea and called for efforts to make the military more powerful. He said China is "blazing a new trail" for developing nations to follow. Under his rule Chinese authorities have clamped on free speech and hit out at NGOs with suffocating government regulations.[47]

Japan's meteoric rise came to a stuttering halt after the US forced it to devalue the Yen upwards under the Plaza Accord in 1985. China is under pressure to revise upward the value of its currency. Both China and Japan have to restructure their economic policies and go for major reforms, if Japan is to escape deflation and China an irreversible slowdown.[48] Shinzo Abe's energetic campaign for internal revival has given him victory at the polls. He cited the Meiji Restoration of the 19th century, which made Japan the leading power in Asia as his inspiration. Both Xi Jinping and Shinzo Abe have stoked the nationalist fire and both are in untenable position.

The Japanese and Chinese Coast Guard ships are in eye ball contest with each other near the Senkaku/Diaoyu islands for the first time ever a Chinese Y-8 reconnaissance plane flew between the Okinawa and Miyako islands, in ostensible airspace, triggering the Japanese ASDF fighters to scramble. Each will find it harder to de-escalate, for fear of being accused by their respective domestic critics of pusillanimity. No leader donning the colours of nationalism can politically afford such a charge.[49]

The current liberal leaders in many parts of the world have to find answers to their people's economic woes. Immigration of Muslim refugees is a cause of growing insecurity. Governments have to deftly deal with the situation. The menace of terrorism which drove the Syrians out of their own country has to be effectively handled by United Nations. Now more than ever the world has to unite to deal with the menace and somewhere the Muslim countries need to take responsibility of Muslim immigration. Terrorism and immigration to Western countries and liberal democracies both cannot be exported simultaneously by the Muslim world. The liberal affluent economies attract both the immigrants and terrorist. Since both the problems are inextricably linked with the Muslim world of Asia, therefore answers and solutions too have to come from the same region.

Notes

1. Guy de Jonquieres, "The world turned upside down: the decline of the rule-based international system and the rise of authoritarian n nationalism", *Springer,* vol. 54, issue. 5, September 2017, pp. 552-560.
2. Satnamand Virdee, Brenden McGeever, *Ethnic and Racial Studies: Racism, Crisis, Brexit,* Taylor and Francis Online, 21 August 2017, pp. 1-18.
3. Audrey Sheehy, "The Rise of the Far Right", *Harvard Political Review,* 11 February 2017.
4. Detrow Scott, "From 'Brexit' to Trump; Nationalist Movements gain momentum around the world," *NPR Politics,* 25 June 2016.
5. "Vladimir Putin's Rise To Power – Full Documentary", Advexon TV, http://m.youtume.com>watch

6. Pal Kolsko, Hegel Blakkisrud, eds., *The New Russian Nationalism, Imperialism, Ethnicity and Authritarianism 2000-2015*, Edinburgh University Press, 2016.
7. Angela Monaghan, Julia Kollewe, "Russia to fall into recession amid sanctions and plunging oil price", *The Guardian,* 2 December 2014.
8. "Russia Under Vladimir Putin," *The Economist,* Moscow, 2 June 2014.
9. "Vladimir Putin's Rise to Powere", Documentary, Advexon TV, YouTube, http://m.youtube.com>watch
10. Dmitry Alexander Simes, "5 Things you need to know about Putin's popularity", *The National Interest*, 21 July 2015.
11. "Russian Presidential election", 2012, Wikipedia 12 n. 9.
13. Andrew Roth, "Vladimir Putin secures record win in Russian presidential election, *The Guardian*, 19 March 2018.
14. Pawel Ireneusz Karolewski, "Neo-Nationalism in Central and Eastern Europe", *21st Century Global Dynamics,* vol. 10, issue 18, 16 March 2017.15 ibid.
16. "Five Star Movement", Wikipedia
17. Marco Bertorello, "Italt's Five Star Movements gain momentum around the world," *The Globe and the Mail World,* 24 March 2017, www.npr.org
18. Steven Erlanger, "Britain Votes to Leave E.U: Cameron Plans to Step Down", *The New York Times,* 23 June 2016.
19. Satnam Virdee and Brenden McGeever, *Ethnic and Racial Studies, Racisim, Crisis, Brexit,* Taylor and Francis Online, 21 August 2017, pp 1-18.
20. *Ibid.*
21. *Ibid.*
22. John Fonte and John O'Sullivan, "The Return of American Nationalism", *National Review,* 18 November 2016, http://hudson.org
23. *Ibid.*
24. Mirren Gidda, "How Donald Trump's Nationalism won over white Americans", *Newsweek,* 15 November 2016, www. Newsweek.com
25. *Ibid.*
26. Christain Pazzanese, "In Europe, nationalism rising", *HARVARDgazette,* 27 February 2017.
27. Zack Beauchamp, "The French elections showed the strength of the European far right – and its limits," *Vox*, 24 April 2017.
28. Chris Harris, "Five takeaways from Germany's election", *euronews,* 25 September 2017.
29. Amanda Taub, "What the Far Right's Rise May Mean for Germany's Future", *The New York Times,* 26 September 2017.
30. Jon Stone, "Germany's new far-right party AFD says it will fight an invasion of foreigners", *INDEPENDENT,* 25 September 2017.
31. Sam Edwards, "Thousands protest in Barcelona against Catalan independence", *Reuters,* 8 October 2017.
32. *Ibid.*

33. "Why the referendum on Catalan independence is illegal", *The Economist*, 26 September 2017.
34. "Hundreds of thousands to rally for Catalon independence from Spain", *The Indian EXPRESS,* 10 September 2017.
35. Scott Detrow, "From 'Brexit' to Trump Nationalist Movements gain momentum around the world", *npr politics,* 25 June 2016, www.npr.org
36. Amanda Taub, "What the Far Right's Rise May Mean for Germany's Future", *The New York Times,* 26 September 2017.
37. "France and the ban on burkini", *The Hindu,* 26 August 2016.
38. Amanda Taub, "What the Far Right's Rise May Mean for Germany's Future", *The New York Times,* 26 September 2017.
39. "What is populism and how is it shaping global politics?", YouTube.
40. Zoe Sands, "Sands: the rise of Hindu Nationalism", *The Dartmouth*, 3 September 2017.
41. "The NDTV Dialogues: The Rise of Neo Nationalism", YouTube.
42. Myshka Chandran, "How Turkey's leader used a failed coup to step on the opposition", *CNBC WORLD ECONOMY,* 17 July 2017.
43. "Rohingya refugees are a security threat: Govt's 'unfinalised affidavit", *Hindustan Times*, 15 September 2017.
44. "Aung San Suu Kyi", *BBC NEWS*, 5 December 2016.
45. Jonah Fisher, "Myanmar's Rohingyas: Truth, lies and Aung San Suu Kyi", *BBC News,* 27 January 2017.
46. R.S. Kalha, "The Rise of Nationalism in Japan and China", New Delhi: *IDSA Comment*, 29 July 2013.
47. Zeeshan Aleem, "Chinese President Xi Jinping just managed to secure himself Mao-like power', *Vox*, 25 October 2017.
48. Rachman Gidean, 'Trump, Putin, Xi, and the rise of nostalgic nationalism", London, *ProQuest*, 2 January 2017.
49. Kalha, n. 46.

Chapter - 10

NSG Exemption for Pakistan? ... No

— ***Reshmi Kazi***

For years now, Pakistan has been expressing its aspirations for an India comparable exemption from the 48-member Nuclear Suppliers Group (NSG). Pakistan's specified objective is intimately linked to its desire to gain access to global commerce of nuclear technology alike India. Experts[1] advocate that America could initiate nuclear cooperation with Pakistan based upon a criteria-centric civilian nuclear deal. The experts support conferment of nuclear legitimacy to Pakistan by granting it an India-alike civilian nuclear energy deal. Any such conferment principally involves the process of granting an NSG waiver for facilitating global nuclear trade. The principal strategic logic embedded in this waiver is that nuclear legitimacy would effectively imply a more sympathetic consideration of Pakistan's nuclear record. In reciprocity, Pakistan would be expected to be more tractable on crucial non-proliferation measures like the Fissile Material Cut-off Treaty (FMCT) at the Conference of Disarmament (CD) and accept the Comprehensive Nuclear-Test-Ban Treaty (CTBT)).

The nuclear non-proliferation regime encourages the proposed strategic goals of resuming negotiations on the FMCT and ensuring nuclear stability in the Indian-subcontinent. However, the suggested pathway[2] – NSG exemption and a civilian nuclear deal – is problematic. While many questions about the AQ Khan proliferation network still remain unanswered,[3] Pakistan's nuclear security remains vulnerable to critical threats from elements within its political and military establishments adhering to radical Islamist ideology.[4] The unstable political situation reeling under persistent terrorist attacks further bear direct impact upon Pakistan's nuclear security.

Given this backdrop, the author attempts to explore the complexities involved in an NSG exemption for Pakistan. The author seeks to objectively assess whether Pakistan has addressed concerns over nuclear proliferation concerns emanating from therein. The paper concludes by raising essential questions on the efficacy and legitimacy of NSG exemption for Pakistan.

Pakistan's Rationale for an NSG Exemption

Following the declaration of the India-United States Civilian Nuclear Cooperation Initiative in 2005, Pakistan has been expressing its desire to access civilian nuclear technology for meeting its energy requirements. Pakistan is an underdeveloped country with a GDP growth rate of 5.28 percent in 2016-17.[5] With a burgeoning population of over 199 million, Pakistan believes that nuclear energy is the potential answer to the prevailing energy crisis in the country. However, several experts believe that Pakistan's energy crisis is attributable to problems of energy mismanagement and corruption rather installed capacity in the country. Pervez Hoodbhoy proclaims that "non payment of electricity bills by the military and various government departments to other government departments"[6] [those managing electricity governance] creates 'circular debt'.[7] This means electricity producers [in Pakistan] are not paid on time and hence cannot import fuel oil.[8] Pakistan's electricity crisis is further intensified by pilferage and faulty gridlines that cause inefficient distribution leading to wastage. The complex energy situation in Pakistan led former US Ambassador Anne Patterson to remark that "the complex maze of GOP policymakers who cannot coordinate Pakistan's energy policy due to overlapping and contradictory authorities....A lack of coordination and absence of any clear line of authority hampers any formulation of policy efforts to address the current energy crisis in Pakistan."[9]

However, Pakistan believes that an India alike NSG exemption can suitably address the prevailing energy crisis. Debatably, nuclear power is not the panacea Pakistan wishes it to be.[10] Perhaps the way out for Pakistan's prevailing acute energy crisis is to commence short and long term policies for addressing the ills in the energy sector. These may include policies like clearing the existing debt to the government department managing electricity production and distribution. Pakistan may also consider energy cooperation dialogues with willing partners to deal with energy shortage. Prime Minister Nawaz Sharif has sought assistance to resolve the energy crisis in the country. In a bid to address Pakistan's acute energy shortage,[11] India has jointly "announced several initiatives to accelerate cooperation in the oil and gas sector."[12] In June 2014, Pakistan has sought as much as 500 MW of electricity from India by laying a transmission line from Punjab into Lahore.[13] According to Indian Government sources, "India is willing to help and is exploring the points which can be used to hook-up to the grid in Pakistan through a high-voltage direct current (HVDC) line."[14]

Complexities Involved in NSG Exemption for Pakistan

Pakistan's quest for an India comparable civilian nuclear deal is beyond simple reasons of meeting its energy requirements. According to Pakistan, the 2008 NSG exemption to India virtually amounts to nuclear apartheid and has disturbed the nuclear balance in the region. An NSG exemption would not only provide Pakistan access to global trade in nuclear technology but also confer significant symbolic value. Since 2005, Pakistan has consistently raised the need to reverse the India-Pakistan nuclear imbalance by seeking parity with India and demanding a similar NSG exemption. Pakistan believes that an NSG exemption might enhance Pakistan's global reputation that remains tainted by its nuclear proliferation record for ten years now.

Islamabad's aspiration for nuclear legitimacy through a NSG exemption similar to India is largely premised upon political rivalry and desires for nuclear parity with New Delhi. The non-proliferation discourse in Pakistan perceives the policies pursued by the NSG cartel toward nuclear proliferation as essentially discriminatory and is prejudiced against the nuclear nation. The 2008 NSG exemption to India is primarily viewed as encouraging nuclear apartheid against Pakistan and aiding India's *de jure* nuclear status. Prominent nuclear expert Shireen Mazari argues it was unfortunate that first US bulldozed unique IAEA safeguard agreement for India and then proceeded to force NSG to create a country specific waiver for India.[15] This waiver has facilitated India to enter into nuclear commerce with France, United Kingdom, Russia, Japan Australia, Canada, Kazakhstan and Argentina.[16] Pakistan apprehends that the NSG waiver has not only augmented India's nuclear status as a responsible nuclear power in the global sphere but has upped New Delhi's overall nuclear clout *vis-à-vis* Islamabad. The political-psychological impact of the nuclear imbalance weighs heavily with many in the Pakistani political and military establishments reckoning that Islamabad is gradually losing influence in the region. The Indo-US civil nuclear deal is viewed by Islamabad as "US condemnation of Pakistan's for its nuclear programme."[17] The lack of empathy from the international community including the US to grant Pakistan an India-alike NSG exemption further intensifies Pakistan's insecurity over its nuclear status. Additionally, Pakistan's dismal proliferation record, poor economic development, political instability, rampant terrorism and steep divergences between the political and military institutions generates lack of international confidence in Pakistan's capacity to undertake responsibilities of nuclear commerce.

The China Factor

Despite the lack of international confidence in Pakistan for an NSG exemption, China has been an ardent supporter. China has acquiesced to relax the NSG rules and provide two reactors (Chashma-3&4) to Pakistan under a "grandfather clause".[18] Inspite of global concerns, China and Pakistan have agreed to proceed with the nuclear reactor trade. China has already supplied two 300 MWe pressurized water reactor (PWR) at Chashma.[19] According to the International Atomic Energy Agency (IAEA), the official constructions of a third 340 MWe nuclear powered PWR Chasma-3 commenced on May 28, 2011 and a fourth unit of Chasma-4 begun in 2012 both under Chinese assistance.[20] The main construction contract for units 3&4 – a project costing some $2.37 billion – was signed in June 2010 by the Pakistan Atomic Energy Commission (PAEC) and Shanghai Nuclear Engineering Research and Design Institute (Snerdi).[21] Additionally, the China National Nuclear Cooperation (CNNC) has approved a loan of at least $6.5 billion to finance the construction of a major nuclear power project in Karachi.[22] However, the primary drivers behind the controversial the Sino-Pakistan reactor sales constitutes Pakistan's desire of purchasing reactors on soft loans provided by China and an India alike civil nuclear deal.

India's NSG Exemption and China-Pakistan Nuclear Trade: A Comparison

The China-Pakistan nuclear trade, criticized from several quarters[23] is believed to be a fallout of the India-US civilian nuclear deal. This is a fallacious assumption and is defensible in the face of documented records. The India-US nuclear deal was a closely guarded government secret till its official declaration in a public statement issued on July 18, 2005 by both the George Bush and Manmohan Singh Governments. (See Table 1) However, as early as April 10, 2005, well before the USA-India nuclear deal, Pakistani officials had announced that Pakistan and China had reached an agreement whereby Beijing would provide two 300-megawatts-electric-capacity nuclear power reactors to Pakistan in the next ten years.[24] Additionally, on May 5, 2004, China signed a contract to build a second nuclear power reactor (Chashma-2) in Pakistan.[25] The agreement was apparently made during the visit of the Chinese Prime Minister Wen Jiabao to Pakistan in early April 2005.[26] Corroborative evidence to support this is the admission made by the Pakistan Atomic Energy Commission in one of its documents that "In the context of South Asia, this project will also help to unshackle the Nuclear Supplier Group's embargos on Pakistan in a very short time frame, and prompt other NPP suppliers to follow suit."[27] Hence, none of the Chinese nuclear transfers to Pakistan has anything to do with the July 2005 US-India nuclear deal.[28]

Table 1: Chronology of India-US and China-Pakistan Nuclear Trades

5 May 2004	China signed a contract to build a second nuclear power reactor (Chashma-2) in Pakistan
10 April 2005	Pakistan and China had reached an agreement on two 300-megawatts-electric-capacity nuclear power reactors effective for the next ten years
18 July 2005	Official declaration of the India US nuclear deal

The India-US civilian nuclear deal has been a game changer for China and Pakistan. The two nuclear neighbours have conveniently used the India-US civilian deal as a pretext to intensify bilateral nuclear trade. China-Pakistan nuclear technology sales have increased in the last five years following 2008 grant of NSG waiver to India. During this period, the NSG engaged with Pakistan and sought its formal commitment to the supplier cartels export guidelines. In April 2005, the NSG representatives visited Pakistan and held discussions on further checks on unauthorized exports. The visit was an "outreach" programme to states that were not members but were heavily involved in technology.[29] These discussions indicate the possibility that intensified NSG co-operation with Pakistan could develop into a formal arrangement concerning Pakistan's access to the global nuclear market.[30]

However, at a time when the NSG is considering options on how to proceed with non-NPT members having NSG exemption like India, prospects of an exemption for Pakistan appears dim. Unlike India, the prospect of an NSG exemption for Pakistan faces the critical challenge of lacking US support. Pakistan faces the disrepute of illicitly proliferating sensitive nuclear technology and materials. There are specific concerns about Pakistan's formal access to global nuclear commerce which arguably poses risks to the status of the non-proliferation regime. An NSG exemption for Pakistan bears the risk of NSG members casting doubt on the decisions of a select few in the cartel group as weakening the edifice of the NPT.

Though an informal body with no enforcement mechanisms, the NSG is viewed as a important tool of the non-proliferation regime to halt the spread of nuclear weapons.

Concerns over Sino-Pak Nuclear Trade

Concerns over China's assistance to Pakistan's nuclear facilities have existed since the 1990s. In 1992, China began to build a nuclear power plant at Chashma and was suspected in 1994 of helping Pakistan to build an unsafeguarded, plutonium-producing reactor at Khushab.[31] Operational since 2001, the Chashma reactor has facility-specific IAEA safeguards (as distinct from full-scope safeguards covering the entire country).[32] Referring specifically to Pakistan's efforts to acquire equipment, materials, and technology for its nuclear weapons program, the DCI's June 1997 "Section 721 report" for the last half of 1996 (after China's May 1996 pledge)[33] stated that China was the "principal supplier."[34] Following Pakistan's 1998 nuclear tests, the Arms Control and Disarmament Agency's annual report on arms control for 1998 stated that "there continued to be some contacts between Chinese entities and Pakistan's unsafeguarded and nuclear weapons program."[35]

The recent Sino-Pakistan nuclear collaboration over the Chasma nuclear deal launched in the mid-1990s is remains ambiguous. The Free Beacon report confirms that in February 2013, China compromised the 'grandfather clause' (relates to building only Chashma-1&2) and entered into a formal agreement with Pakistan for the construction a third 1000 MWe nuclear reactor in Chashma. The transfer of additional reactors at Chashma thus appears beyond the purview of Sino-Pakistan nuclear cooperation existing in the 'grandfather clause'. It further breaches China's commitment made at the time of joining the NSG in June 2004 whereby Beijing specified the list of items it intended to transfer as part of a bilateral understanding to Pakistan. "This list did not include additional power reactors beyond those already agreed to and under construction in 2004."[36] China maintains, "the recent cooperation between China and Pakistan does not violate the relevant norms of NSG."[37] The Free Beacon report has been followed by several other reports highlighting that China has agreed to supply Pakistan with its fifth and possibly sixth Chinese-designed nuclear power reactor since the first joint reactor project was launched in the mid-1990s.[38] The deal, reached in mid-2013, will mark the first time China has exported its new ACP-1000 PWR, which is capable of producing 1,000 megawatts of electricity.[39]

However, no documented record suggests that the deal, which presumably will not be part of the Chashma complex, was either accepted and received the formal approval of the NSG. Neither, has China discussed the sale of the self developed ACP-1000 PWR to Pakistan at either of the NSG plenary meetings in NSG meetings in Christchurch, New Zealand in June 2010, Noordwijk, Netherlands, June 2011, Seattle, US, June 2012, Prague, Czech Republic, June 2013 or Buenos Aires, Argentina in June 2014. According to one account, at the 2010 NSG plenary meeting, even though several member states had requested clarifications from China regarding the deal, Beijing responded that all exports to Pakistan would follow NSG guidelines, implying that the latest round of reactor transactions would be grandfathered through the earlier 2003 agreement.[40] Pakistan has justified the nuclear reactor trade, as not in violation of its commitment to the nonproliferation responsibilities, since it is not related to the strategic side of its nuclear program. China and Pakistan has refrained from discussing concerns on the sale of the new reactors at the Nuclear Security Summit of 2014.

As compared to the ambiguities surrounding the China-Pakistan nuclear reactor trade, the negotiating process of the India-US civil nuclear deal was open to public domain. The NSG exemption granted to India was after long debates and deliberations on the factual information relating to India's nuclear facilities. As part of the agreement, India agreed to "assume the same responsibilities and practices and acquire the same benefits and advantages as other countries with advanced nuclear technology such as the United States." Further 'responsibilities and practices' accepted by India envisaged speak volume.[41]

The China-Pakistan nuclear power reactor trade unlike India-US nuclear deal is not premised upon detailed guidelines. There is not enough information in the public domain regarding the Sino-Pakistani negotiating process and lacks transparency before its official announcement in 2010. Besides, the opacities surrounding the Sino-Pakistan nuclear commerce fails to establish whether the specifics of the agreement is in conformity with the principles of non-proliferation commitments and complies with the NSG guidelines on global nuclear export. Contrarily, the underlying strategy behind the intensified Sino-Pakistan trade is to draw global attention towards the demand for an India comparable civil nuclear deal. However, as much as the NSG supports Pakistan's adherence to the export guidelines, there is no unanimity within the nuclear cartel to provide Islamabad access to global nuclear commerce.

Does the Chinese supplied nuclear technology provide Pakistan the much coveted international status and nuclear technology at par with India? The complexities inherent in the Sino-Pakistan civil nuclear agreement can never confer upon Pakistan the same nuclear benefits and international status, as that of India-US Civil Nuclear Cooperation Initiative of 2005 has provided to India. The nuclear commerce with China can help Pakistan to obtain vintage power reactors that may not be able to redress the energy crisis of the country.[42] Hence, Sino-Pakistan nuclear power agreement is not the desired pathway for Pakistan's desire to seek an NSG exemption similar to India. China-Pakistan nuclear trade has brought the non-proliferation regime and the goals of disarmament at a crossroad. The controversial nuclear engagement generates global distrusts and diminishes the status of the NPT.

Pakistan is a Global Concern

Terrorism

Pakistan remains the core of instability and political disorder in South Asia. Given the prevailing political instability, it remains an unfeasible proposition to initiate nuclear commerce with a nation plagued with widespread terrorism. Pakistan bears the brunt of terrorism from two sides – both as target and as safe haven for deadly terrorists. The frequency and ferocity of terrorist attacks on government forces led Khawaja Khalid Farooq, the former head of Pakistan's National Counter Terrorism Authority, to say in July 2013 that the country was 'bleeding'.[43] In 2013, Pakistan's former Army Chief General AP Kayani had conveyed 'concerns' to President Zardari, about the 'rapidly deteriorating law and order' in Pakistan.[44] In 2012, over 2,000 Pakistani civilians and 680 security forces personnel were killed in terrorist-related incidents.[45] In recent years, the Tehrik-e-Taliban Pakistan (TTP) launched lethal attacks on Pakistan's critical installations including its airports and naval bases. The TTP has attacked numerous heavily-guarded State installations in Pakistan including the the Mehran naval base in 2011, the Minhas airbase (possibly a nuclear weapons storage base) and the Peshawar airport in 2012. The TTP's continuous attacks on airports and naval bases have successfully exposed the capacity gaps in Pakistan's security apparatus.[46] It cannot be ignored that TTP militants might next be emboldened to target Pakistan's nuclear weapons installations. The results of such an attack can be globally catastrophic. Rampant terror incidents have raised concerns about the security of nuclear arsenal in Pakistan.

Non-proliferation experts like Mark Fitzpatrick's have empathized with the prevailing situation stating, "Pakistan does not control all groups that perpetrate terrorism."[47] Pakistan's intransigence to reattribute terrorists masquerading as political leaders has led the international community to question, Islamabad's intentions to address terror concerns emanating from the country. As observed by George Perkovich, "a state cannot be a responsible possessor of nuclear weapons if it does not have sovereign control over organized perpetrators of international violence operating from its territory."[48] Hence, there remain concerns whether it is a pragmatic decision to grant an NSG exemption to Pakistan and thereby facilitate vertical proliferation of its nuclear assets and technology through global nuclear commerce.[49]

Proliferation Record

Pakistan's nuclear proliferation record seriously questions the credibility to deserve an NSG exemption. Pakistan's intransigience on the AQ Khan case has impeded efforts to investigate and enquire the status of the illicit nuclear network. The world remains far from convinced about its proliferation record. Recent news of Saudi Arabia seeking nuclear weapons from Pakistan[50] opened fresh speculations about Pakistan's proliferation activities. Riyadh has reportedly financed Islamabad's nuclear programme including its missile and nuclear laboratories.

Presently, there is no credible evidence to confirm any existing nuclear cooperation pact between Saudi Arabia and Pakistan. But there is considerable evidence to suggest that Riyadh and Islamabad in the early seventies and possibly thereafter have at least discussed such an understanding.[51] Sources indicate the existence of an enduring Saudi-Pakistan military connection for decades and may have an unrecognized nuclear partnership to provide the Kingdom with a nuclear deterrent on short notice, if ever required. The *Nucleonics* in the late seventies reported that Riyadh offered to finance the construction of a reprocessing facility at Chashma in exchange for Pakistani training of Saudi scientists on nuclear power.[52] The state visit of Crown Prince Abdallah to Pakistan in October 2003 was rife with speculations about an undisclosed nuclear agreement "detailing Pakistani support to Riyadh in case of a nuclear threat from any third party." Recent sources confirm that Saudi Arabia provided generous financial support to Pakistan that enabled the nuclear program to continue, especially when the country was under sanctions.[53] Arguably, there is no indicator to disprove these reports though they have been denied by Pakistan.

China-Pakistan nuclear proliferation remains a concern. Earlier on December 21, 2010, PPG Paints Trading Company in Shanghai pled guilty in a US court to illegally exporting high-performance coatings from the US through the PRC to the Chashma-2 reactor in Pakistan from June 2006 to March 2007.[54] Later, on June 16, 2011, authorities in Atlanta arrested Wang Xun, a PRC national and U.S. resident.[55] On November 16, the Commerce Department ordered sanctions against Wang.[56] The "Section 721 Report" for 2011 continued to report that PRC entities have been associated with Pakistan's nuclear programs.[57] Pakistan must undertake to establish a responsible nuclear record and refrain from future proliferation activities as credentials for an India-alike civil nuclear deal.

In a recently published report prepared by Project Alpha of the Centre for Science and Security Studies at King's College, it has been founded that Pakistan has a "deliberate strategy of using deceptive methods to obtain dual-use goods" evident from its "systematic use of front companies to supply its strategic industries".[58] The report claims "Pakistan's strategic industries rely on a network of at least 20 trading companies in mainland China, Hong Kong, Dubai and Singapore which funnel dual-use goods to its strategic programmes."[59] It is believed that witting and unwitting suppliers "probably purchase goods from manufacturers in China, Europe, the United States and elsewhere and then arrange their export to Pakistan."[60] Pakistan's continued proliferation activities seriously undermines global effort towards strengthening the edifice of nuclear security worldwide.

Is Pakistan Contributing to Regional Stability?

A responsible nation promotes domestic stability and further consolidates it by fostering strong ties with neighbours and external powers. Unfortunately, Pakistan lacks the distinction of being a good neighbor to India.[61] Pakistan does not promote stability; it uses a sub-conventional strategy in the region to pursue its revisionist interests at the expense of regional peace and security.[62] Unlike India as pledged in the India-US 2005 Joint Statement to "combat terorism relentlessly" Pakistan has been selective in its approach to extend unremmitting efforts towards counterterror operations. To coerce India to make concession to Pakistan on the disposition of Kashmir, Pakistan has supported an array of Islamist militant proxies that operate in Kashmir and throughout India.[63] Terrorist groups like Lashkar-e-Taiba[64] and its leader Hafiz Saeed opposing stable India-Pakistan relations and regional peace continues to call for violent attacks against India.[65]

Over the years the LeT has received wide-ranging cooperation from the ISI to conduct proxy terror activities in Kashmir. LeT oversees terrorist training camps that have produced between 100,000 and 300,000 fighters over the past two decades.[66] Leaders of the group have gone so far as to call for nuclear jihad against India.[67] In January 2011, LeT leader Saeed said it would be 'no problem' if fighting over Kashmir led to nuclear war between Pakistan and India.[68] Pakistan has practically done nothing to prevent these opponents from destabilizing regional peace and harmony. Pakistan's revisionism persists in regard to its efforts not only undermine the territorial *status quo* in Kashmir but also to undermine India's position in the region and beyond.[69] "Pakistan will suffer any number of military defeats in its efforts to do so, but it will not acquiesce to India."[70]

Pakistan's introduction of tactical nuclear weapons (TNWs) has lowered the nuclear threshold and further corroded regional stability. Pakistan defends its lowered nuclear threshold posture as a response to India's Cold Start doctrine. However, the Cold Start doctrine is a work in progress and would have a stabilizing influence in the sense that it will build confidence in the Pakistan Army that India has no desire to dismember Pakistan through large-scale Strike Corps-led offensive operations deep into the country.[71] India has no plans to use the Cold Start doctrine as is quite evident from the Manmohan Singh Government stand. Following the provocative 2008 Mumbai attacks perpetrated by Pakistan-based terrorists, India resisted mounting pressures from several quarters and refrained from any operational use of the Cold Start Doctrine against Pakistan. However, assurances that India has no intentions of launching any offensive attacks against Pakistan[72] through its non-operational Cold Start Doctrine has failed to assuage Islamabad's concerns. Pakistan continues to engage in proxy wars at the sub-conventional level, which has seriously affected regional peace and stability. Additionally, Pakistan's nuclear build-up affects the regional stability in the region. Any offer of NSG waiver must be preceded with Pakistan validating the reasons for its growing nuclear build-up particularly against India. Pakistan must abort India-centric nuclear strategy as a demonstration of its good faith and a responsible nuclear state.

Should the NSG Grant Pakistan an Exemption?

Pakistan's quest for nuclear legitimacy faces complications galore. The non-proliferation advocates have underlined the importance of integrating the difficult nuclear state within the non-proliferation regime through the incentive of an NSG exemption. Their underlying belief is nuclear legitimacy would induce Pakistan to sign the CTBT and accept the FMCT. Former

Ambassador to the CD, Zamir Akram, has affirmed that if Pakistan had an NSG waiver like India, it would be willing to enter negotiations on an FMCT.[73] The ambassador's views have been reverberated by former diplomat Tariq Osman Hyder stating that "normalisation of Pakistan's relations with the NPT on a *de facto* basis as done for India, NSG exception and membership, and nuclear parity with India to allow access to safeguarded nuclear technology and to remove existing barriers" should be the essential conditions for Pakistan resuming negotiations on FMCT in the CD.[74] However, it must be ensured that the FMCT negotiations are not confined to another round of diplomatic glib ending in an impasse. The international community must be assured that Pakistan is willing to modify its position on the issue of "scope" of the treaty and facilitate its negotiations in the CD.[75] Noteworthy, in June 2014, Pakistan's Ambassador to the CD, Zamir Akram declared that Pakistan would continue to block resumption of the FMCT negotiations over the expected scope of such a treaty.[76]

Any consideration for an NSG exemption for Pakistan must conform to the highest standards of nuclear security to strengthen the objectives of the non-proliferation regime. It is imperative that Pakistan takes adequate steps to assuage the concerns of the NSG members and strengthen global confidence in itself. It must take additional steps to inspire the confidence of the NSG members and the non-proliferation regime.

These Steps Include

- Signing and ratifying the International Convention for the Suppression of Acts of Nuclear Terrorism.
- Ratifying the Amended Convention on the Physical Protection of Nuclear Materials.
- Improve transport security by implementing the recommendations on physical protection of nuclear materials and facilities contained in INFCIRC 225/rev.5.
- Inviting International Physical Protection Advisory Service missions to the existing nuclear facilities and implementing the suggested recommendations.
- Commit not to build any more unsafeguarded fissile material production reactors.
- Commit to put any new reactors built under IAEA safeguards.
- Allow IAEA operational safety review and related teams to conduct routine inspection in cooperation with the IAEA Department of Nuclear Safety and Security.

- Adhere to the Australia Group, Wassenaar, NSG, and MTCR export control regimes.
- Render cooperation to the IAEA and other international authorities to resolve past cases of illicit transfers of nuclear technology.
- Support global counterterrorism efforts.
- Stop providing state support to terrorist groups threatening regional peace and stability by piloting attacks in neighboring states.
- Initiate nuclear dialogue with India for regional nuclear stability.

Conclusion

Several experts have opined that a criteria-based[77] NSG waiver might be a preferred method for seeking formal commitments from Pakistan towards strengthening non-proliferation objectives. The criteria-based approach must be strengthened by making it incumbent upon Pakistan to put one or more of its unsafeguarded reactors under IAEA safeguards and not to block the FMCT negotiations in the CD. However, even if Pakistan agrees to restart the FMCT negotiations it can still block the FMCT text. Therefore, Pakistan must assure that it will not oppose the FMCT text when being negotiated in the CD.

Further, any consideration for an NSG exemption for Pakistan must initiate only after the CD adopts the FMCT text without it being subjected to any potential obstruction from Pakistan. Given Pakistan's dismal political and nuclear non-proliferation record, any suggestion for an NSG exemption for Pakistan is premature and harmful for the global nuclear non-proliferation order.

Notes

1. Mark Fitzpatrick, "Overcoming Pakistan's Nuclear Dangers," *Adelphi Book 443*, IISS, 11 March 2014. Christine Fair argues that a condition-based civilian nuclear deal could be offered to Pakistan if it agrees to abandon support for terrorism. C. Christine Fair,"Should Pakistan Get a Nuke Deal?", *Foreign Policy*, 23 March 2010,http://www.foreignpolicy.com/articles/2010/03/23/should_pakistan_get_a_nuke_deal?wp_login_redirect=0 (Accessed on 14 February 2018). Michael O Hanlon suggests a civilian nuclear deal to Pakistan would constitute an incentive for better cooperation on the Afghanistan issue. See Michael O Hanlon, "How to Win Back Pakistan," *Foreign Policy*, 08 November 2010, http://www.foreignpolicy.com/articles/2010/11/08/how_to_win_back_pakistan (Accessed on 14 February 2018).
2. *Ibid.*
3. David Albright and Corey Hinderstein, "Unraveling the A.Q. Khan and Future Proliferation Networks," *Washington Quarterly*, vol. 28, no. 2, Spring 2005, pp. 118-119.

4. "Pervez Hoodhbhoy, "Post Bib-Laden: The Safety and Security of Pakistan's Nuclear Arsenal," in Pervez Hoodbhoy (ed.), *Confronting the Bomb Pakistani and Indian Scientists Speak Out*, Pakistan: Oxford University Press, 2013, pp. 168-203.
5. "Overview of the Economy," *Pakistan Economic Survey 2013-14,* Ministry of Finance, Government of Pakistan at http://www.finance.gov.pk/survey/chapters_17/overview_2016-17.pdf, p. i (Accessed on 17 February 2018). (Accessed on 06 February 2018).
6. Hoodbhoy, n. 4, p. 342.
7. Ansar Abbasi, "The monster raises its ugly head again: circular debt is back," *The ews*, 22 August 2013, *http://www.thenews.com.pk/Todays-News-13-24918-The-monster-raises-its-ugly-head-again-circular-debt-is-back* (Accessed on 10 February 2018). According to Khawaja Muhammad Asif, Pakistan's Minister for Water and Power, due to shortage of power the country had sustained a huge loss of Rs. 1,000 billion in the last five years. See "Pak Minister to visit India to tackle energy crisis," *The Hindu*, 30 June 2013, *http://www.thehindu.com/news/international/south-asia/pak-minister-to-visit-india-to-tackle-energy-crisis/article4866068.ece* (Accessed on 14 February 2018).
8. Hoodbhoy, n. 4, p. 343.
9. "Haphazard mix" of Pakistan's energy bureaucracy," *Dawn*, 06 July 2011, *http://www.dawn.com/news/641928/secret-us-cables-accessed-by-dawn-through-wikileaks-us-examined-haphazard-mix-of-pakistans-energy-bureaucracy* (Accessed on 04 February 2018).
10. Toby Dalton, (et.al.), "A Criteria-Based Approach to Nuclear Cooperation with Pakistan," *Carnegie Endowment for International Peace, 22* June 2011 at carnegieendowment.org/files/nsgcriteria.pdf, p. 2 (Accessed on 14 February 2018).
11. Pakistan is currently facing a power deficit of 4,000-5,000 megawatts per day. See "Pak Minister to visit India to tackle energy crisis," *The Hindu*, 30 June 2013, *http://www.thehindu.com/news/international/south-asia/pak-minister-to-visit-india-to-tackle-energy-crisis/article4866068.ece* (Accessed on 31 January 2018).
12. Rakesh Sharma and Santanu Choudhury, "India, Pakistan Announce Joint Energy Initiatives," *The Wall Street Journa*l, 25 January 2012, http://online.wsj.com/news/articles/SB10001424052970203806504577182301242396574 (Accessed on 14 February 2018).
13. A Power Ministry delegation led by Joint Secretary Rita Acharya visited Pakistan, earlier this week, and discussed the broad contours of the proposed arrangement. See "Pakistan seeks 500 MW power supply from India," *The Economic Times*, 14 June 2013, http://articles.economictimes.indiatimes.com/2013-06-14/news/39976660_1_transmission-line-joint-secretary-rita-acharya-transmission-network (Accessed on 31 January 2018).
14. "Pak Minister to visit India to tackle energy crisis," *The Hindu*, 30 June 2013, *http://www.thehindu.com/news/international/south-asia/pak-minister-to-visit-india-to-tackle-energy-crisis/article4866068.ece* (Accessed on 31 January 2018).

15. Shireen Mazari, "Nuclear Suppliers Group and Pakistan: Victim of Nuclear Apartheid," Conference Report on "Pakistan and Peaceful Uses of Nuclear Energy," CISS, 19 March 2013, *http://www.ciss.org.pk/publicationinner.php?publicationid=4* (Accessed on 31 January 2018).
16. India and Australia have completed negotiations for a civil nuclear agreement likely to be implemented in September 2014. It will pave the way for uranium imports from Australia, making it one of India's top strategic partners. See Indrani Bagchi, "India-Australia nuclear deal likely next month," *The Times of India*, 07 August 2014, http://timesofindia.indiatimes.com/india/India-Australia-nuclear-deal-likely-next-month/articleshow/39779542.cms?utm_source=NSSPI+News+Digest&utm_campaign=382dbb0c1c—407565265 (Accessed on 31 January 2018).
17. David E Sanger, "Sanctions Could Badly Bruise Fragile Pakistan," *The New York Times*, 29 May 1998, http://www.nytimes.com/1998/05/29/world/nuclear-anxiety-the-economy-sanctions-could-badly-bruise-fragile-pakistan.html (Accessed on 05 February 2018) as stated in Stephen J. Cimbala (ed.), *Deterrence and Nuclear Proliferation in the Twenty-first Century* (USA: Praegar Publishers, 2001), p. 106; Warren Hoge, "Wealthy Nations Cut Aid to Pakistan Over Nuclear Tests," *The New York Times*, 29 May 1998, http://www.nytimes.com/1998/05/29/world/nuclear-anxiety-reaction-wealthy-nations-cut-aid-pakistan-over-nuclear-tests.html (Accessed on 10 February 2018) as stated in Cimbala, n. 17.
18. The '*grandfather clause*' refers to the agreement to construct two nuclear reactors Chashma-1 and -2 in *Pakistan* before *China* joined the NSG in 2004.
19. Chasnupp 1 started operating in June 2000, while Chasnupp 2 began operating in May 2011. Chasnupp 3 is expected to start commercial operation in 2016. "Construction of New Pakistani Reactor," *World Nuclear News*, 15 June 2011, http://www.world-nuclear-news.org/IT-Construction_starts_of_fourth_Pakistani_reactor-1506114.html (Accessed on 10 February 2018).
20. *Ibid.*
21. Ibid.
22. The project includes two large Chinese-supplied nuclear reactors with a capacity of 1,100 MWe each. Mehreen Zahra-Malik, "Exclusive: China commits $6.5 billion for Pakistani nuclear project," *Reuters*, 24 December 2013, http://www.reuters.com/article/2013/12/24/us-pakistan-china-nuclear-idUSBRE9BN06220131224 (Accessed on 10 February 2018).
23. Sharon Squassoni, "The U.S.-Indian Deal and Its Impact," *Arms Control Association*, 02 July 2010, https://www.armscontrol.org/act/2010_07-08/squassoni (Accessed on 10 February 2018); Nick Cunningham, "Why China's nuclear plans in Pakistan draw global criticism," *The Christian Science Monitor*, 11 March 2015, http://www.csmonitor.com/Environment/Energy-Voices/2015/0311/Why-China-s-nuclear-plans-in-Pakistan-draw-global-criticism (Accessed on 10 February 2018).
24. G. Balachandran and Kapil Patil, "China's Reactor Sale to Pakistan: The Known Unknowns," *IDSA Issue Brief*, 15 November 2013, http://www.idsa.in/issuebrief/ChinasReactorSaletoPakistan_gbalachandran_151113.html (Accessed on 10 February 2018).

25. Shirley A Kan, "China and Proliferation of Weapons of Mass Destruction and Missiles: Policy Issues," *Congressional Research Service*, 07 November 2012, http://www.law.umaryland.edu/marshall/crsreports/crsdocuments/RL31555_11072012.pdf, p. 5 (Accessed on 10 February 2018).
26. Balachandran and Patil, n. 24; Zhao Huanxin, "China, Pakistan sign cooperation treaty," *China Daily*, 06 April 2005, http://www.chinadaily.com.cn/english/doc/2005-04/06/content_431695.htm (Accessed on 10 February 2018).
27. "Chashma Nuclear Power Project Units -3 and -4 of 300 MWe Each, PC-I Performa", Pakistan Atomic Energy Commission., Islamabad as stated in Balachandran and Patil, n. 24.
28. *Ibid.*
29. Pakistan has been associated with NSG's outreach programmes since 2002. "Pakistan vow on nuclear exports," *BBC News*, 11 April 2005, http://news.bbc.co.uk/2/hi/south_asia/4434081.stm (Accessed on 10 February 2018).
30. Mark Hibbs, "China provides nuclear reactors to Pakistan," *Jane's Intelligence Review*, January 2014, http://carnegieendowment.org/email/DC_Comms/img JIR1401%20F3%20ChinaPak.pdf (Accessed on 10 February 2018).
31. *Nucleonics Week* (19 June 1997, and 26 February 1998) in Kan, n. 25, p. 4.
32. *Nucleonics Week*, April 26, 2001; and *IAEA, Annual Report 2001*, Kan, n. 25, p. 4.
33. In 11 May 1996 China pledged not to provide assistance to unsafeguarded nuclear facilities. See "China's Nuclear Exports and Assistance to Pakistan," Center for Nonproliferation Studies, August 1999, http://cns.miis.edu/archive/country_india/china/npakpos.htm (Accessed on 10 February 2018).
34. "The Acquisition of Technology Relating to Weapons of Mass Destruction and Advanced Conventions/ Munitions July-December 1996," *Director of Central Intelligence*, June 1997, http://fas.org/irp/cia/product/wmd.htm (Accessed on 10 February 2018).
35. "Adherence To and Compliance With Arms Control Agreements," 1998 Report submitted to the Congress, Washington, DC, US Department of State, http://1997-2001.state.gov/www/global/arms/reports/annual/comp98.html (Accessed on 10 February 2018).
36. Bill Gertz, "China, Pakistan Reach Nuke Agreement," *The Washington Free Beacon,* 22 March 2013, http://freebeacon.com/national-security/china-pakistan-reach-nuke-agreement/ (Accessed on 13 February 2018).
37. "Pak-China civil nuclear coop in compliance with NGS: Spokesman FM," *Associated Press of Pakistan,* http://app.com.pk/en_/index.php?option=com_content&task=view&id=229825&Itemid=2 (Accessed on 13 February 2018).
38. Mark Hibbs, "China provides nuclear reactors to Pakistan," *Jane's Intelligence Review*, January 2014, http://carnegieendowment.org/email/DC_Comms/img/JIR1401%20F3%20ChinaPak.pdf (Accessed on 13 February 2018).
39. *Ibid.*

40. Mark Hibbs, "Moving forward on China, Pakistan, and the NSG," *Arms Control Wonk*, 23 June 2011, http://hibbs.armscontrolwonk.com/archive/228/moving-forward-on-china-pakistan-and-the-nsg (Accessed on 13 February 2018).
41. Identifying and seperating its civilian and military nuclear facilities (since achieved); India has demarcated between its civilian and military nuclear facilities, and voluntarily placed its civilian nuclear facilities under IAEA safeguards. India's 2005 Separation Plan identified 14 thermal power reactors and nine research facilities for the safeguarded side of India's nuclear complex; filing a declaration regarding its civilian nuclear facilities with the IAEA and placing them under its safeguardsby negotiating an Additional Protocol (since completed), India been transparent that the its civilian facilities would not add to India's nuclear weapons program; continuing India's unilateral moratorium on nuclear testing (being adhered to); assuring that its companies will conform to India's international commitments to not engage in any illicit transfer of sensitive technologies to countries of concern; agreed to secure its nuclear materails and technology through comprehensive export control regulations and harmonized its national export controls with the control lists and guidelines of the Nuclear Suppliers Group and the Missile Technology Control Regime (enabling legislation has been enacted); agreed to work with the U.S. to conclude a multilateral FMCT. See PR Chari (ed.), *Indo-US Nuclear Deal: Seeking Synergy in Bilateralism*, New Delhi: Routledge, 2009, pp. 6-7; Geoffrey Pyatt, "Taking Stock of the U.S.-India Nuclear Deal," US Department of State, 30 September 2011, http://www.state.gov/p/sca/rls/rmks/2011/174883.htm (Accessed on 13 February 2018).
42. In the 1990s, China designed and built a prototype nuclear reactor at Qinshan. An accident in 1998 due to a design flaw shut it down for a year. Initially the Chinese nuclear designers and operators could not understand or fix the problem, and had to contract a U.S. company for the repair work. One part of the reactor had to be redesigned. After this China did not build any more reactors of the Qinshan design for itself, but happily sold this type of reactor to Pakistan; four such reactors will eventually operate at Chashma. Pakistan was lucky that the reactor accident happened before the first Chashma plant went online. There was enough time for it to be redesigned to avoid the problem that led to the breakdown at Qinshan. But will Pakistan's luck always hold? See Pervez Hoodbhoy, Zia Mian and A.H. Nayyar, "The Nuclear Shadow over Karachi," *Newsweek*, 17 March 2014, http://newsweekpakistan.com/the-nuclear-shadow-over-karachi/ (Accessed on 13 February 2018).
43. '"Pakistan is bleeding" - ex counter terrorism chief,' *BBC News*, 09 July 2013, http://www.bbc.co.uk/news/world-23242399 (Accessed on 13 February 2018).
44. Pakistan is experiencing an increasing loss of political control in every sphere of governance. "Pakistan Assessment 2013," *South Asia Terrorism Portal*, http://www.satp.org/satporgtp/countries/pakistan/index.htm (Accessed on 13 February 2018).
45. Pakistan's institutional and organizational system like its military units, police stations, and border checkpoints, and military installations has been subject to bombings. The Tehrik-e Taliban Pakistan (TTP) often claimed responsibility for attacks targeting civilians and security personnel in Pakistan.

46. Reshmi Kazi, "Pakistan's nuclear security faces insider threat," *Hindustan Times*, 19 June 2014, http://www.hindustantimes.com/comment/analysis/pakistan-s-nuclear-security-faces-insider-threat/article1-1231378.aspx (Accessed on 13 February 2018).
47. Fitzpatrick, n. 1, p. 164.
48. George Perkovich on "The Non-Unitary Model and Deterrence Stability in South Asia", *Stimson Center*, 13 November 2012, http://www.stimson.org/images/uploads/research-pdfs/George_Perkovich_-_The_Non_Unitary_Model_and_Deterrence_Stability_in_South_Asia.pdf, p. 17 (Accessed on 13 February 2018).
49. Any decision for an NSG exemption and a consequent civil nuclear energy deal with Pakistan could potentially help accelerate production of bomb materials. This might impact upon internal Pakistani demands to conduct more nuclear tests and cause vertical proliferation escalation. The same concerns were also indicated during the negotiations of the India-US nuclear energy cooperation initiative. However, India has not violated any of its commitments made in the deal agreement.
50. Mark Urban, "Saudi nuclear weapons 'on order' from Pakistan," *BBC News*, 06 November 2013, http://www.bbc.com/news/world-middle-east-24823846 (Accessed on 15 February 2018); Naser al-Tamimi, "Will Riyadh Get the Bomb? Saudi Arabia's Atomic Ambitions," *Middle East Quarterly*, Spring 2013, http://www.meforum.org/meq/pdfs/3509.pdf, p. 51 (Accessed on 15 February 2018).
51. Bruce Riedel, "Enduring Allies: Pakistan's Partnership with Saudi Arabia Runs Deeper," *Brookings Institution*, 09 December 2011, p. 20, http://www.brookings.edu/~/media/research/files/articles/2011/12/09%20saudi%20arabia%20pakistan%20riedel/1209_saudi_arabia_pakistan_ riedel.pdf (Accessed on 15 February 2018).
52. Christopher Clary and Mara E. Karlin, "The Pak-Saudi Nuke, and How to Stop It," *The American Interest*, 10 June 2012, http://www.the-american-interest.com/articles/2012/06/10/the-pak-saudi-nuke-and-how-to-stop-it/ (Accessed on 15 February 2018).
53. Feroz Hassan Khan, *Eating Grass: The Making of the Pakistani Bomb*, Stanford, CA: Stanford University Press, 2012, p. 383.
54. Shirley A. Kan, "China and Proliferation of Weapons of Mass Destruction and Missiles: Policy Issues, *Congressional Research Service*, 07 November 2012, http://www.law.umaryland.edu/marshall/crsreports/crsdocuments/RL31555_11072012.pdf, pp. 5 (Accessed on 15 February 2018).
55. *Ibid.,* p. 6.
56. *Ibid.*
57. *Ibid.*
58. "Pakistan's strategic nuclear and missile industries," Project Alpha at the Centre for Science and Security Studies (CSSS) at King's College, London, September 2016, http://projectalpha.eu/wp-content/uploads/sites/21/2016/11/20160929-Pakistan-public-version.pdf, p. 28 (Accessed on 15 February 2018)
59. *Ibid,* p. 25.
60. *Ibid,* p. 7.

61. "Sharif regrets Pakistan's bad relations with India," *The Hindu*, 30 January 2014.
62 Toby Dalton, et al., "A Criteria-Based Approach to Nuclear Cooperation with Pakistan," *Carnegie Endowment for International Peace, 22* June 2011, *carnegieendowment.org/files/nsgcriteria.pdf,* p. 12 (Accessed on 15 February 2018).
63. Sumit Ganguly, *Conflict Unending: India-Pakistan Tensions Since 1947*, New Delhi: Columbia University Press, 2001.
64. Lashkar-e-Taiba was responsible for both the 2001 attack on the Indian Parliament and the 2008 Mumbai massacre.
65. "India Assessment – 2013", South Asia Terrorism Portal, http://www.satp.org/satporgtp/countries/india/index.html (Accessed on 15 February 2018).
66 Mariam Abou Zahab and Olivier Roy, *Islamist Networks: The AfghanPakistan Connection*, London: Hurst, 2002, p. 39 as stated in Mark Fitzpatrick, "Overcoming Pakistan's Nuclear Dangers," *Adelphi Book 443*, IISS, 11 March 2014, p. 135.
67. 'Would not mind Indo-Pak N-war: JuD Chief', *Zee News*, 06 February 2011, http://zeenews.india.com/news/south-asia/would-not-mindindo-pak-n-war-jud-chief_685470.html (Accessed on 15 February 2018).
68. Graham Allison, 'Nuclear Terrorism Fact Sheet', Policy Memo, Belfer Center for Science and International Affairs, Harvard Kennedy School, April 2010, http://belfercenter.ksg.harvard.edu/publication/20057/nuclear_terrorism_fact_sheet.html (Accessed on 15 February 2018).
69. Christine Fair, *Fighting to the End: The Pakistan Army's Way of War*, UK: Oxford University Press, 2014, p. 4.
70. *Ibid.*
71. Gurmeet Kanwal, "India's Cold Start Doctrine and Strategic Stability," *IDSA Comment*, 01 June 2010, http://www.idsa.in/idsacomments/IndiasColdStart DoctrineandStrategicStability_gkanwal_010610.html (Accessed on 15 February 2018).
72. "US embassy cables: India 'unlikely' to deploy Cold Start against Pakistan," *The Guardian*, 30 November 2010, http://www.theguardian.com/world/us-embassy-cables-documents/248971 (Accessed on 15 February 2018).
73. "The South Asian Nuclear Balance: An Interview with Pakistani Ambassador to the CD Zamir Akram," *Arms Control Today*, December 2011, https://www.armscontrol.org/act/2011_12/Interview_With_Pakistani_Ambassador_to_the_CD_Zamir_Akram (Accessed on 15 February 2018).
74. Tariq Osman Hyder, "FMCT – facts and fiction," *The News*, 28 March 2012, http://www.thenews.com.pk/Todays-News-9-99914-FMCT-%E2%80%93-facts-and-fiction (Accessed on 15 February 2018).
75. A similar position has been suggested by Mark Fitzpatrick who "sets a high bar for a nuclear normalization deal, requiring Pakistan to agree to end fissile material production, drop its veto over initiating FMCT negotiations in Geneva, sign the CTBT, and cease its support for groups that conduct terrorism."See Fitzpatrick, n.1.
76. Pakistan provided new details about the kind of FMCT that it seeks. See "On the issue of Scope," Statement by Ambassador Zamir Akram, Permanent

Representative at the Conference on Disarmament, Informal discussions on agenda items 1 and 2 with a general focus on the ban of the production of fissile materials for nuclear weapons and other nuclear explosive devices, 5 June 2014 at http://fissilematerials.org/library/pk14b.pdf (Accessed on 15 February 2018)

77. Toby Dalton, et al., "A Criteria-Based Approach to Nuclear Cooperation with Pakistan," *Carnegie Endowment for International Peace, 22* June 2011, *carnegieendowment.org/files/nsgcriteria.pdf,* p. 12 (Accessed on 22 July 2014); Fitzpatrick, n. 1.

Chapter - 11

India-Pakistan Collaborative Framework on Nuclear Security: Inquiring the Rationale and Exploring the Possibilities

— *Manisha Chaurasiya*

Introduction

The recent history of both India and Pakistan shows that the worst attacks on these two nations originates from the non-state terrorist actors operating in the region. India and Pakistan are among a handful of countries that possess advanced nuclear capabilities and delivery mechanisms but are not members of the Nuclear Non-Proliferation Treaty (NPT). Both countries envision expansion of civilian nuclear energy programs in the near future. The security of nuclear facilities and materials thus becomes paramount due to the global and active threat of nuclear terrorism acknowledged by a majority of world countries. Both states are vulnerable due to their geographical proximity to the breeding grounds of most notorious and dangerously active terrorist organizations of the present century, including Al Qaeda, the Islamic State of Iraq and the Levant (ISIL), Lashkar-e-Taiba, and Jaish-e-Mohammed, Tehrik-i-Taliban, among others. India and Pakistan share not only the same neighbourhood, but also a historical animosity that has resulted in several wars between the two states. Prolonged unhealthy political relations have led to the diplomatic linkages between them shaky with a trust deficit.

This paper proposes a collaborative framework on nuclear security between India and Pakistan given the fact that both states possess nuclear weapons, use nuclear energy and expect expansion of their respective nuclear energy production. This also remains a brute fact that they are located in a volatile region suffering from a continued growth of international terrorism. The threat to nuclear materials and infrastructure through nuclear terrorism cannot be met by efforts of individual states in isolation. That was the very reason the Nuclear Security Summit (NSS) process launched by the United States (US) government prioritized multilateral initiatives and promoted collaborative efforts to secure nuclear materials all over the world through cooperation with the various national governments. This paper reinforces the belief in a synergic approach to the threat of nuclear terrorism and suggests collaboration, specifically between India and Pakistan. However, the paper does not look into the military aspects of nuclear technology and the associated security but focuses only on the civilian nuclear materials and infrastructure. This particular concern regarding prioritizing nuclear security is actually global. It has become more important after the conclusion of the NSS in 2016. The majority of countries that participated in the NSS process believe that an urgent need remains to sustain the momentum of the summits after its conclusion. The spirit of prioritizing nuclear security matters should not be defeated and compromised, necessitating collaboration on nuclear security either through bilateral, regional or multilateral levels.

Why Nuclear Security is Salient?

There are many valid reasons why nuclear terrorism is treated as one of the most salient threats facing mankind. The possibilities of nuclear terrorism lead to a concerted effort to ensure nuclear security. Nuclear terrorism can become a reality with dire results, if there is any leniency in the nuclear security infrastructure and efforts. Terrorists have been eager to utilize nuclear and radiological sources for their ambitions. In 1995, a group of Chechen rebels in Moscow hid a crude dirty bomb containing radioactive cesium in a Moscow park.[1] Though it never exploded and was discovered in a timely manner, media broadcasts generated panic and psychological fear. The events of 9/11 marked the audacity and reach of the non-state terrorist actors ready to cause unacceptable damage. In January 2001, Howard Baker and Lloyd Cutler in their official review briefed President Bush that the most urgent unmet national security threat to the US was "the danger that weapons of mass destruction or weapons-usable material in Russia could be stolen, sold to terrorists or hostile nation states and used against American troops abroad or citizens at home."[2] The same year during the investigation, they speculated that a 'second shoe'[3] of the attacks on the World Trade Centre and the Pentagon had been planned by Al Qaeda terrorists that possessed a ten-kiloton nuclear bomb on the US soil.[4] In addition to these, the capabilities and possibilities of new emerging non state terror groups like ISIL, with much more advanced technological sophistication and network, to blackmail the world through nuclear terrorism or a dirty bomb remains largely uncovered and unanticipated.

According to the International Atomic Energy Agency (IAEA), nuclear security comprises the prevention and detection of, and response to unauthorized removal, sabotage, unauthorized access, illegal transfer or other malicious acts involving nuclear or radiological material or their associated facilities. Any bilateral or multilateral effort to ensure greater security of nuclear materials in this light can be beneficial for the cause.

'State responsibility' in the international law context emphasizes that each state remains responsible for the activities on its soil, including the security and safety of one's nuclear assets, facilities, plants, and materials. The IAEA recognizes that "the responsibility for nuclear security rests entirely with each State and that appropriate and effective national systems for nuclear security are vital in facilitating the peaceful use of nuclear energy and enhancing global efforts to combat nuclear terrorism."[5]

However, this does not in any manner discount the power and capacity of achieving nuclear security through multi-stakeholders and parties. Nuclear terrorism is an immediate and urgent threat that deserves to be addressed through efforts that surpass any individual state's domestic efforts.

In this regard, the Nuclear Security Summit process can be cited as an important multilateral initiative to revisit nuclear security matters. The NSS process aimed to increase global awareness and prioritization on nuclear security. President Barack Obama initiated the Nuclear Security Summit Process in 2010. According to Obama, it is of utmost salience that terrorists never acquire a nuclear weapon as it is the most immediate and extreme threat to global security.[6] The NSS process aimed at providing high-level attention to nuclear security through prioritized efforts. However, the conclusion of the NSS process in 2016 after six years of its existence has left a vacuum.

Nuclear Security: Analysis of Contemporary South Asia

Historically states tend to guard technological innovations and developments from sharing, especially in the nuclear realm. However, states have remained more open in the area of nuclear security. The success of NSS, achieved in a comparatively limited time of only six years, suggests that the issue of nuclear security has transcended the typical inclination of many states to guard everything related to nuclear matters. Secrecy on the matters of security makes less sense in the face of global challenges like nuclear terrorism, where collective action and efforts remain vital.

Nuclear terrorism has become a more prevalent threat since 9/11, which marked a serious change in the type, scope, and magnitude of terror attacks all over the globe. As Ambassador H.E. Marcel de Vink stated at the third Nuclear Security Summit:

> Terrorists or other criminals need relatively small amounts to manufacture a nuclear explosive device...the most difficult hurdle to building a bomb is acquiring sufficient quantities of these materials."[7] Sophisticated nuclear technology and the desire to widen the damage and cause impact in both physical and psychological terms has been a priority of terrorist groups. Sitakanta Mishra warns though that "fabricating and/or pilfering a full-fledged nuclear bomb is difficult for them, sabotaging a nuclear facility by a suicide attack or by using a 'dirty bomb' is undoubtedly within their reach.[8]

In the context of South Asia a bilateral approach between India and Pakistan to nuclear security would be possible through shared safety procedures, technology in detection equipment, forensics, and overall 'best practices' and experiences in transferring and in enforcement and managing spent fuel. Though there are a number of political differences between India and Pakistan, the approach of the leadership on both sides is somewhat similar towards nuclear security as a pressing concern.

Before a terrorists attempt to utilize nuclear or radiological materials for their purposes, both India and Pakistan should invest their energy and take cooperative initiative towards preventing nuclear terrorism. The NSS brought the issue of nuclear security to the multilateral table to prioritize and devise a habit of cooperation on best practices: bilateral efforts in the same direction post-NSS should be considered a continuation of those efforts.

Both India and Pakistan have been suffering from terrorism. In Pakistan, there has been a loss of around 1457 civilian and security personnel lives in 2015-2016 alone due to terror attacks.[9] India has also suffered considerable human life losses in hands of non-state terror groups. The Mumbai terror attacks in 2008, the multiple serial bombings of the capital and the Pathankot Air Force Base attack in 2016 prove the threats posed by terror groups are a continued security threat. In the midst of already mounting multiplicity of traditional and non-traditional threats to state security, nuclear security has become the next threat to face. The task confronting states who are utilizing nuclear technology is to dedicate serious attention towards collaboration. Both India and Pakistan are in possession of nuclear weapons and the related military nuclear material is not taken up by this paper. The NSS process has also concentrated specifically on the unsecured civilian nuclear materials around the world with an exception to the military uses and facilities for all the participating countries.

Nuclear Security and India

Jawaharlal Nehru, the founding father of the state as well as a chief architect of the country's nuclear programme stated that, 'the source materials for nuclear energy, not an ordinary commodity and needed to be handled with care.'[10] Nuclear security is a journey, a process and not simply a destination. Therefore, states should take continuous strides and avoid complacency.

Nuclear security is important for India as a country which embarks on an ambitious civil nuclear expansion plan.[11] It has fairly large infrastructure related to nuclear technology which remains dispersed countrywide, and given that radiological materials are used in many sectors, the probability of their use in an unauthorized manner cannot be completely ruled out. Finally, India is situated in a volatile region, and hence, remains vulnerable to nuclear terrorism.[12]

In fact, India's nuclear security culture accepts that a credible threat exists and that global initiatives to strengthen nuclear security infrastructure and related practices serve Indian interests.[13] India joined the Nuclear Security Summit Process at its initiation in 2010. At the 2014 NSS India stated that, 'Nuclear terrorism and clandestine proliferation continue to pose a serious threat to international security. India fully shares the continuing global concern on possible breaches of nuclear security'.[14] Since then India participated in all four NSS. The threat of nuclear and radiological terrorism is real and in the opinion of Sitakanta Mishra, nuclear security involves a broader set of threats which includes sabotage, cyber and conventional attacks on nuclear and radiation facilities and breaches of regulations governing transfers of technology and radiological materials including during transport apart from the obvious nuclear terrorism and RDDs.[15] "Unlike nuclear weapons which inflict mass causalities and destruction through blast, searing heat, and the release of massive amounts of radiation, a RDD or 'dirty bomb' in common parlance...uses conventional explosives to disperse small, perhaps vial-size amounts of radioactive material that are attached or placed next to the explosive," said Mishra.[16]

India has the benefit of experience in nuclear security as the first nuclear research reactor in India, *Apsara* went critical in 1956 and India thus has been well aware of the responsibility that comes along with enjoying the benefits of nuclear technology. The Bhabha Atomic Research Center (BARC) designed and built the reactor with the assistance from the United Kingdom. In 1962 India adopted the Atomic Energy Act, which provided the legal framework for all aspects related to development of nuclear and radiation technologies, including their security. The rules and guidelines issued under this Act include those related to export controls. They are continuously updated to include controls on export of related technologies.[17]

India is party to thirteen legal instruments regarded as the benchmarks for a State's commitments to combat international terrorism.[18] These include the International Convention for the Suppression of Acts of Nuclear Terrorism (ICSANT) and the Convention on the Physical Protection of Nuclear Materials (CPPNM). In 2014, India also ratified the Additional Protocol between India and the IAEA for the Application of Safeguards to Civilian Nuclear Facilities.[19]

Nuclear Security and Pakistan

At the most recent NSS summit in Washington, Tariq Fatemi, acting Special Assistant to Pakistan's Prime Minister on Foreign Affairs, said that "Pakistan is committed to the objective of nuclear security and has been proactively engaged with the international community to promote nuclear safety and security."[20] It remains in Pakistan's interest that nuclear and radioactive materials and all related facilities are well secured. Over the last few decades it encountered terrorism on its soil, with continued escalation in the magnitude and damage involved in the attacks. The state has remained volatile as it harbours various forms of Islamic fundamentalism and shares a porous border on the western side of the country.

Pakistan's first acquaintance with nuclear technology was in 1972 when it established the Karachi Nuclear Power Plant (KANUPP). Since then the state has been involved in nuclear activities. Presently Pakistan has been encountering energy shortfalls in face of a growing population and economy thus has shown inclination towards safe and sustainable civilian nuclear energy as an option. Pakistan envisages a of 40,000 MW energy generation through nuclear.[21] This means that a robust nuclear security infrastructure and regime on nuclear security becomes a necessary requirement which can be furthered by the national legislative, regulatory and administrative framework.

As part of the NSS, Pakistan has announced the establishment of the centre of excellence called the National Institute of Safety and Security (NISAS) to facilitate national and regional courses on nuclear security and training in various nuclear security disciplines including physical protection and personnel reliability.[22] Pakistan has committed to adopt the international guidelines of the IAEA and accepted best practices on nuclear security and safety. It cannot be denied that Pakistan has taken the overall issue of nuclear security seriously as it recognized that the effects of nuclear terrorism would have disastrous impact. Pakistan signed and ratified the amendment to the International Convention on the Physical Protection of Nuclear Materials (CPPNM) in March 2016.

Cooperative Framework on Nuclear Security

A cooperative framework on nuclear security would be beneficial for both Pakistan and India. This multifaceted collaboration, (a) has the potential to synergise the existing individual approaches led by both India and Pakistan on nuclear security, (b) could assist and benefit Pakistan to strengthen itself against existing vulnerabilities, a product of volatility in its geo-political location, (c) would help India to better understand a variety of nuclear security techniques and get acquainted with the probable challenges and scenarios, and (d) would promote a stronger bilateral and joint solution to the herculean task of nuclear security, an effort that would originate from the South Asian region itself. Both New Delhi and Islamabad are yet to pay the required attention to cooperate in the nuclear domain. In 2015 the joint statement of Prime Minister Modi and Prime Minister Sharif touched on several issues such as the release of fishermen in each other's custody, facilitating religious tourism, means to expedite the Mumbai case trial and others. However, any future-oriented and mutually beneficial joint efforts on nuclear security remained absent.[23]A stalemate that hurts both countries could be overcome by a diplomatic breakthrough. Cooperation on issues of mutual interest, including on nuclear security, is a necessity. Cooperation on nuclear security between India and Pakistan and a collaborative framework could include the following components:

1. A Bilateral "Gift Basket"

Gift Basket Diplomacy is a collective action agreed by a small group of participants that goes beyond the lowest common denominator consensus that larger groups reach in multilateral forums. In the NSS context the 'gift basket' was initiated at the 2012 summit in Seoul. After the conclusion of the NSS process, the idea of sharing best practices could be formalized through an Indo-Pakistan framework on nuclear security. Two countries could reach an agreement on preventing nuclear terrorism through coordinated efforts. The platform for the exchange can initiate through a ministerial level meet which can then lead to initiatives involving a multitude of members ranging from atomic agencies, security agencies and specifically the trained personnel of civil nuclear facilities of both the countries. Although, a annual review on the ministerial level is desirable and can prove productive.

The 2016 NSS produced several multilateral initiatives under a 'gift basket' umbrella. Twenty seven countries plus the INTERPOL signed a statement on "Mitigating the Insider Threats". It called to establish national-level measures to mitigate the insider threat in the nuclear infrastructures and facilities against the possibility of nuclear terrorism. The broad aim was to lead to "an integrated, graded approach to mitigating insider threats (and that the) nuclear and radiological security programs should include national-level and agency- or facility-specific Insider Threat Mitigation policies and programs, training and awareness activities, and collaboration between facility-level organizations".[24] Unfortunately, both India and Pakistan did not join this initiative.

India did express willingness to join a 'contact group,' a smaller subset of NSS participating countries. It will be instrumental in monitoring the implementation of the various outcomes from the summit.[25]New Delhi has also communicated its intent to join two other 'gift baskets' on countering nuclear smuggling and on training and support centre.[26] The scope of numerous 'gift baskets' are relevant to the challenges India and Pakistan face in the region.

'Gift baskets' can certainly enhance state's own preparedness through complementing it with the benefit of international best practices and expertise. Pakistan believes that with the help of the IAEA its centre of excellence can one day become a regional and international hub.[27] This brings us closer to another venture worth collaboration on nuclear security between the two states – their respective newly created centres of excellences.

2. Centre for Excellence in Nuclear Security

The centre of excellence is an institution that conducts specialized courses in nuclear security, physical protection, material control and accounting, transport security and personnel reliability, and other. Under the auspices of the Nuclear Security Summit both India and Pakistan developed their respective centres of excellence. Unfortunately, there has been no connection or formal communication between the two institutions which undertake identical tasks and goals in the same region.

The Indian centre of excellence is known as the Global Centre for Nuclear Energy Partnership (GCNEP). It bases its design on a holistic vision of nuclear energy and has five schools on: advanced nuclear energy systems, nuclear security, radiological safety, nuclear material characterization, and applications of radioisotopes and radiation technologies. The institution has signed MOUs with the IAEA, United States, France, Russia and the United Kingdom.[28]

The Pakistani centre for excellence shares similar goals. It is called the National Institute of Safety and Security (NISAS). In Pakistan two institutes – the National Institute of Safety and Security (NISAS) and Pakistan Institute of Engineering and Applied Sciences (PIEAS) – worked together on nuclear security education and training as well as in the areas including physical protection, material control and accounting, transport security, cyber security and personnel reliability.[29]

The GCNEP conducted the 4th National Training Course on Physical Protection of Nuclear Material and Nuclear Material and Nuclear Facilities in March-April 2016 at the National Fuel Complex, Hyderabad.[30] The GNCEP conducted an International Training Course (ITC) on "Preventive and Protective Measures Against Insider Threats". In 2016 it conducted a workshop on "Medical Response to Radiation Incidents". Yet these initiatives either remained confined to national participation or to some other states with which India has signed related MoU on nuclear security matters. Pakistan conducted the first-ever nuclear security training conference under the auspice of the International Network for Nuclear Security Training and Support Centres (NSSC).[31]A total of 29 countries participated in the initiative, excluding India.[32] Overall both India and Pakistan deliberately avoid cooperating with each other, despite the fact that both countries are working individually to advance nuclear security efforts through their respective centres of excellences in the same region.

3. Cooperation on Nuclear Emergency Management

Pakistan established a Nuclear Emergency Management System to handle nuclear and radiological emergencies. Two institutions – Nuclear and Radiological Emergency Support Centre (NURESC) and National Radiation Emergency Coordination Center (NRECC) – participate in emergency response. As per the National Progress Report presented at the NSS, Pakistan is involved in conducting several training courses and exercises in emergency preparedness for the first responders, emergency response personnel and front line officers to effectively deal with a situation of nuclear emergency.[33] Pakistan has also been involved in several training courses for the first responders and emergency response personnel to raise its emergency preparedness.[34]

The Strategic Export Control Division (SECDIV) in the Ministry of Foreign Affairs of Pakistan has notified second revision of the 'National Export Control List' in 2015. Pakistan also claims that as part of its national detection architecture it has deployed radiation detection equipment at several entry and exit points to deter, detect and prevent illicit trafficking of nuclear and radioactive materials.[35]

In India the Department of Atomic Energy (DAE) supervises the institutional set up on nuclear emergency preparedness. These are Crisis Management Group (CMG), Computer Information & Security Advisory Group (CISAG), etc. These agencies have manpower trained to respond to emergencies including radiological ones. The security of nuclear and radiological material in India is ensured through robust oversight by the India's Atomic Energy Regulatory Board (AERB). The institution deploys a large pool of highly trained and specialized manpower for this purpose. There has been no collaborative framework on nuclear emergency management between India and Pakistan. None of the countries in the South Asian region have yet contemplated joint efforts to mitigate nuclear emergencies.

4. The Physical Security Forces Cooperation

Having engaged in several battles and constant cease-fire violations over the LoC, India and Pakistani forces have hardly been involved in joint exercises of any sort. Thus any deliberation or proposal of collaborative security of nuclear infrastructure is quite bold or courageous a step and thus has hardly been ever debated.

In India, a paramilitary force called the Central Industrial Security Force (CISF) provides security to nuclear facilities. Apart from the CISF, a dedicated institutional mechanism called a Counter Nuclear Smuggling Team has been established at the national level. It is part of a coordinated multi-agency approach to deal with the threat of nuclear or radioactive material reaching individuals and groups for malicious purposes. The team also has representation from concerned ministries, departments, and agencies and meets frequently. It conducts exercises for effective and coordinated response to related threats.[36]

Network of 23 Emergency Response Centres are spread across India for the purpose of physical protection of nuclear material. They were developed to detect and respond to a nuclear or radiological emergency anywhere in the country. All major sea ports and airports were equipped with radiation portals and detection equipment to monitor all vehicular, passenger and cargo traffic.

India acknowledged the reality of nuclear security threats coming from the cyber domain. With the help of a highly technologically specialized team New Delhi addresses the growing challenges of threats to computer, network and information systems. Through extensive expertise available in the country on matters of cyber security, the on-site Cyber security architecture has also been deployed. A secure network access system (SNAS) has been developed and deployed for protection of the cyber infrastructure in the country.[37]

In Pakistan nuclear security has also received serious attention due to the presence of a variety of non-state terrorist groups on its soil. On the international front Pakistan has successfully implemented the IAEA-Pakistan nuclear security cooperation program.[38] This carries several projects for capacity enhancement in nuclear security. The Pakistani security forces have been trained by the United States to deal with acts of nuclear terrorism. Yet as the volatility of the situation in Pakistan suggests (frequent and regular incidences of terrorist attacks), it becomes vital that the forces keep themselves updated and prepared for nuclear terrorism. According to news reports the Pakistan's nuclear facilities have been attacked at least three times by home-grown extremists till date.[39] These incidents include an attack on a nuclear missile storage facility at Sargodha in 2007 and also a homicide bombing at the nuclear airbase at Kamra the same year.[40] However, Shaun Gregory in his paper titled, "The Terrorist Threat to Pakistan's Nuclear Weapons" has cited the third attack as 'a much more considerable raid' conducted by the Pakistani Taliban in August, 2008 when homicide bombers blew up several entry points to a main armament complex at the country's main nuclear facility, the Wah Cantonment Ordnance Complex.[41]

Collaboration between India and Pakistan in way of an annual or biannual joint training of the forces which are involved in the physical protection of the nuclear facilities and also the transfers of the radioactive materials could be beneficial. On the physical security aspect between both the countries any kind of cooperation has been largely lacking. Reason of geopolitics and a continued rivalry has been responsible for such a scenario. But a renewed approach can add a fresh rigour to both the state's individual and isolated efforts so that they could better fight the great threat of nuclear terrorism. Especially because it is a known secret that vulnerabilities regarding nuclear terrorism are not just exists but also can lead to catastrophic and unacceptable consequences for both the states.

Way Forward

At the dawn of a new century, we find ourselves in a new arms race. Terrorists are racing to get weapons of mass destruction; we ought to be racing to stop them. - Sam Nunn

Two salient lessons of the present century regarding nuclear security remain present. First is the importance of sustaining the efforts, momentum and the nuclear security culture established by the NSS process. Second the necessity to reach some concrete form of cooperation bilaterally between countries or multilaterally through regional efforts.

In this sense an India-Pakistan collaborative framework on nuclear security makes perfect sense. It could be attempted through a wide array of techniques, including an exchange of best practices through 'mutual gift' baskets, annual exchange of reports on the functioning and on the on-ground challenges confronted by the civilian and military forces involved in security of nuclear facilities, and a regular exchange of specialists from both India and Pakistan for co-ordinated training of technicians at the centres of excellence in both countries. Many strategists argue that a democratic government in Pakistan and a strong non-coalition government in India present a healthy possibility of cooperation to flourish. Therefore, Pakistan's Prime Minister Nawaz Sharif and the Indian Prime Minister Narendra Modi present hope and positivity which could shed the old and conventional ways in favour of a more cooperative bilateral relationship.

Cooperation between India and Pakistan could play a great role in offering expertise on nuclear security to 'newcomer' nuclear states in the region and facilitate strengthening of intra-regional expertise to defend the region from the threat of nuclear terrorism. Jointly addressing and systematically reducing the threat of nuclear terrorism in the region is, after all, an area where both states stand to gain.

Notes

1. Jack Caravelli, *Nuclear Insecurity: Understanding the Threat from Rogue Nations and Terrorists*, London: Praeger Security International, 2008, p. 59.
2. Graham Allison, *Nuclear Terrorism: The Risks and Consequences of the Ultimate Disaster*, London: Constable and Robinson Ltd., 2004, p. 9.
3. After the 9/11 there were speculations in the US National security community that these terror attacks were the beginning of a whole new series or set of attacks for which it has to be prepared. As pointed by Allison, 2004, p. 6.
4. Allison, n. 2, p. 1.
5. IAEA, "Nuclear Security Plan-2014-2017", accessed on 04 May 2016, http://www-ns.iaea.org/downloads/security/nuclear-security-plan2014-2017.pdf
6. Barack Obama, "Remarks by President Barack Obama in Prague as Delivered", 2009, https://www.whitehouse.gov/the-press-office/remarks-president-barack-obama-prague-delivered
7. H.E. Marcel de Vink , "3rd Nuclear Security Summit", The Hague, accessed on 18 March 2016, http://pakistan.nlembassy.org/news/2014/03/press-statement-19th-march-2014-3rd-nuclear-security-summit.html
8. Sitakanta Mishra, *The Challenge of Nuclear Terror*, New Delhi: Knowledge World, 2008, p. 15.
9. South Asia Terrorism Portal, "Fatalities in Terrorist Violence in Pakistan 2003-2016", 2016, accessed on 18 March 2016, http://www.satp.org/satporgtp/countries/pakistan/database/casualties.htm
10. Ministry of External Affairs (MEA), "Nuclear Security in India", accessed on 14 June 2016, http://www.human.ula.ve/catedralibreindia/documentos/india_nuclear.pdf
11. India has 21 operational reactors, 6 are under construction, and 16 more are planned based on cooperation with Russia, France, and the US.
12. Sitakanta Mishra and Happymon Jacob, "Nuclear Security Governance in India: Institutions, Instruments, and Culture", 2015, accessed on 15 January 2016, http://www.sandia.gov/cooperative-monitoring-center/_assets/documents/sand2015-0233.pdf
13. *Ibid.*
14. As said by the Indian External Affairs Minister Salman Khurshid at the Nuclear Security Summit 2014.
15. MEA, n. 10.
16. Caravelli, n. 1, p. 59.
17. MEA, "India's National Progress Report, Nuclear Security Summit 2016", accessed on 15 June 2016, http://www.mea.gov.in/bilateral-documents.htm?dtl/26590/Indias+National+Progress+Report+Nuclear+Security+Summit+2016

18. MEA, n. 10.
19. IAEA, "India's Additional Protocol Enters Into Force", accessed on 15 July 2016, https://www.iaea.org/newscenter/news/indias-additional-protocol-enters-force.
20. "Pakistan Committed to Objective of Nuclear Security: Fatemi", *The Nation,* accessed on 17 June 2016, http://nation.com.pk/national/02-Apr-2016/pakistan-committed-to-objective-of-nuclear-security-fatemi
21. NSS, "National Statement Pakistan 2016", accessed on 02 October 2016, http://www.nss2016.org/document-center-docs/2016/4/1/national-statement-pakistan
22. NSS, "National Statement Pakistan 2014", accessed on 15 June 2016, http://www.state.gov/documents/organiza1tion/235403.pdf
23. "Full Text of India-Pakistan Joint Statement on PM Narendra Modi-Nawaz Sharif Talks in Russia", *The Hindu*, accessed on 15 June 2016, http://www.thehindu.com/news/resources/full-text-of-the-joint-statement-by-the-foreign-secretaries-of-india-and-pakistan-in-russia/article7407431.ece
24. The White House, "Gift Basket on Mitigating Insider Threats", accessed on 15 June 2016, https://www.whitehouse.gov/the-press-office/2016/04/01/gift-basket-mitigating-insider-threats
25. Devirupa Mitra, "India to Join Three 'Gift Baskets' at Final Nuclear Security Summit", accessed on 17 June 2016, http://thewire.in/26497/india-to-join-three-gift-baskets-at-final-nuclear-security-summit/
26. The circle on countering nuclear smuggling aims at stopping the illicit trafficking of nuclear and other radioactive materials through an exchange of information and through aggressive prosecution through effective domestic legislation.
27. NSS, n. 21.
28. MEA, "India's National Progress Report, Nuclear Security Summit 2016", accessed on 15 June 2016, http://www.mea.gov.in/bilateral-documents.htm?dtl/26590/Indias+National+Progress+Report+Nuclear+Security+Summit+2016.
29. NSS, n. 21.
30. GNCEP, 4th National Training Course on Physical Protection of Nuclear Material and Nuclear Facilities *PROSPECTUS*, accessed on 15 June 2016, http://www.gcnep.gov.in/programs/details/2016/Prospectus%20NTC4%20on%20PP%20of%20NM%20and%20NF%202016.pdf.
31. "Pakistan Hosts International N-security Training Workshop", *The News*, accessed on 17 June 2016, http://www.thenews.com.pk/print/107135-Pakistan-hosts-international-N-security-training-workshop.
32. Twenty nine countries namely, Afghanistan, Brazil, Bulgaria, Chile, China, Djibouti, Ecuador, Ghana, Indonesia, Japan, Jordan, Kazakhstan, Kenya, Korea, Lebanon, Lithuania, Morocco, Myanmar, Romania, Russia, Senegal, South Africa, Sudan, Thailand, Indonesia, UK, Ukraine, USA, and Vietnam.
33. NSS, n. 22.
34. *Ibid.*
35. *Ibid.*
36. *Ibid.*

37. MEA, n. 10.
38. NSS, n. 21.
39. "Report: Pakistan Nuclear Facilities Attacked at Least Three Times by Terrorists", *Fox News*, accessed on 3 April 2017, http://www.foxnews.com/story/2009/08/11/report-pakistan-nuclear-facilities-attacked-at-least-three-times-by-terrorists.html
40. *Ibid.*
41. *Ibid.*

Chapter - 12

Illegal Cross-Border Migration in South Asia: Impediments to Regional Peace and Stability

— Sitakanta Mishra

Cross-border migration, legal or illegal, in South Asia is a much older phenomenon. Prior to 1947, migration from and within South Asia was rooted in British colonial expansion and labour requirements across its colonies. Therefore, one can find cross-border cross-cultural ethnic presence in every nook and corner of the region. However, the recent discourse on cross-border migration in the region is burdened with fears – casting negative impact on regional cohesion, peace and stability.

Although common history, geographical proximity, cultural and kinship linkages were major reasons early days for 'irregular' or undocumented cross-border migration,[1] such process has become a serious concern today for its socio-political and strategic implications. Absence of any dialogue for appropriate legal framework, and inability of the regional platform – South Asian Association for Regional Cooperation (SAARC) – to address the issue has allowed it to pose as a major impediment to regional security today.

The Nomenclature

In retrospect, South Asia has a massive experience in mass exodus and associated problems. Interestingly, there is no overarching legal regime to regulate illegal migration in South Asia, therefore, quite often the categories of migration in this region gets mixed up – "migrants, refugees, illegal settlers or stateless persons become one and the same. Sometimes even the nomenclature of a single category changes over time, say, from refugee to new refugee to new entrants; from illegal settlers to undocumented migrants to infiltrators."[2] According to the International Organization for Migration (IOM), migration is "a process encompassing any kind of population movement regardless of length, composition, or cause, from one part of location to the other that may be perceptibly or relatively stable, safe, or prosperous."[3] It includes the migration of refugees, displaced persons, uprooted people, and economic migrants. This phenomenon is common to many parts of the world (about 3% of the world's population live outside their place of birth)[4] including South Asia and the perceived reasons being poverty, overpopulation, family reunification, wars and war problems, unemployment, etc.

Many South Asian countries are suffering from the wave of, so called, 'illegal' migration, which has reached an "alarming" stage. However, scholars question the description of certain migrants as 'illegal'; instead they like to use the term "'irregulars', and not 'illegals', because human beings cannot be illegal. They might have crossed a border in an irregular way without papers, without documents, but they are no illegal human beings."[5] In the United States, a campaign named "Drop the I-word" was launched in 2010 "dedicated to ending the mass criminalization of communities of color."[6]

Whether 'illegal' or 'irregular', migration in South Asia is unique in many ways for the presence of multiple corridors of exodus, nexus between security-migration, and the complex geopolitical discourse. First, the major migration corridors in the region are between Afghanistan-Pakistan, Bangladesh-India, India-Pakistan, and Nepal-India. Out of these, cross-border migration is legal between India-Nepal, India-Bhutan, Bhutan-Nepal, and Pakistan-Afghanistan as a result of special bilateral treaties arrangements. But the actual flows of population are found to be larger than the official figures due to the huge undocumented flows.

Second, the major issue related to cross border migration in this region is the links between illegal migration and human trafficking, drug trafficking, smuggling, terrorism, crime, etc., often facilitated by brokers and middlemen. Those who enter through illegal channels, including those who are smuggled, trafficked, or enter with forged or no papers, suffer abuse and terrible death or punishment. They are prone to the target of criminal networks of organized people smugglers resulting in 'double victimization'.

Even some countries in the region are believed to have adopted cross-border 'intrusion' and clandestine smuggling as state policy.

Third, the geopolitical realty of Indo-centricism makes it extremely challenging for India to manage multiple exodus. Geographically India is contiguous to every country in the neighbourhood; whereas no other country, except Pakistan and Afghanistan, is contiguous to any other country except India. The relative political and economic stability in India vis-à-vis neighbours make India an attractive destination for the migrants.

Interestingly, statistics says that intra-regional registered migration in South Asia is consistently declining since 1990.[7] The volume of cross-border migration is decreased from 13.81 million in 1990 to 9.65 million during 2015. Why then the migration in South Asia remains a contentious issue when many other countries use it for their national advantage? Whether migration is a risk or a chance for South Asia? According to Steffen Angenendt, "migration is one of main driving forces of economic and human development. From a historical perspective it is obvious that most of the countries that tried to avoid migration were not too successful in economic, social and cultural terms. Overall, migration should be considered as a chance, and therefore open border policies should be fostered."[8] Has any country in South Asia accrued benefits out of intra-regional migration?

As per the World Bank's *Migration and Remittance Fact Book 2016* data, out of the top 10 migration corridors (2013) in the world, three belong to South Asia: Afghanistan–Pakistan, Bangladesh–India, India-Pakistan. Also, India ranks among the leading migrant destinations in SAARC, with a stock of 5.3 million in 2013. The India-Bangladesh migration corridor ranked as the third largest corridor in 2013 accounting for a stock of 3.2 million persons.[9] The number of people from Nepal working in India is actually between 2-3 million, "2 to 5 times higher than official statistics."[10] India also provides access to citizens of Bhutan in education and employment opportunities. There is also significant movement of people between India and Sri Lanka.

Partha S. Ghosh in *Migrants, Refugees and the Stateless in South Asia* (2016) narrates that "Seven out of the eight South Asian countries are both migrant-sending and -receiving countries."[11] The only exception is Maldives that does not send or receive many migrants/refugees largely because of its archipelagic nature and Sunni Muslim concentration. Afghanistan is primarily a refugee-sender country since 1970s. Bangladesh, before 1971 East Pakistan, has a long history of both receiving and sending migrants in which both India and Pakistan are involved. Subsequently, Bangladesh is hosting large amount of Rohingya migrants from Myanmar. Bhutan has received migrants from India's Nepalese-majority areas and from Sikkim, and has sent refugees to both Nepal and India as well. Pakistan has received migrants from India, Afghanistan (which is still continuing), and a few from Bangladesh before partition. Nepal has received migrants from India and Bhutan, and sent migrants to India and Pakistan. Sri Lanka has sent two distinct categories of migrants – Indian Tamils and Sri Lankan Tamils – to India throughout the LTTE crisis.

In recent years, Myanmar forces a mass exodus of migrants/refugees from its Rakhine state which has become a rising concern in South and Southeast Asian region. In South Asia, Rohingya refugees are fleeing to Sri Lanka, India, Pakistan, and Bangladesh, leading to an increase in anti-Muslim and anti-refugee sentiments in the region. Almost 500,000 Rohingya refugees have fled to Bangladesh, and over 40,000 to India and Pakistan respectively.[12]

India, being located at the center of South Asia and contiguous to all countries, has received migrants from all neighbours. Meanwhile, it has also sent migrants to Nepal and to undivided Pakistan earlier. In the wake of India and Pakistan independence in 1947, about 5 million Hindus and Sikhs left Pakistan for India, and about 6 million Muslims moved to Pakistan from India. At present, there are 50,000-100,000 Burmese Chin immigrants residing in India, mostly in Mizoram and a small number is found in Delhi.[13] India has thousands of people from Pakistan, living illegally, according to one study; from 2009 it is above 7,700.[14] By 2009, India had over 13,000 illegal immigrants from Afghanistan.[15] As far as Pakistan is concerned, according to some studies, it hosted the most refugees of any country in 2008, around 1.8 million, largely from Afghanistan.[16]

In the flipside, interestingly "South Asian countries have displayed a unique hospitality and unusual empathy towards refuge seekers and migrants in comparison to other parts of the world. By and large, migrants in South Asia [legal or illegal] have been tolerated if not actually welcomed."[17] As most of the ethnic communities are dispersed within the region, in times of crisis, migrant population always finds some sympathy from a section of population of the host country. Until recently, no South Asian states have ever been unwilling to provide shelter and relief to migrant guests even though it is a financial burden for them.

However, the history of tolerance and welcome to migrants seems wearing off these days, and tensions have surfaced along with variety of political and social responses across the region. Reportedly, Indian Minister of State, Home Affairs, Kiren Rijiju, announced that India would deport entire Rohingya population living in India illegally.[18] With the intervention of the Supreme Court of India the deportation idea has been temporarily stayed. Bangladesh has also followed a policy of making the country unwelcome for Rohingyas and has signaled the Myanmar government to take them back.[19] As far as Pakistan is concerned, it is not willing to give further extension to 1.4 million registered Afghan refugees for their stay in the country. According to Human Rights Watch, Pakistan has carried out campaigns to drive out nearly 600,000 Afghans since July 2016.[20]

The Root Causes

Many view that both state- and nation-building process are incomplete in South Asia. Religion, caste, creed, race, ethnicity, nationalism, etc., still determine the South Asian discourse along with segmental economic deprivation. Discrimination against minorities, religious and ethnic hatred, state repression against demands for self-determination, etc., are other causes for aggrieved people to look for succor in the other side of the border. Therefore, no single cause can be attributed to illegal migration in the region.

Partha S. Ghosh asserts that "collective violence", amongst others, is the prime factor behind mass exodus in South Asia.[21] Around 50 million people have scrambled across national borders ever since the emergence of modern nation-states in this region. Be it India-Pakistan partition, Bangladesh crisis, Maoist insurgency in Nepal, Sri Lankan Tamil or Rohingya refugees of Myanmar, 'collective violence' based on 'collective memories' of oppression and relative deprivation – failure of nation-building – runs through each process of exodus.

Myron Winer has listed 12 important flows of 'rejected people and unwanted migrants' in South Asia, particularly into India, which would reveal that "violence was the chief characteristic feature of the process."[22] They are:

> (i) India-Pakistan refugee flow, 1947-48 involving 15,000,000 Hindus and Muslims, (ii) exodus of Burmese Indians numbering about 1,000,000 during 1948-65, (iii) exodus of Srilankan Indians and Tamils to the tune of about 1,000,000 from 1954 which is still continuing, (iv) flight of almost 10,000,000 Bangladeshis to India in 1971, (v) "stranded" Pakistanis in Bangladesh numbering about 300,000, (vi) flight of 200,000 Burmese Muslims to Bangladesh in 1978, (vii) flight of 100,000 Chakmas into India in 1981, (viii) some 300,0000

Afghans moved to Pakistan during 1978-93 of which about 200,0000 have since returned, (ix) flight of Tibetans to India from 1958 to 1963 numbering about 100,000, (x) exodus of nearly 60,000 Bhutanese of Nepalese origin to Nepal in 1990-91, (xi) unestimated and unaccounted immigration of Nepalese into India; and lastly (xii) the massive, controversial and unwanted population flow from Bangladesh to Assam, West Bengal and Tripura in particular, and other parts of India in general.[23]

Failure of state-building process in many South Asian countries is equally a strong cause for illegal migration from economic downtrodden regions to lucrative destinations across the boundary. Abysmal economic performance and consequent deprivation of specific religious-social groups, along with collective violence perpetrated, compels many to flee. Supported by porous borders and poor border management, illegal migration takes place along with smuggling and trafficking. As "migration is a socially embedded process", "social networks often guide the aspirants into or through specific places and occupations."[24] In addition, documented/legal migration as a cumbersome and costly affair, many in South Asia find it easy and profitable to slip into the neighboring country clandestinely. Similar physiological features and cultural habits of the migrants help them intermingle easily in the destination country without fear of easy detection or social seclusion.

Another intriguing cause of illegal migration is the state repression against dissent groups or self-determination aspirants, may not large in numbers, sometime find safe-heavens across the border. Fissiparous tendencies are ubiquitous in South Asia and in many countries, dissent groups in direct conflict with their central authority, escape to other side of the border in times of state action of suppression. For example, the Sri Lankan LTTE cadres in Tamil Nadu or southern India; Indian Naxalites (Maoists) in Bangladesh and Nepal; Jihadists in Pakistan and Afghanistan; northeast separatist groups in Myanmar, etc.

The oft-emphasized cause of illegal migration and the root cause of the problem are socio-economic; for example, the reason for which Bangladeshi and Nepali migrate to India. Most of them are engaged in household menial work in the urban centres which requires no documentation. Deprived of basic amenities in their domicile countries, they opt for undocumented migration to stay indefinite duration, escaping legal restrictions. There are around 20 million illegal Bangladeshi migrants in India.[25] The current status shows a rise of around 67% over the 1.2 crore estimate in 2004.[26]

Nepalese migration to India cannot be termed as illegal.[27] As per the Treaty of Friendship and Peace 1950, people from both countries can legitimately move into each other's territory without any documentation. However, open border arrangement has given rise to unique problems as well. First, there are many Nepalese migrants who have settled permanently in India and have enrolled as Indian voters. In a sense, these migrants hold dual citizenship which is illegal, contradicting the 1950 Treaty which does not permit dual citizenship. Second, many illegal migrants from Bangladesh enter Nepal as Indians, and from there to India as Nepalese.

Suffice it to say, "South Asia represents an amazing and complex phenomenon of human migration; South Bhutanese of Neaali origin have fled to Nepal; Chakmas of Bangladesh have fled to India, and Tamils of Indian origin have sought shelter in India from Sinhalese persecution in Srilanka."[28] When it comes to deportation, there is no definite and amicable strategy yet to identify and deport them. The Illegal Migrants (Determination by Tribunal) Act, 1983 (IMDT Act) was found to be insufficient in the identification and deportation of illegal migrants. Furthermore, deportation is continuous process and the powers of identification, detention and deportation of illegal foreign nationals...have been delegated to the Indian State governments and Union Territories under the Foreigners Act, 1946.

The Security-Migration Nexus

Migration is generally viewed through the lenses of national security mainly in two ways. On the one hand, as an international security matter, it affects border-crossing and border control policies. Border management comes under serious stress owing to trafficking and smuggling along with migration. On the other hand, as an internal security matter, migrants are often seen as a threat to the host place demographic composition, cultural assimilation, availability of jobs, social services or law and order. Indeed, migration is often represented as a challenge to the welfare state and a 'danger' to society.[29]

Specifically, the illegal migration is posing at least five threats to countries in South Asia. They include demographic threats, social threats, economic threats, political threats, and security threats to defense.[30] "For the Indian state, the security implications of large-scale migration from both Bangladesh and Nepal are varied but inter-related, given the complex nature of migration and the multiple identities that migrants profess. They cover demographic changes, growth of radicalism, particularly Islamic fundamentalism, regionalism, and, more importantly, involvement and even encroachment of foreign powers on the country's 'sovereign space'".[31]

In South Asia, those migrants follow the path of illegal migration, often become prone to international criminal networks of organized people smugglers. In addition there is large-scale trafficking of women and children across border from Bangladesh and Nepal into India. Continuous irregular migration from Bangladesh into India, and the presence of a large number of Bangladeshi illegal migrants in the border states of India such as West Bengal, Assam and Tripura, creates social and political tension in the region, and is one of the major current security concerns for India.[32] A large numbers of smugglers cross the border along West Bengal into India. They are being engaged in smuggling goods from India into Bangladesh to avoid high tariff imposed on some Indian goods by Bangladesh government. Bangladeshi women are trafficked to India, Middle East for labour and sexual goods.[33]

In an affidavit to the Supreme Court of India, the Government of India has told that Rohingyas pose a serious threat to national security as many of them "figure in the suspected sinister designs of ISI/ISIS and other extremists groups who want to achieve their ulterior motives in India including that of flaring up communal and sectarian violence in sensitive areas of the country."[34] The affidavit also accused the Rohingyas of taking advantage of the porous borders in the east with organised smuggling of people, human trafficking, mobilisation of hawala and many of them have managed to acquire fake Indian identity cards. The affidavit categorically says that Rohingyas with militant background are found to be very active in Jammu, Delhi, Hyderabad and Mewat which may culminate in violence. Besides, it is feared that the "illegal immigrants" would exhaust the national resources of India and deprive Indian citizens "of their legitimate share in the employment sector, subsidised housing, medical and educational facilities".[35]

According to the Group of Ministers Report on National Security (2001), "Both the external and internal environment are changing at an incredibly fast" with developments in various strategic issues including 'illegal migration' that have "gravely impacting upon the security of the country."[36] It further observes that illegal migration "has generated a host of destabilizing political, social, economic, ethnic and communal tensions. Politically, the Bangladeshi migrants in India are in a position to influence the results of the elections in a large number of constituencies in the North East (about 32% of the constituencies in Assam). Economically, increased pressure on land, resulting in depletion of forest wealth, undercutting of wages of unskilled jobs, forcible occupation of Government land by the migrants and a host of other such issues, generate a ripple effect in the entire North East."[37]

The other country in the neighbourhood that suffers from similar security threat owing to illegal migration is Pakistan. More than 2 million registered and undocumented Afghan refugees remain in Pakistan, and Pakistani officials argue that it has become too expensive and too risky for them to stay.[38] Pakistan's former Chairman Joint Chief of Staff Committee General Zubair Mehmood Hayat is quoted saying: "Afghan Refugees have become security threat for Pakistan."[39] Many of them are found to be involved in smuggling and trafficking, kidnapping, killings for ransom and snatching. Most importantly, Pakistani authorities claim that they "have been used in different proxy wars by agencies of other countries from a long time now."[40]

Therefore, security concerns involving illegal migration is paramount in South Asia which has given rise to mutual suspicion and blame-game instead of mutual cooperation for lasting solution. Illegal migration issue has been a contentious issue in South Asia requiring a special attention devoid of bilateral blame game.

Absence of Cooperative Framework

Surprisingly, despite having massive migration related experience, South Asia is lacking a comprehensive legal regime or cooperative framework to govern illegal migration. Barring Afghanistan, no South Asian country has signed the UN Refugee Convention of 1951 and its 1967 Protocol. No country has ratified the ILO conventions on migrant workers either. It is true that the UN Convention and Protocol may not be relevant as they are the product of Cold War context where refugees were largely political, distinct from current trend. Each South Asian country has only specific domestic labour and border laws covering certain aspects of migration related issues. The SAARC is averse to discuss the issue as its charter mandates not to take up any bilateral contentious issue.

But management and deportation of refugees to their home country cannot just be a bilateral affair; rather it demands a multilateral approach involving other stakeholders from SAARC. The SAARC Social Charter 2004 only emphasizes enhancing cooperation in the social development to "carefully, diligently and effectively" manage "unsustainable population changes, internal migration, homelessness...," etc.[41] However, the charter has not been very effective in solving the problems related to migrants because it does not include commitments from SAARC countries to respect ILO core labour standards. Moreover, SAARC has irregularly faced hiccups due to bilateral tensions between its member states, especially between India and Pakistan.

The Colombo Process, a ministerial-level consultative forum initiated in 2003, is meant to share experiences and promote dialogue with destination countries where top South Asian countries like Bangladesh, India, Nepal, Pakistan, Sri Lanka are involved. In its first three meetings, concerns were raised regarding irregular migrants and recommended to ensure their human rights. In its Dhaka declaration 2011, recommendations were made to address effectively the specific needs of vulnerable groups especially women domestic workers, low-skilled and low-wage workers. However, the achievements of Colombo Process have been modest so far.[42]

It would be prudent for the region to arrive on a consensus early for a regional or sub-regional Convention on Migration as the problem cannot be addressed single-handed. For example, India's IMDT Act for facilitating effective action against illegal migrants ironically found to be "the biggest hurdle and is the main impediment or barrier in the identification and deportation of illegal migrants."[43] How strong a country may be, cross-border issues bound to create ripples and extremely difficult to manage single handedly. Most of South Asian countries have high density of population with medium level human development and limited capacity to cope with huge influxes of migrants. Second, some migrations have implications on countries beyond the region; for example, migration from Afghanistan on Iran and migration of Rohingyas from Myanmar. Equitable distribution of responsibilities in managing the illegal migration in the region and beyond is an imperative.

Impediments to Regional Cooperation

South Asia may be politically divided but it faces a common security challenge of illegal migration which has reached an alarming stage. Along with illegal migration, issues like cross-border smuggling, foreign aided-insurgency, human trafficking, etc. form a vicious circle that outweighs any individual effort. Mutual suspicion and blame-game has made the matter worse to which ad-hoc policies and measures by individual nations are advanced.

The first casualty of mismanaged migration in South Asia is the regional cohesion. Every country points fingers toward the other for illegal migration and related problems culminating in sufferings of innocent people. Thriving mutual suspicion is eroding every prospect of regional cooperation for developmental projects. Onus of internal strife and consequent displacement of civilians is consciously avoided by respective governments.

Second, as most of migrations are induced and based on bitter sense of history, the age-old historical social fault-lines get reverberated. Any bilateral conflict riddled with bitter sense of history, religious differences and conflicting claims over territory bound to perpetuate. This is one of the reasons why Indo-Pak conflict over Kashmir will not resolve peacefully in foreseeable future.

Third, extreme sense of deprivation and uproot germinate tremendous anger and violence in the minds of the migrants. Any perpetrated displacement bound to follow illegal route and culminate in destructive mode. As some migration in South Asia seem to be intentional, no regional cooperative framework would succeed, except highhanded border management and threat of punishment / sanctions on the source country which has negative repercussions.

Fourth, the amount of resources, energy and time spent by affected countries in managing the illegal migration are sheer wastage which could have been channeled for developmental activities in the region as a whole. As migration management involves huge economic burden, no country in the region would like to involve in the process except pointing fingers and washing their hands off.

Lastly, the worst sufferer of illegal migration in South Asia is India for its central location, economic attractiveness, and porous borders. Its prospect of becoming a global power will be seriously marred for it cannot take along its neighbours who are yet to get rid of historical baggage of ethnicity, territory, authoritarianism, etc. When nothing much can be expected from the regional grouping, India can assume the responsibility to manage the refugee conundrum in a consorted manner with like-minded neighbours, if possible drawing lessons from other regions and groupings. India needs to initiate and devise innovative schemes of border management and introduce effective scheme of 'Work Permit for Foreigners'. Only security-heightened border management, stringent legal framework, or avoidance of the issue would serve no purpose.

Notes

1. Ravi Srivastava, Arvind Kumar Pandey, "Internal and International Migration in South Asia: Drivers, Interlinkage and Policy Issues, UNESCO, 2017, unesdoc.unesco.org/images/0024/002494/249459e.pdf, p. 6.

2. Partha S. Ghose, *Migrants, Refugees and the Stateless in South Asia*, New Delhi: SAGE Publications India, 2016.
3. Vartika Sharma, et al., *Migration in South Asia: A Review*, Population Council, June 2015, p. 1.
4. *Ibid.*
5. Jerry Sommer and Andrea Warnecke, "The Security Migration Nexus Challenges and Opportunities of African Migration to EU Countries", https://www.bicc.de/uploads/tx_bicctools/brief36.pdf, p. 16.
6. "Drop the I word campaign", https://www.colorlines.com/droptheiword/resources/en/toolkit.html
7. Srivastava and Pandey, n. 1.
8. Steffen Angenendt, "International Migration—Just a Matter of State Security?", in Jerry Sommer and Andrea Warnecke, eds., *The Security Migration Nexus*, https://www.bicc.de/uploads/tx_bicctools/brief36.pdf, p. 19.
9. The World Bank, *Migration and Remittances Factbook 2016*, http://www.worldbank.org/en/research/brief/migration-and-remittances, p. 33.
10. Refugee Review Tribunal, Australia, http://www.refworld.org/pdfid/4b6fe2bf0.pdf, p. 20.
11. Ghosh, n. 2.
12. Angel Sharma, "How South Asia is Failing its Rohingya Challenge",https://thediplomat.com/2017/12/how-south-asia-is-failing-its-rohingya-challenge/
13. "India – Close the Gap for Burmese Refugees", Refugees International, http://aprrn.info/india-close-the-gap-for-burmese-refugees/, 9 December 2009.
14. "More illegal immigrants from Afghanistan than Pakistan', *Hindustan Times*, 14 November 2011.
15. *Ibid.*
16. Stephen Castles, Mark J. Miller, "Migration in the Asia-Pacific Region", https://www.migrationpolicy.org/article/migration-asia-pacific-region, 10 July 2009.
17. *Ibid.*
18. Krishna N. Das, "India in talks with Myanmar, Bangladesh to deport 40,000 Rohingya", https://www.reuters.com/article/us-myanmar-rohingya-india/india-in-talks-with-myanmar-bangladesh-to-deport-40000-rohingya-idUSKBN1AR0MH
19. "Exile island", https://www.economist.com/asia/2015/07/23/exile-island, 23 July 2015.
20. Zulfiqar Ali, "No more extension in stay of Afghan refugees", https://www.dawn.com/news/1383493, 17 January 2018.
21. Ghosh, n. 2.
22. Myron Winer, "Rejected Peoples and Unwanted Migrants in South Asia", *Economic and Political Weekly*, 21 August 1993.
23. The list is compiled in paper presented by Rajeev Sharma and Ankita Bhushan on "Illegal Immigration of Bangladeshis into India" at 23rd World Congress of IPSA, 19-24 July 2014, Montreal, Canada, http://paperroom.ipsa.org/papers/paper_42931.pdf, p. 3.

24. Sharma et al., n. 3, p. 10; S. Thieme, "Social networks and migration: Far West Nepalese Labour Migrants in Delhi", NCCR North South Dialogue, NCCR North-South, Berne, 2006.
25. Bharti Jain, "Two crore Bangladeshi immigrants illegally staying in India, Centre informs Rajya Sabha", *Times of India*, 17 November 2016.
26. Ibid.
27. Sangeeta Thapliyal, "Movement of Population Between India and Nepal: Emerging Challenges", https://www.idsa-india.org/an-aug9-6.html
28. Rajeev Sharma and Ankita Bhushan, "Illegal Immigration of Bangladeshis into India", paper presentedat 23rd World Congress of IPSA, 19-24 July 2014, Montreal, Canada, http://paperroom.ipsa.org/papers/paper_42931.pdf, p.
29. D. Bigo, E. Guild (eds.), *Controlling Frontiers: Free movement into and within Europe*, Hants/Burlington: Ashgate, 2005.
30. Vinod K. Bhardwaj, "Migration and Security in South Asia: Emerging Challenges and Concerns", https://www.academia.edu/6856846/Migration_and_Security_in_South_Asia_Emerging_Challenges_and_Concerns
31. S. Behra, "Trans-border Identities: A study on the impact of Bangladeshi and Nepali Migration to India", *ICRIER Policy Series*, No. 1, May 2011, p. 12.
32. Pushpita Das, *Illegal Migration From Bangladesh Deportation, Border Fences and Work Permits*, New Delhi: IDSA Monograph Series No. 56, December 2016, https://idsa.in/system/files/monograph/monograph56.pdf
33. Saheli Naik, "Illegal Migration - A Threat To India", *IOSR Journal Of Humanities And Social Science*, Volume 21, Issue 7, July 2016, http://www.iosrjournals.org/iosr-jhss/papers/Vol.%2021%20Issue7/Version-6/C2107061720.pdf
34. Krishnadas Rajagopal, "'Illegal', Rohingya refugees pose security threat, Centre tells SC", *The Hindu*, 19 September 2017.
35. *Ibid.*
36. "GoM Report on National Security, 2001", Chapter II, http://www.vifindia.org/sites/default/files/GoM%20Report%20on%20National %20Security.pdf, p. 6.
37. N Manoharan, "Illegal Migration as a Threat to India's Internal Security", http://www.vifindia.org/article/2012/august/06/illegal-migration-as-a-threat-to-india-s-internal-security, 6 August 2012.
38. Valerie Plesch, Naila Inayat, "Pakistan wants millions of Afghan refugees gone. It's a humanitarian crisis waiting to happen", https://www.pri.org/stories/2017-03-30/pakistan-wants-millions-afghan-refugees-gone-its-humanitarian-crisis-waiting, 30 March 2017.
39. "Afghan Refugees have become security threat for Pakistan: CJCSC", *Times of Islamabad*, 03 June 2017.
40. Hamza Ahmad, "Afghan Refugees A Threat to Pakistan Security", https://www.scribd.com/document/322966167/Afghan-Refugees-a-Threat-to-Pakistan-Security
41. "Social Charter of the South Asian Association for Regional Cooperation (SAARC)", http://www.jus.uio.no/english/services/library/treaties/02/2-03/saarc-social-charter.xml, 04 January 2004.

42. Srivastava and Pandey, n. 1, p. 40.
43. IMDT Act is the biggest barrier to deportation, says Supreme Court", http://www.thehindu.com/2005/07/14/stories/2005071405551200.htm

Chapter - 13

China in Latin America: The Evolving Asymmetric Relations

— E. Dilipraj

Latin American and Caribbean (LAC) – one of the most dynamic regions of the world, yet comparatively remains a least prioritized region of discussion among the academic and political circles due to various misconceptions. The first and foremost being the geographical disconnect between the region which is situated in the western hemisphere and the rest of the world across the pacific. This physical divide has created a sense of ignorance towards the region and a widespread belief that the political and other aspects of this region has not directly affected the rest of the world and vice-versa except in few big instances like Cuban Missile Crisis and Falklands War. However, the historical facts and evidences are contrary to this idea where the European powers have played an influential role in shaping the region during the colonial era and the European politics, economy and culture have a deep rooted influence in the region.

Moreover, the presence of the current super power of the world, the US, geographically situated to the north of LAC has forced many scholars to call the region as the backyard of the US, which is true to some extent in the past. However, in recent years, this factor of US hegemony in the region has reduced drastically owing to various reasons like globalization, revival of the 'Pink Tide'[1] in Latin American countries, etc. This change in the LAC geopolitics coincided with the new found interest towards the region from the developing countries like India and China have increased the importance of LAC in the 21st century.

The LAC which stretches from Mexico in the north to Chile and Argentina in the south has 33 sovereign countries of various sizes with a total population of more than 532.18 million[2] and cumulative GDP at market prices of approximately $4.911 Trillion[3]. Moreover, LAC is a resource rich region filled with resources like precious metals, sugar, rubber, grains, coffee, copper, oil, etc and it is this abundance of resources that had attracted the European colonists in the past and the developing nations like India and China in the recent years. The availability of profusion of resources, the value of the market and the associated economic benefits are the important factors which has made LAC as a favourable attraction for rapidly developing country like China.

China – this Asian giant which thinks and claims to be the 'Middle Kingdom' on earth is undoubtedly one of the fastest growing economies of the world and is even predicted to surpass the US in the near future. With the backing of a strong economy, China is flexing its muscles in all directions in order to expand its influence and to support its economic and political interests at the global stage. In this quest, for China to gain its supremacy, the regions of Africa and LAC play an important role owing to its resource richness and market factors. LAC especially is more important as China directly enters into the zone of influence of the US. Moreover, with a new form of multi-polar global order shaping up, many developing countries in LAC are looking for partners from rest of the world which has created a natural competition around the world between countries like China, India and many European countries.

Therefore, based on the above arguments, it would be prudent to study the involvement of China in LAC to understand and evaluate the nature and depth of the relation between the resource rich LAC and resource hungry China.

China in Latin America

Post economic reforms which started in late 1970s and continued through 1980s, China gained significant change in its economic firepower not only in its near abroad but also in a global level. Domestic reforms and transitions rapidly changed China's economic presence while fundamentally altering its global commercial dynamics. In fact, China's reforms in the 1980s, followed by rapid integration to the world markets - culminating with its admission to the World Trade Organisation (WTO) in 2001- precedes its relationship with Latin America. Thus, it could be stated that China's relations with LAC is a product of domestic developments within the country since reforms began in late 1970s.[4]

China identifies in its official white paper, four broad areas for cooperation between LAC – namely political, economic, cultural & social aspect and peace, security and judiciary affairs.[5] However, China's interest in LAC is highly prioritized on the aspects of gaining political support and economic returns from the region over the other two.

Political Aspects of China's Interest in LAC

China's attempt to gain political support of the LAC countries is not only to supplement its current global ambitions but also lies in the country's historical baggage. The historical conflict between the mainland - People's Republic of China (PRC) and Republic of China (ROC) or Taiwan, for their recognition as the real China has reached till the LAC countries. Table 1 shows the difference of opinion between the different LAC countries in recognizing the real China.

Table 1: Difference of opinion in Recognition of China between LAC Countries

Countries in the Latin American and Caribbean region according to PRC[6]	Latin American and Caribbean countries that recognize Taiwan
• Antigua and Barbuda • Argentina • Bahamas • Barbados • Bolivia • Brazil • Costa Rica • Chile • Colombia • Cuba • Dominica • Ecuador • Grenada • Guyana • Jamaica • Mexico • Peru • Suriname • Trinidad and Tobago • Uruguay • Venezuela	• Belize (1989) • El Salvador (1961) • Guatemala (1933) • Honduras (1941) • Nicaragua (1962–1985, 1990) • Panama (1909) • Dominican Republic (1957) • Haiti (1956) • Saint Kitts and Nevis (1983) • Saint Lucia (1984–1997, 2007) • Saint Vincent and the Grenadines (1981) • Paraguay (1957)

Source: Author's compilation of data from Ministry sources.

Table 1 clearly shows the dilemma in the foreign policy of LAC countries while identifying and recognizing the real China. It is to be noted that PRC does not have official relations with those countries that have recognized Taiwan but only has cultural and trade relations with few. However, PRC's quest for garnering recognition for itself and de-recognition for Taiwan among the LAC countries is an ongoing process. It is for this purpose and more, China published its first White Paper on LAC region titled "China's Policy Paper on Latin America and the Caribbean" in 2008. The White Paper established long-term goals for China based on the existence of "abundant raw materials", growing economic linkages and the five Principles of Peaceful Coexistence.[7]

Moreover, since the beginning of 21st century there have been regular visits by the Chinese Premiers and Presidents to the LAC region (See Table 2). And the number of visits to China by LAC Heads of States is on much higher scale.

Table 2: Number of visits of China's Premier and President to LAC, 2001-2015

Year	Total No. of Visits
2001	6
2002	0
2003	1
2004	4
2005	0
2006	0
2007	0
2008	3
2009	0
2010	1
2011	0
2012	5
2013	3
2014	4
2015	4
Premier Total	9
President Total	22
Combined Total	31

Source: Enrique Dussel Peters, "China's Evolving role in Latin America: Can It Be a Win-Win?", *Atlantic Council* Report, Latin American Center, September 2015.

Such frequent bilateral visits result in increased engagement of China with the region's multilateral institutions. China became a permanent observer in the Organisation of American States (OAS) in 2004 and in 2009 it became a member of the Inter-American Development Bank (IDB) and has also actively participated in the functioning of Economic Commission for Latin American and the Caribbean (ECLAC) in the recent years.[8] China is also enhancing its relations with LAC through participating in the multilateral organization, Community of Latin American and Caribbean States/ *Comunidad de Estados Latinoamericanos y Caribeños* (CELAC). As a result of China's persistent pressure, China-CELAC First Ministerial meeting was held in January 2015 and a plan for cooperation was charted. The highlighting points mutually agreed during the meeting are:

- China would invite 1,000 party leaders from CELAC members to visit China.
- Both sides would strive to achieve a trade volume of $500 billion and investment of at least $250 billion within a decade.
- China promised 6,000 government scholarships for CELAC members from 2015 to 2019.[9]

Thus through different channels of bilateral and multilateral engagements China has politically and diplomatically moved closer towards various LAC countries in the recent years thereby creating a smooth environment for pursuing its real interest of economic engagement.

Economic Aspects of China's Interest in LAC

Since the end of 20th century, the economic relations between LAC and China have grown strongly. According to ECLAC, bilateral trade between LAC and China has expanded over 22 times between 2000 and 2014.[10] In 2000, bilateral trade between China and LAC was worth $12 billion and in 2013 that figure had risen to $289 billion.[11] China's consumption of LAC exports rose from 2% in 1993 to 9% by 2013[12]And China's exports to LAC countries also saw a steep rise from 2% in 2000 to 16% in 2014.[13]

China has also increased its financing to the LAC countries since 2000. Chinese gross financing commitments to LAC countries from 2005-2015 is more than $125 billion. China Development Bank and China Export Import Bank have provided these loan commitments to the LAC countries and their State-Owned firms. Venezuela leads the list of LAC that has taken loan from China with a total sum of $65 billion. Chinese loans to LAC countries worth $70.2 billion, $40.3 billion and $1.7 billion are mainly focused on the areas of Energy, Infrastructure and Mining respectively.[14]

Year	*No. of Loans*	*Amount*
2005	1	$30 million
2007	4	$4.8 billion
2008	1	$356 million
2009	8	$15.7 billion
2010	11	$35.6 billion
2011	6	$7.9 billion
2012	7	$7 billion
2013	10	$14 billion
2014	6	$10 billion
2015	14	$29.1 billion

Source: Kevin P.Gallagher and Margaret Mayers, "China-Latin America Finance Database", Washington: *Inter-American Dialogue*, 2015, http://www.thedialogue.org/map_list/, accessed on 25 May 2016.

Unlike the financing aspect, China's Foreign Direct Investment (FDI) in LAC region was very limited until 2010. ECLAC data suggests that China's FDI in LAC in 2 decades preceding 2010 would total just around $6 billion. And most of this amount was invested in oil and mining projects which were started in the 1990s and continued over the years. However FDI flow from China started swelling from 2010 – the year in which China's FDI totalled $13 billion.[15]

Country Name	1990-2009	2010	2011	2012
Argentina	143	3100	2450	600
Brazil	255	9563	5676	6066.33
Chile	N/A	5	N/A	76
Colombia	1677	6	293	996
Ecuador	1619	45	59	86
Mexico	146	9	2	74
Peru	2262	84	829	1306.84
Venezuela	240	900	N/A	N/A
Total	6342	13712	9309	9206

Source: "Chinese foreign direct investment in Latin America and the Caribbean", China-Latin America Cross-council Taskforce, *ECLAC*, Prepared for Summit on the Global Agenda world Economic Forum, Abu Dhabi, 18-20 November 2013.

Also, as mentioned earlier, China has plans of investing $250 billion in LAC countries within the time period of 2015-2024, which would bring more investment into the Latin American countries. However, the Chinese investments are all heavily focused only on energy and infrastructure sectors. For instance, out of the $13 billion FDI in 2010, three quarters of the amount were invested in two very large oil acquisitions by Sinopec in Brazil and CNOOC in Argentina. Chinese companies are among the most important foreign players in the oil and gas industry in Argentina, Venezuela, Brazil, Colombia and Ecuador and a have a smaller presence in Peru.[16] Latin America holds an estimated 336 billion barrels of oil – one fifth of the global total; with Venezuela alone accounting for an estimated 298 billion barrels. China's investments in the energy sector in LAC are focused only in extracting maximum amount of oil from the region to supply for its huge demand.

In the mining sector, Chinese firms have concentrated their investments in Peru and, to a lesser extent in Brazil. China buys one third of the iron ore sold on the world markets and one fifth of the copper, most of which coming from LAC. Also the largest presence of Chinese companies outside the natural resources sector is in Brazil, where there are a number of manufacturing companies operating and at least one large company in electricity services.[17]

Despite being the fourth largest country by landmass and housing 20% of world's population, China only has 8% of arable land. This deficiency of land for cultivation leads to huge imports of food products from abroad. Therefore, China imports 40% of global production of Soybeans, taking 75% of its supplies from Brazil and Argentina.[18] With one third of the world's fresh water resources and more than a quarter of its good quality farmland, LAC has everything that China needs in the agricultural sector.

Brazil, LAC region's largest economy, is now the world's biggest exporter of foodstuffs like sugar cane, orange juice, meat and soybean and much of it is destined for Asia especially China.[19] In fact Brazil is China's largest trade partner in LAC, with China accounting for over 40% of Brazilian exports and imports. And 70% of Brazil's exports to China comprises of iron ore and soybeans. Apart from Brazil, China imports soybeans from Argentina, oil from Venezuela, copper from Chile and fishmeal and copper from Peru. From 2000 to 2013 LAC exports to China has increased 25 fold, reaching approximately $100 billion a year.[20]

However, China is still behind the US in overall trade with LAC as there is a huge difference of percentage between the US-LAC trade and China-LAC trade. For instance in the year 2010 alone LAC exports to the US was 41% and imports from the US was 31% whereas LAC exports to China was 8% and imports from China was 13%.[21] This difference in percentage between the US and China has not reduced much in the years later, though the amount of trade between LAC and China has risen to an extent.

China being the second largest trade partner of the LAC region second only to the US, it has signed free trade agreements (FTA) with three of the countries in the region namely – Chile in 2006, Peru in 2010 and Costa Rica in 2011.[22] However, it could be said that China is following the US in this aspect of FTAs with LAC as the US has an elaborate list of agreements with the region. In fact out of the total 20 FTAs of the US globally, 11 are with the LAC countries; Chile in 2004, Colombia in 2012, Costa Rica, Dominican Republic (DR), El Salvador, Guatemala, Honduras, Nicaragua under Central American FTA-DR in 2004, Panama in 2012, Peru in 2009 and Mexico under North American FTA in 1994.[23]

During the Chinese President Xi Jingping's visit to LAC in 2014 for the China- CELAC summit, China promised to comprehensively launch the China-Latin America Cooperation Fund with a commitment to invest $5 billion in the region.[24] During the state visit of Chinese Premier *Li Keqiang* to Brazil, it was announced that China would set up a $30 billion special fund for industrial cooperation between LAC and China.[25]

Infrastructural Development and Security Aspect of China in LAC

It should be noted here that the resource export boom of 2002-2012, one of the longest in the history of LAC did good for the region by lifting millions out of poverty as many more millions joined the burgeoning urban middle classes. Also there was some sort of a major coincidence during the period, as the boom in the China trade coincided with the rise of the Left across much of LAC which is dubbed as 'Pink Tide'. This coincidence combined with the commodity export surpluses underwrote the '21st century Socialism' especially in countries like Venezuela, Ecuador and Bolivia.

Owing to the economic growth a new wave of infrastructural development started in full swing in LAC region and China took active participation in this aspect too; however with the reservation of selection of projects that would benefit its interests in the region. In 2015, during

Chinese Premier *Li Keqiang*'s state visit to Brazil, he put forward a "3x3 Model" of cooperation with LAC in which the first 3 refers to cooperation in building three arteries for LAC in the fields of logistics, power and information, second 3 refers to interaction among businesses, the society and the government and the third 3 refers to the three financing channels of fund, credit and insurance.[26] Out of this, the first three refers to the overall infrastructural development aspect in which China is keen in the region. Apart from participating in different construction projects like building rails, roads, dams, ports, and airports across LAC, China has also initiated and conceptualized few strategically ambitious projects that would benefit China on a longer run.

The first and foremost was the ambitious "Atlantic-Pacific Railway", a concept which was promoted even during Chinese Premier *Li Keqiang*'s visit in 2015 to Brazil.[27] The Premier signed an agreement for a feasibility study for the railway project during this visit with both Brazil and Peru. This 3,300 miles long railway project will go across the Amazon, connecting from Brazil's Atlantic coast to Peru's Pacific coast. Some political leaders in both Brazil and Peru have welcomed this Chinese proposal and many scholars who study China's ties with LAC opine that the proposed railway would go well beyond cutting shipping costs, reflecting Beijing's efforts to secure raw materials, improve China's food security and find new markets for its engineering and rail firms at a time when the country's economy is slowing down.[28]

On the flip side, the project has attracted lot of criticism from environmental activists and many indigenous tribal activists and indigenous groups living in the Amazon region as a project of this magnitude will lead to huge environmental destruction to the world's largest rainforest and other agricultural lands around. Especially in Peru, while the Peruvian officials favour a northern route through virgin forests rich in biodiversity, the environmentalists prefer a southern route to Matarani.[29]

In fact the Chinese government in 2011 had proposed a similar railway project connecting Colombia's Pacific coast and Atlantic coast and the announcement regarding the proposal was made by Colombia's President Juan Manuel Santos during an interview to The Financial Times. However, in 2014, the project was cancelled and forced to drop due to controversies that arouse in the bidding process.[30]

In Venezuela, the Chinese companies are in construction of a 290 mile high-speed railway system; however the project is facing financial issues due to monetary shortfalls on the Venezuelan side. Similarly, in Mexico a Chinese led bid to build a $4.3 billion worth high-speed railway system was cancelled after accusation that the Mexican government had favoured contractors.[31]

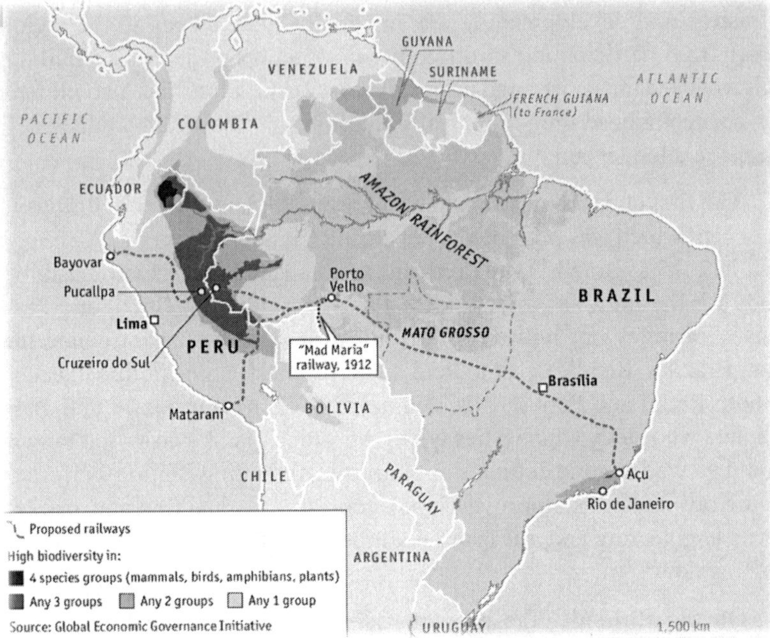

Source: "The Chinese Chequebook", *The Economist,* 23 May 2015, http://www.economist.com/news/americas/21651889-latin-america-needs-be-more-hard-headed-its-big-new-partner-chinese-chequebook, accessed on 27 May 2016.

Image 1: Proposed Atlantic-Pacific Railway Across the Amazont

Another transcontinental infrastructure project, but more strategically important, was floated by a Chinese telecommunications tycoon, *Wang Jing* – the principal owner of Beijing Xinwei, in 2013 for construction of a 172 mile long canal across Nicaragua, which is seen as a rival project to the existing Panama Canal. Although, the feasibility study and other process are underway, yet the project is surrounded by huge scepticism, albeit support from Daniel Ortega's government in Nicaragua for this project.[32]

It can be said that China's push for constructing channels of transportation across the continent connecting the Atlantic and Pacific coast lies in the region's escalating trade with China – which needs raw materials to fuel its economy and new markets for its exports. Also, currently, all Chinese imports from South America have to travel through the Panama Canal where the cost of transporting a ship through it has tripled over the last few years. And it is estimated that overland routes from Brazil, from where China imports billion of dollars worth of iron ore, soybeans, oil and other commodities, to the Pacific could lower shipping costs.[33]

Source: Carrie Kahn, "A Chinese Man, A $50 billion plan and A canal to reshape Nicaragua", http://www.npr.org/sections/parallels/2014/08/14/340402716/nicaragua-banks-on-its-own-canal-to-boost-economy, accessed on 28 May 2016.

Image 2: Proposed Nicaragua Canal

Other infrastructure projects include the Chinese up gradation of the Argentinean dilapidated cargo network, for which imports of railroad materials and trains from China reached around $700 million in 2014. In Ecuador, state owned Chinese banks have already invested nearly $ 11 billion in building a dam, roads, highways, bridges and hospitals.[34]

It should be noted here that, though China proposed many infrastructural projects that would favour itself on a longer run in the LAC region, however many major projects like rail or highway links either gets cancelled or comes to standstill in the middle due to the factors of local conflicts, concerns on environmental degradation, concerns about disturbances to indigenous livelihood, monetary issues with the host country, change of governments, corruption scandals, and most importantly lack of proper understanding of the region's needs by the Chinese. However, China is persistent in enlarging its footprint in the region and hence seeks all opportunities to fulfil its interests.

It is in this interest, China is expanding its presence through cooperation in the security sector with the LAC region. Chinese arms companies which have close association with the Chinese military, such as the Aviation Industry Corporation of China (AVIC), China shipbuilding Industry Corporation (CSIC), China National Electronics Import & Export Corp (CEIEC) and China's North Industries Corporation (NORINCO), all have developed their positions in LAC region. It is estimated that China's military equipment sales to the LAC region have risen from virtually meagre in 2005 to $100 million in 2010 to a new high of $130 million in 2014. However, 90% of these arms sales go to Venezuela and the rest to Ecuador and Bolivia.[35]

China's cooperation in the security sector of LAC region includes the sale of small arms, clothing, construction of field hospitals, trucks, munitions co-production of light helicopters; Multiple Launch Rocket Systems (MLRSs) to Peru; Surface to air missiles (SAMs) to Bolivia and Ecuador; Towed guns to Bolivia and Anti-tank missiles to Ecuador. Venezuela, in particular, has purchased a variety of Chinese military equipments since 2000s including infantry fighting vehicles, short range air to air missiles, training aircraft and radar, Shaanxi y-8 medium transport and Harbin Z-9C anti-submarine helicopters. Another area other than sales where China cooperates with LAC region in the defence sector is through exchange of senior military officials between China and different LAC countries like Brazil, Mexico, Suriname, Chile, Venezuela, Bolivia, Colombia, Cuba, Ecuador and Paraguay. In late 2012, Beijing even hosted the first "China-Latin America High-Level forum on Defence", which was continued in 2014 too.[36]

Examining China's interest in Latin America

China's entry into the LAC region as an alternative to the US, and the Chinese investments as an alternative to the west dictated IMF and World Bank has been embraced by many Latin American governments in the past, but this Chinese boon has its own pitfalls. The trade relationship between China and LAC is asymmetrical, while China matters a lot to LAC countries; the reverse is really not the case. For instance, China is Brazil's largest trading partner however Brazil is only ninth most important source of overall imports for China. China might be the largest buyer of Venezuelan oil, however much of it is peddled by China on the re-export market.[37] Moreover, the balance of trade between China and LAC countries remains imbalanced and totally leans in favour of China (See Image 3).

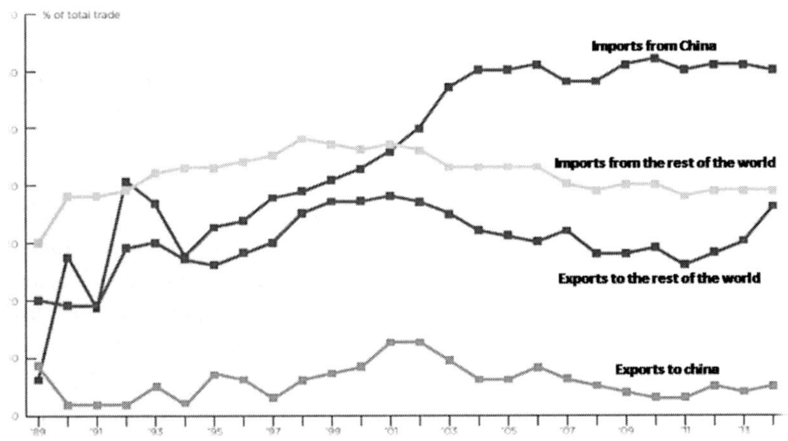

Source: Enrique Dussel Peters, "China's Evolving role in Latin America: Can It Be a Win-Win?", *Atlantic Council Report*, Latin American Center, September 2015

Image 3: LAC Medium and High Technology Goods Trade with China (1989-2014)

Regional statistics reveal that LAC region's trade deficit with China has skyrocketed from below $20 billion until mid-2000s to over $75 billion in 2012 and has only increased in the later years.[38] The main reason for this asymmetry lies with the way China conducts trade with LAC. China's active

Table 5: Top 5 Exports between LAC and China, 2009-2013

Top LAC exports to China		Top Chinese exports to LAC	
Item	**Share of total export**	**Item**	**Share of total export**
Iron ore and concentrates	20%	Telecom equipment, parts	10%
Soybeans and other oil seeds	18%	Data processing equipment	4%
Copper	14%	Ships, boats, floating structures	4%
Copper ores, concentrates	10%	Optical instruments	3%
Crude petroleum	9%	Refined petroleum products	3%
Total percent	69%	Total percent	23%

Source: Rebecca Ray and Kevin Gallagher, "China-Latin America Economic Bulletin 2015 Edition", Global Economic Governance Initiative, 2015.

trade engagements with the LAC region are restricted only to 7 to 8 countries from where it imports the most. Also there is lack of export diversification for LAC countries in its trade with China. More importantly, LAC exports to China continue to be heavily concentrated in primary goods.

Table 5 clearly shows how exports of LAC to China is driven majorly by raw materials and that of China to LAC involves finished goods like cell phones, laptops, textiles, shoes, and a wide array of various low-tech, low-cost manufactured items. Also, the fact that the top 5 exports from LAC to China together makes 69% of the total exports shows the lack of diversification, whereas on the other side the top 5 exports of China to LAC together makes only 23% shows how China has a diversified trade with LAC. This existing trade pattern between China and LAC is referred by scholars and analysts as the return of historic 'raw material dependency' relationship that once existed between LAC countries and the European powers. Also it could be stated that this sort of asymmetric trade relations and raw material dependency would only lead to the collapse of economies in the LAC region on a longer run. However, diversification of export goods with China and increasing trade partners with rest of the world are the pragmatic approach available for LAC countries in order to continue on the path of economic growth.

Additionally, China's engagement with LAC countries especially in the infrastructural development aspect and also in mining and raw material trade has lead to a series of social and environmental conflicts. Undoubtedly, the 'China-boom' in LAC has lead to the construction of a number of roads, canals and railroads for the transportation of trade goods and dams to provide hydro power to mines and oil fields. However, all these infrastructural projects have emerged with the expense of damaging the environment and forest eco-system of the region as well as by displacing thousands of indigenous population denying them of their homelands. Also LAC exports to China are almost twice as carbon intensive and three times as water intensive than average economic activity in LAC.[39] For instance, the volume of Lake Nicaragua is approximately 108 billion cubic meters. In other words, if LAC had not conducted trade with China in 2012 alone (by producing domestically everything it imported from China and consuming locally everything it exported to China), it would have saved roughly 90% of the volume of Lake Nicaragua. The depletion of water resources has major ramifications not only environmentally but also socially as competition for water has become a frequent source of social conflict between communities practicing peasant agriculture or small-scale ranching and large–scale plantation and mines.[40] Therefore, it could be stated that if LAC countries do not change their trade pattern with China and if they do not realize the amount of damage being caused to their environment, then on a longer run the LAC countries would destroy themselves from within.

Apart from these pitfalls, the over dependence of LAC region on China for trade and other economic reasons has its own disadvantages. First China has the potential and demand to trade LAC dry of its resources. Second, China will flood the LAC markets with its low-tech and low-quality products that are rejected in the Western markets eventually making it a dump yard. Finally, post 2013 Chinese economy is slowing down which the enthusiasts of China-LAC relations view as a mere blip in China's rise in LAC, whereas moderate analysts suggest that this flux in Chinese economy will reflect heavily on the LAC countries for the next few years especially on the countries like Venezuela, Ecuador and Brazil.

In conclusion, the 'pink tide' which emerged in early 2000s with which Chinese-boom in the LAC region strengthened is slowly on the retreat coinciding with the slowing Chinese economy. Therefore, the time is right for countries like Russia and India to partner with LAC countries not only in multi-lateral political forums but also in serious economic engagements. It is only through such overall partnerships between the emerging and developing nations a truly multi-polar world order could be established.

Notes

1. Pink Tide is a phrase used in contemporary 21st century political analysis in the media and elsewhere to describe the perception that anti-Americanism, leftist ideology and left-wing politics in particular, were increasingly becoming influential in Latin America primarily between 1998 and 2009.
2. The World Bank, "Data for Caribbean small states, Latin America & Caribbean (developing only)", http://beta.data.worldbank.org/?locations=S3-XJ, accessed on 20 May 2016.
3. *Ibid.*
4. Enrique Dussel Peters, "China's Evolving role in Latin America: Can It Be a Win-Win?", *Atlantic Council* Report, Latin American Center, September 2015.
5. White Paper by The State Council of The People's Republic of China, "China's Policy Paper on Latin America and the Caribbean", 2008, http://www.gov.cn/english/official/2008-11/05/content_1140347.htm, accessed on 22 May 2016.
6. Official Website of Ministry of Foreign Affairs of the People's Republic of China, "Latin America", http://www.fmprc.gov.cn/mfa_eng/gjhdq_665435/3447_665449/, accessed on 22 May 2016.
7. n. 5.
8. n. 4.

9. "China, CELAC deepen cooperation with major documents", *Xinhua*, 09 January 2015, http://news.xinhuanet.com/english/china/2015-01/09/c_133909004.htm, accessed on 23, May 2016.
10. "Export Diversification Is the Main Challenge for Latin America and the Caribbean in Its Trade Relationship with China", ECLAC, 25 May 2015, http://www.cepal.org/en/pressreleases/export-diversification-main-challenge-latin-america-and-caribbean-its-trade, accessed on 24 May 2016.
11. Katy Watson, "What will china's Investment do for Latin America?", *BBC*, 07 July 2015, http://www.bbc.com/news/world-33424532, accessed on 24 May 2016.
12. Rebecca Ray, *et. al.*, "China in Latin America – Lessons for South-South Cooperation and Sustainable development", *Boston University Report*, April 2015.
13. n. 4.
14. Kevin P. Gallagher, Margaret Mayers, "China-Latin America Finance Database", Washington: *Inter-American Dialogue*, 2015, http://www.thedialogue.org/map_list/, accessed on 25 May 2016.
15. "Chinese foreign direct investment in Latin America and the Caribbean", China-Latin America cross-council taskforce, *ECLAC*, Prepared for Summit on the Global Agenda world Economic Forum, Abu Dhabi, 18-20 November 2013.
16 *Ibid.*
17. n.15.
18. Ronn Pineo, "China and Latin America: What You Need to Know", *Council on Hemispheric Affairs*, 29 July 2015, http://www.coha.org/china-and-latin-america-what-you-need-to-know/, accessed on 25 May 2016.
19. n.11.
20. n. 18.
21. Juan de Onis, "China's Latin Connection: Eclipsing the US?", *World Affairs Journal*, January/February 2014, p. 63.
22. Carol Wise, "China's Free Trade Agreements in South America", Economics Brief, *Inter-American Dialogue*, November 2012.
23. Office of the United States Trade Representatives, Executive Office of the President, government of the United States of America, https://ustr.gov/trade-agreements/free-trade-agreements, accessed on 26 May 2016.
24. "Xi Jinping Attends China-Latin America and the Caribbean Summit and Delivers Keynote Speech, Comprehensively Expounding China's Policies and Propositions Toward Latin America, Announcing Establishment of China-Latin America Comprehensive Cooperative Partnership of Equality, Mutual Benefit and Common Development, and Establishment of China-CELAC Forum", Ministry of foreign affairs of the People's Republic of China, 18 July 2014,

http://www.fmprc.gov.cn/mfa_eng/topics_665678/xjpzxcxjzgjldrdlchwdbxagt wnrlgbjxgsfwbcxzlldrhw/t1176650.shtml, accessed on 26 May 2016.

25. "Premier Li Keqiang: Upgrade Practical Cooperation Between China and Latin America and the Caribbean Under the "3×3 Model"", Ministry of Foreign Affairs of the People's Republic of China, 22 May 2015, http://www.fmprc.gov.cn/mfa_eng/wjb_663304/zzjg_663340/ldmzs_664952/xwlb_664954/t1266202.shtml, accessed on 27 May 2016.
26. *Ibid.*
27. *Ibid.*
28. Simon Romero, "China's ambitious Rail Projects Crash Into Harsh Realities in Latin America", *The New York Times*, October 3, 2015, http://www.nytimes.com/2015/10/04/world/americas/chinas-ambitious-rail-projects-crash-into-harsh-realities-in-latin-america.html?_r=1, accessed on 27 May 2016.
29. "The Chinese Chequebook", *The Economist,* 23 May 2015, http://www.economist.com/news/americas/21651889-latin-america-needs-be-more-hard-headed-its-big-new-partner-chinese-chequebook, accessed on 27 May 2016.
30. n.11.
31. n. 28.
32. *Ibid.*
33. Lily Kuo, "Why China wants to build a railway across South America", http://qz.com/236220/why-china-wants-to-build-a-railway-across-south-america/, accessed on 27, May 2016.
34. n. 28.
35. Paul Coyer, "China's Pivot To Latin America: Beijing's Growing Security Presence In America's Backyard", *Forbes*, 20, February 2016, http://www.forbes.com/sites/paulcoyer/2016/02/20/chinas-pivot-to-latin-america-beijings-growing-security-presence-in-americas-backyard/#72657956d915, accessed on May 29, 2016.
36. *Ibid.*
37. n. 18.
38. United Nations COMTRADE Database, http://comtrade.un.org/db/, accessed on 28 May 2016.
39. Rebecca Ray and Kevin Gallagher, "China-Latin America Economic Bulletin 2015 Edition", Global Economic Governance Initiative, 2015.
40. Rebecca Ray, et. al. "China in Latin America – Lessons for South-South Cooperation and Sustainable development", *Boston University Report*, April 2015.

Gender Typecast

Chapter - 14

Forced Marriage Law in Britain: Predicament of Indian Women

— *Parvathy Poornima*

Increased restrictions imposed by many of the west European countries on marriage related migration opened discourses on cultural integration of minority ethnic groups, socio economic consequences of transnational marriages and related immigration issues.[1] The issue of forced marriage was debated in the backdrop of rising media reports in several instances and their links with migration to Britain. Forced marriage is a commonly found feature of cultural practices of especially South Asian communities in Britain and majority of the victims usually belong to families of South Asian origin.

In spite of a controversial debate that took place on criminalization; forced marriage is recognized as a criminal offense in Britain with the penalty being imprisonment under the Anti-Social Behaviour, Crime and Policing Act 2014. However risks to women seeking legal redress in related cases are still existent and their problems are yet to be resolved. This study focuses on the predicament of Indian women who are at risk of forced marriages in Britain in the context of 'criminalization of forced marriages'. The paper argues that criminal legislation on forced marriage in Britain has not been able to provide redress to Indian women seeking justice. The first section of the paper traces the context and features of legislation on forced marriage in Britain whereas the second section examines the challenges of Indian women seeking legal redress in Britain. Though the study is limited by emphasis on quantitative data on estimates on Indian victims of forced marriage (due to conditions of anonymity), it invariably outlines the challenges they face, which require immediate and rigorous attention of activists, academia and policy makers.

Forced Marriage Law in Britain

The debate on forced marriages began in the British Parliament in February 1999, when the case of Zena Briggs,[2] who went into hiding after fleeing an arranged marriage was raised in the House of Commons by the former Labour party MP Ann Cryer. Several such instances of forced marriage including honor killings for resisting the forced marriages have been reported in Britain since the 1990s. The stories of Jasvinder Sanghera, Rukshana Naz, Shafilea Ahmed, Humayra Abedin and Zufia Ahmedare are well known among the cases related to families of Asian origin.

Recognizing the gravity of the issue, the British government appointed a group, consisting of Asian women's associations and concerned individuals in 1999 to examine and investigate the issue in detail. The report titled *A Choice by Right: The Report of the Working Group on Forced Marriage;* published by Home Office in 2000 categorically condemned forced marriages as a violation of human rights. Subsequently the legislation on forced marriage was passed in British Parliament. As the Government of UK[3] observes, "Forced marriage is when you face physical pressure to marry (e.g. threats, physical violence or sexual violence) or emotional and psychological pressure (e.g. if you're made to feel like you're bringing shame on your family)."[4]

A legal solution to forced marriages in Britain was brought through various stages. The Forced Marriage Unit was set up by the government preceding the enactment of legislation. The criminal offense was introduced in 2014. The course of legal solution to forced marriage through different stages can be summarized as follows.

1. Forced Marriage Unit

The Forced Marriage Unit (FMU), a joint venture of Foreign and Commonwealth Office and Home Office, set up in 2005 has been facilitating Britain's policy on forced marriage by providing support services including safety advice and rescue measures for victims. Trained professionals of FMU offer confidential advice and assistance to those who have been forced into marriage, those at risk of being forced into marriage and professionals working with actual or potential victims of forced marriage.[5] FMU provides a wide range of information for victims and professionals including statistics, case studies, documentaries, statutory guidance for agencies safeguarding children and vulnerable adults.

2. The Forced Marriage (Civil Protection) Act

The Forced Marriage (Civil Protection) Bill was introduced in the House of Lords by the Liberal Democrat peer, Lord Lester of Herne Hill in November 2006. The autobiography of Jasvinder Sanghera,[6] titled *Shame* was cited in the House of Lords. The Forced Marriage (Civil Protection) Bill received Royal Assent on 26 July 2007 and the Act came into force on 25 November 2008.[7] The Act applies to England and Wales and Northern Ireland. Scottish government has specific jurisdiction and protection act to combat forced marriage.[8]

The Forced Marriage (Civil Protection) Act aimed at providing civil remedies for those who face the threat of forced marriage. The Act permits the victims of forced marriage, or a relevant third party to apply for a Forced Marriage Protection Order (FMPO) and the breach of an order is treated as a contempt of court. Any person can apply for FMPO if he/she or someone else is being threatened with a forced marriage. The court is authorized to order the behavior or conduct of those forcing another person into marriage to change or stop, or impose requirements upon them. If a person fails to comply with the court order they will be dealt with by the court and may be sent to prison.

3. Criminal Offense of Forced Marriage

The British government launched a consultation in 2011 seeking views on criminalization of forced marriage from key partners, concerned parties including victims, police, legal practitioners, and various other government departments and organizations.[9] *Forced Marriage: A Consultation Summary of Responses* published in 2012 summarized arguments for and against criminalization and highlighted that majority of the respondents were in favor of criminalization.

Forced marriage is recognized as a criminal offense since June 2014 with a maximum penalty of seven years imprisonment (Home Office, UK 2014) as incorporated in part 10 of the Anti-social Behavior, Crime and Policing Act 2014. The Act explains the amendment of Family Law Act 1996 to insert section 63C that indicates offense of breaching Forced Marriage Protection Order.[10] According to the law, a person commits the offense of forced marriage if he or she:

(a) Uses violence, threats or any other form of coercion for the purpose of causing another person to enter into a marriage.

(b) Believes, or ought reasonably to believe, that the conduct may cause the other person to enter into the marriage without free and full consent.[11]

FMPOs can be made ex-parte also as one can get an emergency order (ex-parte or without notice order) to protect someone immediately without having to involve the respondent.[12] The law is also applicable for UK nationals overseas who are at risk of becoming victims of forced marriages. The law makes it illegal to 1) take someone overseas to force them to marry (whether or not the forced marriage takes place) 2) marry someone who lacks the mental capacity to consent to the marriage (whether they're pressured to or not).[13]

As mentioned earlier, the offense of forced marriage is presumably more rampant and quite regular among South Asian communities. Indians, Bangladeshis and Pakistanis are largely identified as South Asians in Britain.[14] The struggles and achievements of Indians in Britain as a Diaspora community have been manifested in their identity politics and negotiations with British state since pre independence period. The issue of forced marriage is no exception. The following section of the paper summarizes the challenges of Indian women seeking legal redress in the context of forced marriage in Britain.

The Case of India

As far as ethnic minority population of the UK is concerned, 1 in 8 (13.3%) of the resident population of the UK are born abroad, India ranks second to Poland among the most common non-UK country of birth[15]. Notwithstanding the achievements and affluence of Indian diaspora in Britain, the struggles and issues concerning the lives of Indian women there, have been brought to public notice since the onset of the second wave feminist discourse in Britain in the 1960s. Contemporary debates on forced marriage drew considerable attention towards the struggles of South Asian women in Britain.

The Government of Britain ensures lifelong anonymity to victims and alleged victims of forced marriage with the intention to encourage them to come forward in an effort to increase the number of prosecutions for the crime.[16] Names of survivors used in the survivor stories published by charities have been changed to safeguard their anonymity. Lack of accurate data on particular cases related to survivors of Indian origin makes qualitative data analysis difficult. However survivor stories of known cases are accessible and are imperative to struggles of Indian women against forced marriage. Jasvinder Sanghera is the champion of battles against forced marriages in today's Britain. Her experiences of eloping with a man of her choice to escape an arranged marriage and of being disowned by her family during the 1980's inspired Jasvinder for her latter fights against forced marriages in Britain.[17]

Irrespective of the continued assurance of not associating forced marriages with any one country or culture, it is still branded as a South Asian issue in Britain, time and again. *The Right to Choose: A Statutory Guidance for Dealing with Forced Marriage* published by the Department of Finance and Personnel, UK in 2012, observes that, "majority of cases of forced marriage reported to date in the UK involve South Asian families."[18] Hence it is relevant to look into the prevailing statistics and figures to understand the extent of the issue in Britain.

Statistics

The FMU: Forced Marriage Unit dealt with 1220 cases in 2015. India ranks third among the five highest volume countries in which victims were at risk of forced marriage.[19] Pakistan and Bangladesh rank first and second among the focus countries as per the data. The statistics published by FMU in 2016 indicate that, it handled cases involving 67 focus countries, in which a victim was at risk of, or had already been taken to in connection with forced marriages. FMU dealt with 75 cases of Indian origin that constitutes 6% of the total number of cases handled in 2015.

Percentage of Cases of Forced Marriage from India 2012-2015

Year	Total Number of Countries of Cases of Forced Marriage handled by FMU	Percentage of Cases of Forced Marriage from India	Total Number of Cases Handled by FMU
2012	60	8%	1485
2013	74	10.9%	1302
2014	88	7.8%	1267
2015	67	6%	1220

Source: Forced Marriage Unit, Government of UK (Statistics Published, 2012 to 2015).

Regardless of FMU statistics, experts confirmed at the 'International Crime and Policing Conference', conducted by Home Office in 2015, that there are an estimated 8,000 to 10,000 forced marriages or threats of forced marriage in Britain every year.[20] Hence it is required to consider the extent of unreported cases and failed prosecutions along with official statistics to understand the extent of the issue.

Therefore statistics confirm the prevalence of forced marriage among Indian and other South Asian communities in Britain. To analyze the challenges of women at risk of forced marriage, it is crucial to understand the causes and effects of forced marriages, as the perpetrators in majority of the cases are most often immediate family.

Causes and Effects of Forced Marriage

Conflicts between different generations, arising out of clashes between western and non-western values among immigrant communities can be identified as one of the most significant causes behind instances of forced marriage in Britain.[21] Many scholars have identified a 'between cultures' dilemma that the younger generation British Indians experience when the first generation tries to make them forcibly assimilate cultural values which they reject. to The British government has also identified parental pressure as the sole motive for forced marriages.[22] FMU has outlined reasons including, controlling unwanted behaviour and sexuality, preventing 'unsuitable' relationships with people outside their ethnic, cultural, caste or religious group, protecting perceived cultural or religious ideals, family honour or long-standing family commitments, peer group or family pressure, claims for residence and citizenship, etc.[23] Among the reasons mentioned, protection of family honour forms the most significant motive behind instances of forced marriage as per survivor testimonies. Family members, mostly the parents become perpetrators of violence in the majority of the cases and it makes legal redress further difficult as daughters have to choose between remaining in the forced marriages and taking parents to court.

Indian girls who endure forced marriage in Britain often feel isolated within and outside families. Most victims are locked up in their homes and are unable to disclose their fears, as communication with people outside the family is limited due to restrictions. Isolation eventually leads to emotional suffering, depression and self harm.[24] Many times young girls withdrawn from education are powerless to protest due to the fear of disownment by their families. Forced marriage entirely limits prospects of education, career and social development of women. Those women who succumb to the pressures of forced marriage, exerted by family, may subject to repeated sexual abuse and domestic violence within the marriage. Children within marriage witnessing persistent violence may be traumatized or may learn that violence is justified.[25] Survivors who escape forced marriages with the help of police and social service, estrangement from family generates suicide feelings and often end up in hospitals.

Hence the legislation poses significant barriers to women victims of forced marriage to access justice in various forms. The study argues that the legislation on forced marriage in Britain has not been able to tackle the issue of forced marriage and is unable to provide redress to Indian women due to following reasons.

1. Forced and Arranged Marriages: Overlapping Concerns

Several official reports published by Government of UK including *The Right to Choose: Multi-Agency Statutory Guidance for Dealing with Forced Marriage,* 2008, outlines the distinction between forced and arranged marriages. As it observes "in arranged marriages, the families of both spouses take a leading role in arranging the marriage but the choice whether or not to accept the arrangement remains with the prospective spouses. In forced marriages, one or both spouses do not (or, in the case of some adults with support needs, cannot) consent to the marriage and duress is involved. Duress can include physical, psychological, financial, sexual and emotional pressure."[26] The distinction between arranged and forced marriages in Britain is primarily drawn on the basis of consent and coercion.

For validating arguments for consent related to marriages, Britain invokes universal parameters and UN definition on consent to marriage.[27] While considering the limitations of approach of regulation in reconciling the conflicts between cherishing cultural diversity and ensuring women's equality in the context of forced marriage debates,[28] especially the underlying assumption that a particular set of behaviours is right, the Forced Marriage (Civil Protection) Act enforces individualist notions of consent based upon groups where consent is more community based with regard to marriages. For instance, a report by Centre LGS[29] stresses on how understanding of legitimate consent and force across cultures becomes crucial to define forced marriages. Legislation is not able to succeed in recognizing the notion of consent as it is ambiguous cross-culturally. The study further stipulates that the Act is ineffective in helping the current victims facing pressure as it provides them with a 'bargaining chip' either to negotiate with their families or to empower parents who face pressure from their communities. Both are not easy ways for Indian and other South Asian women as it would isolation and psychological pressures.

2. Prosecution of Family Members: The Unbearable Redress

There was common agreement on the offense of forced marriages, though there was severe disagreement among concerned parties on the criminalization. Criminalization was also echoed in the parliamentary debates related to legislation on forced marriage. Arguments for and against criminalization revolves fundamentally around the possibility of forced marriage being driven underground. People in favour of criminalization stress that it will act as a deterrent and send a strong message that forced marriage is not tolerated and the perpetrators will be prosecuted. Those who oppose criminalization assert that criminal proceedings can deter victims, which may lead to fewer criminal proceedings, and may further drive the issue of forced marriage underground due to less possibility of women opting to sue parents and family members. Jasvinder Sanghera, Aneeta Prem, Dr. Nazia Khanum OBE were among staunch supporters of criminalization whereas Dr. Aisha Gill, Pragna Patel (Southall Black Sisters), Baljit Banga (Newham Asian Women's Project), Shaista Gohir OBE (Muslim Women's Network UK) and others are concerned about the implementation challenges of the new criminal offense.[30]

Recent studies confirm that there are few prosecutions happening on forced marriages in UK apparently due to fear of sending parents to jail.[31] A 34-year-old businessman from Cardiff was the first person in UK to be jailed for forced marriage in 2015.[32] Hence few or no criminal proceedings suggest that the legislation is not helping Indian and other women to escape forced marriages. In addition there are several factors identified by studies[33] that hinder criminal prosecution of forced marriages including:

- Requirement of higher standard of proof has negative impact on victims.
- Requirement of prosecution to disclose all evidence including sensitive information gathered by the police, charities etc to the defense restrains the victims from opting for prosecuting their families.
- Requirement of victims and witnesses to give evidence in court, and submit to being cross-examined and sharing and discussion of this information in public which may place them at risk of harm.
- Lack of protection for victims and witnesses of failed prosecutions who face social ostracism generates fears about prosecution.
- Overseas application of the legislation is limited. Many times, victims are taken abroad to get married and the registration of a

criminal offence cannot help due to conflict of laws of different states and/or countries.

3. Inadequate Support Services

The British government has established a multi agency practice for handling cases of forced marriage with the co-operation of the police department, education professionals, health professionals, the crown prosecution service and the local housing authority.[34] As soon as a case is reported, police enquiry begins regardless of ethnicity and citizenship of the victims. Civil protection and support services offered by FMU are readily available as soon as the FMPO is issued. Housing option for survivors who are estranged from families include Refuges in UK, local authority homeless persons units, etc. Health professionals and educational professionals are trained to generate awareness among victims about the risk of forced marriages. Nevertheless victim testimonies expose the need of more training about the understanding of psychological costs of forced marriage including the increased risk of suicides and impact of family estrangement to support service professionals.[35] Research studies point out that the victims of forced marriage are not able to afford the required legal assistance. Lack of additional resources announced to meet these needs along with cuts to legal aid poses challenges to victims.[36] Lack of foster homes and professionals with appropriate training and cultural sensitivity further aggravates the plight of the victim.[37] Consequently Indian and other Asian victims of forced marriage who opt for prosecution are subject to risk of further persecution due to inadequate support services.

Furthermore, the British Home office was subject to a controversy in December 2016 for ordering a victim of forced marriage to repay the British government the costs of her repatriation. Newspaper reports indicate that the 17 years old victim of forced marriage was issued a bill for £814 as the cost of her repatriation from Pakistan and even had to surrender her passport before she was flown back to the UK. Women activists criticized the move as morally wrong and counter-productive as victims cannot be expected to afford to pay for their escape. Besides, having already becomes estranged from their families, victims have no option but to remain in the forced marriage since they cannot afford their escape.[38]

4. Cultural Stereotypes

Criminalization reinforces stereotypes, particularly toward South Asian communities who have frequently been portrayed in media as monolithic and primitive whereby forced marriage is an accepted cultural norm.[39] Apprehensions raised by legislators like former MP Anne Cryer[40] regarding involvement of South Asian Muslim communities in relation to instances of forced marriages becomes relevant in this context. Women activists have refuted similar assumptions as racial profiling of communities. As statistics confirms prevalence of forced marriage among non-Muslim communities also, it is discriminatory to typecast South Asian Muslims as violent parents and daughters as mere victims.

Culturally insensitive usage of misleading campaign images constitutes another significant arena that reinforces cultural stereotypes. For instance there is repeated usage of mehndi/henna[41] clad hands of a woman where forced marriage is illustrated in the BBC website (Ethics Guide, BBC and BBC News). Despite continuous efforts made to draw distinction between arranged and forced marriages to pledge the anti-racist stance by the government of UK, the campaign images mis-represents one thing for the other. Usage of similar images impart misleading information about forced marriage for viewers who are unaware of the *mehndi* ritual in the majority of Indian marriages, (whether arranged or not) and what appears in the image is apparently construed as forced marriage by the majority of Britons.

Pakistanis (44%), Indians (6%) and Bangladeshis (7%) who are clubbed as South Asians by Britain constituted 57% of the cases handled by FMU in 2015. Rest 43% included survivors from various other parts of the world. Therefore, forced marriage is not a sole South Asian issue. However there are less accounts of involvement of people from other ethnicities and countries in British national documents despite the nominal mention.

5. Linking Forced Marriage with Immigration

UK 'Visas and Immigration agency' links forced marriage with immigration as most of the cases falls in visa category. Chapter 8 of the immigration directorate instructions that deals with family applications underlines that "there is an allegation or other information suggesting that the marriage may not be genuine, that the marriage is a forced marriage or the couple are not living together"[42] Immigration fear of Britain is manifested as clearly seen in the recent initiatives of restrictive regulatory clauses on spouse visas through probationary period (5 years) for foreign spouses before applying for Indefinite Leave to Remain (ILR) in the UK; No Recourse to Public Funds (NRPF) for foreign spouses, mandatory English tests for foreign spouses etc. While there is no established evidence to prove the link between forced marriage and immigration, the logic of using immigration restriction to tackle this issue is dubious at most.

Restrictive clauses for overseas spouses expose the immigration panic and the irrational claims to cut down the numbers of immigrants. Given the fact that the majority of the survivors of forced marriage are women, constant emphasis on overseas brides by British state and the media outcry upholds the view that Indians and other Asian women are silent victims who are in need of the protection offered by the savior state. They are denied the services of any agency and their potential for self-realization and empowerment is undervalued. Consequently, Indian women at the risk of forced marriages suffer the treatment as victims of their culture and it essentially diverts the attention away from the other fundamental issues affecting them including socio-economic empowerment, which is essentially denied by the UK government based on their immigration policies

Conclusion

Forced marriage is perceived as a grave human rights violation and violence against women and legal and social provisions to address this issue of forced marriage is being scrutinized in Britain and elsewhere. Despite prevalence of statistical evidence and Britain's attempts to dissociate South Asian immigrants from the issue of forced marriage to pledge anti racist stance, forced marriage largely remains as a South Asian affair. Forced marriage legislation in Britain poses significant barriers to Indian and other South Asian women at risk, to access justice. Constraints stem from a variety of reasons ranging from synonymic elucidation of forced and arranged marriages, inevitable prosecution of family members, lack of adequate support services, generation of cultural stereotypes, establishment of incoherent linkage between forced marriage and migration to other factors. Moreover few criminal proceedings indicate incompetence of criminalization of forced marriage.

Hence the forced marriage law is not adequate to eliminate the cultural offense of forced marriage among Indian and other South Asian communities in contemporary Britain. Apparently it is more of an effective immigration control measure than a legal empowerment of women victims or a form of civil protection measure in its present form. While considering the legal, social and cultural hurdles, women at risk of forced marriage encounter, one can say that there is a need for reconsidering the proposition made by activists to treat forced marriage as a form of domestic violence, instead of enacting a separate criminal law. In addition there is an increased need for active women participation in dialogical encounters with community groups to combat forced marriage. Adequate support services including free legal aid, secure shelter homes, sensitization of professionals and provisions for socio economic empowerment of Indian women is also required to combat this issue of forced marriages in Britain.

Notes

1. Katharine Charsley, et al., "Marriage Migration and Integration Report," *Media Library*, Bristol University, 2016, accessed 10 December 2016, bristol.ac.uk
2. Zena a Pakistani girl from Bradford, Britain who eloped with her boyfriend Jack Briggs to escape arranged marriage was chased and threatened by her family and bounty hunters and private detectives hired by them. Martin Weinwright, "Legal Bid by Pair on Run from Forced Marriage" *The Guardian*, 15 August 2000.
3. GOV. UK provides combined source for the website of all government departments and agencies and public bodies.
4. Home Affairs Section, *Forced Marriage, Standard Note: SN/HA/1003*, 21January 2015, accessed 18 December 2016, Research Briefings Parliament, GOV.UK.
5. *Information and Practice Guidelines for Professionals Protecting, Advising and Supporting Victims,* March 2013, accessed 23 December 2016, https://www.gov.uk/guidance/forced-marriage
6. Jasvinder is a survivor of attempted forced marriage and forerunner of among activists of Indian origin who fight forced marriages in Britain. Karma Nirvana in Derby run by her have helped British government to shape policy of legislation on forced marriages.
7. The Bill was considered in Grand Committee on 10 May 2007 and substantial amendments were made including incorporation of the Bill as a new Part 4A of the Family Law Act 1996. Home Affairs Section, *Forced Marriage, Standard Note: SN/HA/1003*, 21 January 2015, accessed 18 December 2016, Research Briefings Parliament, GOV.UK.
8. *Forced Marriage etc. (Protection and Jurisdiction) (Scotland) Act 2011*, accessed 02 January 2017, http://www.legislation.gov.uk/asp/2011/15/part/3/enacted
9. Home Office, *Forced Marriage A Consultation: Summary of Responses*, June 2012, accessed 13 December 2016, https://www.gov.uk/government/uploads/system/uploads/attachment_data/file/157829/forced-marriage-response.pdf
10. *Anti-social Behaviour, Crime and Policing Act 2014*, accessed 23 December 2016, http://www.legislation.gov.uk/ukpga/2014/12/part/10/enacted
11. *Ibid.*
12. *Apply for A Forced Marriage Protection Order,* 13 July 2016, accessed 02 December 2016, https://www.gov.uk/apply-forced-marriage-protection-order/overview
13. *Forced Marriage*, 25 October 2016, accessed 16 December 2016, https://www.gov.uk/stop-forced-marriage

14. *Ethnicity*, accessed 23 November 2016, www.statistics.gov.uk/ downloads/theme _compendia /foe2004/ethnicity.pd
15. *Population of the UK by Country of Birth and Nationality Report*, August 2015, accessed 02 September 2016, https://www.ons.gov.uk/peoplepopulationandcommunity/populationandmigration/internationalmigration/articles/populationbycountryofbirthandnationalityreport/2015-09-27
16. PA Media Lawyer, "Forced Marriage Victims to Have Lifelong Media Anonymity," *Press Gazette*, 14 June 2016.
17. Jasvinder Sanghera runs the charity named Karma Nirvana in Britain. Her autobiography titled *Shame* was mentioned during British parliamentary debates on forced marriage.
18. *The Right to Choose: A Statutory Guidance for Dealing with Forced Marriage*, accessed 02 December 2016, http://www.dfpni.gov.uk/right-to-choose-forced-marriage.pdf
19. Home Office, *Forced Marriage Unit Statistics 2015*, 08 March 2016, accessed 12 December 2016, https://www.gov.uk /government/uploads/system/uploads/attachment _data/file/505827/ Forced_Marriage _Unit_ statistics_2015.pdf
20. *Hidden Victims of Forced Marriages*, http://www.expressandstar.com/news/2015/06/13/hidden-victims-of-forced-marriages/, 13 June 2015, accessed 2 December 2016.
21. Parvathy Poornima, "Contemporary Feminist Discourse and South Asian Women in Britain: A Study of Forced Marriage (Civil Protection) Act 2007", Ph.D Thesis, Jawaharlal Nehru University, 2015. (Unpublished)
22. *The Right to Choose: A Statutory Guidance for Dealing with Forced Marriage*, accessed 02 December 2016, http://www.dfpni.gov.uk/right-to-choose-forced-marriage.pdf
23. "Forced Marriage", accessed 14 December 2016), http://www.basingstokeitec.co.uk/images/pdf/Forced-Marriage.pdf
24. Various interviews of activists working to fight forced marriage in Britain including Jasvinder Sanghera, Aneeta Prem, Refuge Workers and others.
25. Excerpts from survivor stories published by government of UK and other charities working against forced marriage.
26. *The Right to Choose: A Statutory Guidance for Dealing with Forced Marriage*, accessed 02 December 2016, http://www.dfpni.gov.uk/right-to-choose-forced-marriage.pdf
27. *Convention on Consent to Marriage, Minimum Age for Marriage and Registration of Marriages*, accessed 21 December 2016, http://www. ohchr.org/EN/ProfessionalInterest/Pages/MinimumAgeFor Marriage.aspx
28. `"UK Initiatives on Forced Marriage: Regulation", *Dialogue and Exit*, 2004, accessed 22 November 2016, http://eprints.lse.ac.uk/546/
29. Centre LGS, Response to the Home Office Consultation Document, 'Forced Marriage: A Wrong Not A Right', 2005, (accessed 13 November 2016); available from https://www.kent.ac.uk/clgs/documents/pdfs/clgsforcedmarriage response .pdf

30. UK Makes Forced Marriage Illegal as Pursues Campaign of 'British values', *Reuters*, 16 June 2014.
31. Yasminara Khan, "Why are there so Few Forced Marriage Prosecutions?" *BBC,* 10 June 2015.
32. John Bingham "First Ever Forced Marriage Conviction in UK", *The Telegraph*, 10 June 2015.
33. *Criminalizing Forced Marriage has not Helped its Victims*, 2015, accessed 02 January 2017, http://theconversation.com/criminalising-forced-marriage-has-not-helped-its-victims-43351.
34. HM Government June 2014, "Multi-Agency Practice Guidelines: Handling cases of Forced Marriage," https://www.gov .uk/government /uploads/system /uploads/attachment _data/file /322307 /HMG_ MULTI_ AGENCY_PRACTICE_GUIDELINES_1_180614_FINAL.pdf
35. UK is Failing Girls Who Flee Forced Marriage, Says Honour Abuse Survivor, *Reuters*, 11 March 2016.
36. *Evidencing Domestic Violence: A Barrier to Family Law Legal Aid,* 2013, accessed 26 December 2016, http://rightsofwomen.org.uk/wp-content/uploads/2014/10/Evidencing-DV-a-barrier-2013.pdf
37. Katherine Sellgren, "Charity Warns of a Shortage in Foster Carers in UK", *BBC News*, 20 December 2011.
38. Francis Perraudin, "Forced Marriage Victims are Made to Pay to Go Home to UK", *The Guardian*, 26 December 2016.
39. Sabbir Malik, "The Government Must Act Now", 2014, accessed 06 December 2016, https://jantrust.wordpress.com/2014/09/22/the-government-must-act-now-by-sabbir-malik/
40. "MP Cryer to Quit at Next Election", *BBC News*, 21 August 2008.
41. Mehndi ceremony refers to application of henna leaves as a form of skin decoration in Asia and elsewhere.
42. "Immigration Directorate Instructions" https://www.gov.uk/government/uploads/system/uploads/attachment_data/file/287807/section1_1_.pdf

Chapter - 15

Gender Stereotyping on the Basis of Clothes

—Aanchal Jha

> What a strange power there is in clothing.
>
> – Isaac Bashevis Singer

Sex roles are one of the obvious definitions made by dress. In societies such as nineteenth-century England and America, which differentiated greatly between the role of men and women, the clothing of the two sexes also diverged widely. The rather minimal differences between the physical anatomy of men and women are enormously exaggerated by clothed bodies.[1] Samuel Butler describes two children looking at a picture of Adam and Eve in an illustrated Bible: "Which is Adam and which is Eve?" asks one child. "I don't know," answers the other, "but I could tell if they had their clothes on."[2]

This paper lists out the ideas on how women were restricted not only socially, verbally, physically but they were confined on a very shrewd idea which no one would have thought about: fashion / clothing.

The feminine characteristics that are projected by women's dress – frivolity, delicacy, inactivity, and submissiveness – were embodied in the heroines of literature and praised by writers and journalists. John Keats's ideal woman is like "a milk-white lamb that bleats for man's protection.[3]

Clothing transform a person's appearance. When we see a person for the first time we figure out a person more or less by his/her clothes, it could influence the actions and perception of both the wearer and the observer.

For instance, up until now we thought laced corset was a mere fashion accessory, which makes the waist appear thinner and sexier and may be more "feminine". Wearing laced corset was a ubiquitous thing in England and America throughout the 19th century. It was designed to make the body to relate more closely to feminine ideal of smaller waist size, which was worshipped during that time. Women were made to wear this type of tight clothes to restrain and restrict them from growing. What fear did man have or still has in his mind about women's growth?

This may sound intimidating but men from ages are toiling to find out ways to restrict women. The use of corset was basically to make women more submissive to men. Women were made different from men on the basis of their clothing ideas. Men were considered to be serious regarding their work, so they wore dark colours, and women, to be an archetypal feminine, were allowed to wear pretty pastels with a bow and a lace only. Men were meant to be active, so their clothes were comfortable that allowed them much movement as compared to women whose clothes were tight and uncomfortable restricting her movement. In 1830s and 40s, the sleeves of a dress were set so low over the shoulder and so tightly encased the arm that it was virtually impossible for a women to raise her arms in an aggressive manner; not only clothing but some attributes like 'aggression' is believed to be used by men only. The corset was used to make the difference between male and female body by making the waist thinner and hips and bust bigger. Wearing this laced corset constricted the diaphragm, forcing women to breathe from upper part of the chest. Uncomfortableness caused by this laced corset depends on the proportions of waist size, sleeves, and skirt that defined the fashionable silhouette. The tightness of lace corset also depends on social occasion, their age, and marital status.

Many doctors considered this tight lace corset leads to physical deformities. The women also suffered from rib deformities in order to procure an Hourglass figure. Wearing corset also came to be known as a moral imperative. The women who rejected the idea of corsets were accused of having loose morals. As one defender of tight lacing said: "The corset is an ever-present monitor indirectly bidding its wearer to exercise self restraint: it is evidence of a well disciplined mind and well-regulated feelings."[4]

D. Edgar Flinn, in *Our Dress and Our Food in Relation to Health* (1886), affirmed that every woman who tight-laced must be regarded as deformed and noted the many illnesses it caused, including a "general sense of languor and fatigue."[5] Ada Ballin, in *Health and Beauty in Dress*, also noted the weakness caused by tight-lacing and describes the many women going "through life uncomplaining with a sort of dull, negative suffering, the result of low vitality."[6]

Wearing corsets also came to be seen as a moral imperative. The un-corseted women were in danger of being accused of loose morals. As one defender of tight-lacing said: "The corset is an ever-present monitor indirectly bidding its wearer to exercise self-restraint: it is evidence of a well-disciplined mind and well-regulated feelings."[7] One can deduce that "Corset was an item of clothing that directly and graphically disciplined women to their submissive-masochist role."[8]

Along with corset, one more fashion accessory that was in demand is Crinoline, appeared in June 1856, which was used by women to give volume to her dress. It was made of spring steel hoops, increasing in diameter towards the bottom. (Roberts) It was designed to give and create a desired bell-shaped effect. The fashion became so popular that Punch nicknamed the crinoline craze "Crinolinemania".

The new fashion gave ample assurance of immobile submission, a reminder to men of their own superior mobility and to women of the restraint and passivity supposedly inherent in their sex.[9] Mrs Oliphant, writing in the 1870s, deplores "the painful spectacle of the whole female race more or less tied into narrow bags," but doubts that women will overturn the tyranny of fashion. Women call attention to their "bondage," she notes, by a propensity "to embroider our bandages with wreaths of primroses and daffodils." She disapproves of "the stiff lines of embroidery which show where the narrow bag of the skirt is drawn most closely round the confined limbs, or the limbs which appear to be confined whether they are so or not." She describes a skirt with a band of contrasting colour below the knees which had "a perplexing air of having been tied round the legs expressly to confine…movements." This dress and many others in the 1870s, Margaret Oliphant confides, "was artfully contrived to look like the instrument of torture which it was not in reality."[10]

As psychoanalyst Anthony Storr points out, the purpose of abuse is not to inflict pain or to experience it, but to establish relations of dominance and submission. The pain involved is the most convenient and believable sign that one is willing to be truly submissive, that the other will be accorded total dominance.[11]

The dangers and inconveniences of wearing the cage were much publicised at the time, and included being unable to fit into carriages or through narrow doorways. Some satirical images went so far as to pretend that women had to leave their crinolines outside or on top of the vehicle when travelling. Revealing more ankle and legs than was thought proper was another much cited problem. It suggests that women sometimes showed even more underwear by being blown by a sudden gust of wind. The crinoline craze reached its peak during the late 1850s and early 1860s. After about 1862 the silhouette of the crinoline changed and rather than being bell-shaped it was now flatter at the front and projected out more behind.[12]

More seriously, the light material of the crinoline posed the very real danger of inflammability. "Take what precautions we may against fire, so long as the hoop is worn, life is never safe," warned the *Illustrated News of the World* (1863); "all are living under a sentence of death which may occur unexpectedly in the most appalling form."[13] The *Englishwoman's Domestic Magazine* of 1867 reported 3,000 women were burned to death annually and another 20,000 injured because they wore the crinoline.[14]

Along with long run fashion fad of corset and crinolines there came another trend of hobble skirts, these were invented not known by whom but were created when someone thought women were getting more physically active. This was designed mainly to stop women from progressing. This skirt was literally designed to hobble women. And in the 1910s, it was all the rage. Some say, it was inspired by Edith Berg, the first female to fly on an airplane. Before flying on an airplane in 1908 with the Wright Brothers, she tied her skirt so that her skirt is not caught in the machinery. But legendry French designer Paul Poiret got the inspiration for his hobble skirts from the Asian garments that were fashionable at the time, like cocoon coats and kimonos. His hobble skirt was so narrow at the hem that it was difficult for a woman to walk. In fact, as we look down the lane we found that it was Paul Poiret who banished the use of corset. Poiret wrote: "Yes, I freed the bust, but I shackled the legs". The hobble skirt became the rage of that time and it was associated with luxury and was believed that wearing a hobble skirt you are so rich you don't need to move or work or even really move at all. The skirt was so tight fitted that it was nearly impossible for a women to move, and that lead to many hazardous accidents leading to death. *The Englishwoman's Domestic Magazine* recommended in 1875 that "the bodice be as long-waisted and as tight fitting as possible, the skirt as scant and the train as full as maybe."[15]

The Paris correspondent for *The Ladies' Treasure*, reported that "skirts are now so tight that our sitting and walking are seriously inconvenienced;

and the sleeves of our bodices are so closely fitting to the arms that we can hardly raise them, even to half their usual height…." Unfortunately, these very tight dresses are more frequently dis-advantageous to the greater portion of the ladies than they are becoming.

These clothing/dressing sense restrictions can be found in literature prominently as literature and fashion are integrally connected. Reflecting on the relation between fashion and literature, one realizes that there is something substantial that links the two; though different, they might seem similar.

To the nineteenth-century writers, the phrase "clothes make the man" was no empty cliché, but a profound and perceptive truth about the workings of society. For Thomas Carlyle in *Sartor Resartus*, clothes were not mere aesthetic ornament, but emblems of society's hierarchy and symbols of the spirit. "Man's earthly interests," he observes, "are hooked and buttoned together and held up by clothes."[16]

From an historical perspective, in the Western world, by the mid-nineteenth century, clothes and accessories were becoming less stigmatized than they ever had been. In those decades, clothes and accessories started to be looked at as reflections of the individual's self-image, communicating aspects of his or her personality.

Writers used this clothing or dress code to define or to allude the characters' personalities, class and circumstances in their work. To name a few: Gustave Flaubert, George Eliot, Anzia Yezierska, Theodore Dreiser, and Kate Chopin. Being the courageous and innovative artist she was, Chopin, for one, centered some of her stories precisely on clothing (be they stockings or bloomers) and indicated its importance in memorable scenes in *The Awakening* (1899). Toward the end of the nineteenth century, another writer who was very knowledgeable in matters of fashion and paid a undue attention to the way he dressed and accessorized his characters was Henry James, a precursor of modernism. It has been eloquently argued that as an admirer of Balzac and a fine estimator of the visual arts, James understood the significance of apparel in presenting and defining a character, although he never lingered on this aspect too long.[17]

During the transition towards twentieth century, while undergoing basic changes in order to answer their wearers' new demands, women's clothes were employed in literature and/or in critical writings, not only to define characters' personalities or the times' tastes and trends, but also to resist fashion's dictates.

American sociologist and novelist Charlotte Perkins Gilman waged a strenuous battle over the conventionally fashionable female clothes of the beginning of the twentieth century in her pamphlet "The Dress of Women," published in instalments in *The Forerunner* (1915). She judged most contemporary feminine apparel to be preposterous and inimical to women's physical and emotional welfare as well as to their potential tasks—tasks that would be profitable to them and to society. Gilman did not play down the role of clothing; on the contrary, she claimed with notable foresight that "cloth is a social tissue," but fought against its exaggerations and lack of comfort. In her utopian novels *Herland* (1915) and *With Her in Ourland* (1916), she dressed her female characters according to her own principles, based on practicality (skirts, for instance, had to have pockets) and freedom of movement.[18]

In utopian writings, incidentally, clothes play a crucial role: usually plain and unvarying, they are upheld as indexes of rationality and efficiency, implicitly or explicitly stigmatizing those that, either formerly or in those same years, were designed and worn.[19] Another example of stereotyping from clothes can be found in charlotte Gilman's short story *If I Were a Man* (1914); the protagonist Mollie transforms into her husband Gerald, and suddenly the world feels so right to her as in those days were not allowed to work; consequently, she has no experience of going to work, or having her own money, or being around men outside in a social gathering. Charlotte Gilman here uses a piece of example, pockets, that were only meant for men and not for women; women never experienced the joy of having pockets but when the protagonist gets to experience the joy of having pockets, her reaction, expressed by the author as:

> Another impulse fished in a convenient pocket for change-instantly, automatically, bringing forth a nickel for the conductor and a penny for the newsboy. These pockets came as a revelation. Of course she had known they were there, had counted them, made fun of them, mended them, even envied them; but she never had dreamed of how it felt to have pockets.[20]

Clothing differs from place to place; as the geographical area changes the dressing sense of people changes. Now, let us analyse the same thing from earlier Indian era and dynasties, and what was the situation at that period.

During the Mauryan dynasty (322-185 BC) evidence of female clothing is available from the statues of Yakshis; the female epitome of fertility. The most common attire of the people at that time was *Antariya*, which they used to wear as a lower garment that men used to wear the same attire.[21]

Every country has its own erogenous zones. In sculptures from the Maury and Sunga periods (about 300 BC), men and women wore rectangular pieces of fabric, on the lower part of the body and one on the upper part. Little else. In India, unlike in Britain, there are no written codes of conduct or sumptuary laws about what should be worn. What was considered suitable was spread through word of mouth. So today's guardians of the hemline – who no doubt believe they are safeguarding women by prescribing what women should wear – are following in the footsteps of older political overlords.

Indian women now are much freer, at least in the cities, yet we see dress codes being set and women condemned for what they wear. [22] In Ancient India, people wore clothes according to their position and role in society. Soldiers were different from ascetics who were different from prosperous *Setthis* and royalty or common farmers and artisans. Clothes also had ritualistic and a social significance.

This short exposition is but an introduction to the complexities of clothing in Ancient India. Some common features across space and time can be discerned. A very intriguing feature is the gender neutrality of the basic dress. The variations and twists given to dress by women or men cannot hide the fact that the three items of dress — the *Uttariya*, *Antariya* and *Kayabandh* — were common to both the sexes. The same unstitched piece of cloth could be worn equally by a man or a woman – contrary to Victorian England, for instance, where the cumbersome skirts and whalebone stays of women were impediments to free movement in strong contrast to the trousers and breeches worn with waist coats and vests by men.[23]

Clothing has a psychological effect on human being and that can be associated by examples above as well as once appearance, mood, thinking, attitude. Today, clothes mean so many things and their significance has changed so much. For example, in a time when women were submissive, they wore corsets and clothes that fitted the role, but once women decided they do not want a submissive life, the way they looked changed to meet the part.

We might look at distant, so-called "undeveloped cultures" with doubt, claiming we are not similar to them, but are. We see how in many ancient or tribal cultures, clothing played an important part: the way one dressed was a message to the community about their religion, status, lifestyle, interests and so on. In the Western world, we have use clothes to transmit the same messages, just that the code is not a written one.

Alison Lurie, an American Pulitzer Price winner said in *The Language of Clothes*:

> Long before I am near enough to talk to you on the street, in a meeting, or at a party, you announce your sex, age and class to me through what you are wearing – and very possibly give me important information (or misinformation) as to your occupation, origin, personality, opinions, tastes, sexual desires and current mood.[24]

Clothes have both a functional and a psychological use, even though we do not consider or see it minutely but one can tell about a person by just looking at them.

Researchers have identified a series of psychological changes that occur when we wear certain types of clothes. We hear sayings like "dress for the job you want; not the job you have" and "look good, feel good" all the time. Most people do not really believe in them, but we try to match our attire to the occasion nevertheless. The good news is that research into the impact of clothes on behaviour now suggests that there may actually be a grain of truth in these sayings. Science says that the clothes we wear affect our behaviour, attitudes, personality, mood, confidence, and even the way we interact with others. This is "Enclothed Cognition". The term Enclothed Cognition is used to describe the effect that our clothes seem to have on various psychological processes like emotions, self-evaluations, attitudes, and interpersonal interactions. Clothes affect our behaviour and our moods because of the symbolic meaning that we (as a society) ascribe to different types of attire.[25]

There is a reason why formal clothing a well-tailored jacket/suit a white crisp shirt are associated with the term "decked up for opulence". It seems that wearing formal and designed clothes puts us in right temperament to carry out our work. Wearing this type of clothing makes one feel powerful, and hence should be called "power clothing". Wearing a formal dress has psychological effect on person's mind, and that affects his mood, abstract thinking, decision making and this thing is scientifically proved.

A paper in August 2015 in *Social Psychological and Personality Science* asked subjects to change into formal or casual clothing before cognitive tests. Wearing formal business attire increased abstract thinking – an important aspect of creativity and long-term strategizing. The experiments suggest the effect is related to feelings of power.[26]

For example, a person is not motivated to exercise but putting on gym clothes may generate some interest in person's mind to exercise. "Clothes can actually make you smarter." Dressing, that is associated with intelligence, like doctor's coats or pilot's uniforms, may not only make you look smarter but may actually make you act smarter too, according to a study published in the *Journal of Experimental Social Psychology*. Researchers gave doctor's lab coats to subjects (none of whom were doctors) and then asked them to perform a series of complex tasks. Those in white coats made significantly fewer mistakes than the people in their street clothes. The scientists then repeated the experiment but this time gave lab coats to all the participants. However, they told half the people they were doctor's coats while the other half were told they were paint smocks. Again, the people in the "doctor's coats" performed better on the tests, which shows that it is not just what you wear but also what you think of what you wear that matters.[27]

As we search the topic and look deep into its realm, we further see that things apply to men and women differently. Women were constricted by her dress so that she cannot move and work equally as men. So to slow down her pace many attempts were made by fashionist as of those times. But today in 2017 as we put an attempt to analyse women and their clothing we see that women now are much bolder in their choice they even opt for suit, coats, jackets, pants, skirts, pencil skirts, etc. But situation in India is quite different then other places, the women is expected to dress according to situation, place, circumstances. For example, a women in any institution is expected to wear Indian clothes such as *saree* and *salwar kameez* which have been passed down somewhere from Mughal dynasty. For a party women can put a formal dress like men suit, coat, pants but no, she is expected to wear something according to the situation.

The time is changing and women are comfortable in wearing a formal dress pairing it with pencil or hobble skirt, but still they are expected to make it feminine by choosing light pastel colours as block colour or dark shades have been associated with men. Women have to include a feminine hint in their attire or else they are termed as "Tomboyish". Tomboy is a term associated with a woman having attributes like men.

Even if a woman manages to handles the formal look, again footwear is a problem for her, like men a women can't wear a pair of black formal shoes which again makes the look more tomboyish, a women has to wear heels, sandals, stilletoe which comes with a wide varieties of problem. On the other hand, wearing heels makes it very difficult and uncomfortable for a woman to walk. If a woman manages to walk, she may suffer from diseases like Metatarsalgia, bunions, Tailor bunions, Hammer toes, etc.

The same topic can be analysed by keeping films in mind, there have been many movies that showcase the above given issues related to dressing sense I would like to analyse some of movies here. In the movie Cinderella the protagonist is dressed by her fairy godmother in blue gown which has a corset top which makes the waist of the protagonist slim and tiny.

In another movie, which has established its mark in film world is *Titanic*, the protagonist of the movie actress named Kate Winslet who was known by the name Rose is seen travelling in an unsinkable ship called *Titanic* and as being a royalty women often dress in ball gowns, corsets, hats and umbrellas in the movie. The most famous scene from the movie is rose standing in the room clutching to bedposts while a mistress is tightening her laced corset.

The image from the film *Gone with the Wind* sums up many people's view of Victorian women - clutching to bedposts while their maid pulls and pulls at the corset strings to achieve the desirable and highly restrictive tiny waist. The woman battles against the restriction of her undergarments but to no avail. She is doomed to her position in society: a slave to fashion, cosseted and striving to be pleasing to men, whatever the cost.[28]

Helena Bonham Carter has captivated us all with her haunting, quirky and often corset-wearing characters. The list of movies including her tight-laced looks is exhaustive. Sweeney Todd, Alice in Wonderland...pretty much any of her period piece movies; all corsets. She loves them so much, most of her red carpet appearances and press photos are corset dresses. Dark, bold, mysterious and deliciously weird – her style has steampunk written all over it.

Jessica Rabbit is a fictional character in *Who Censored Roger Rabbit* and its loose film adaptation, Who Framed Roger Rabbit, from her tiny teeny waist we can definitely make out tat she is wearing something under that red attire of hers. Along with this, here comes new type of corsets which are displayed in movie *The Wonder Women* the Gal Godot may have mesmerised all of us but Lynda carter will always remain the most favourite character. And yes, *The Wonder Women* manages to display new type of corset very well.

We have seen women being stereotyped in many ways but through clothing was a thing which could not have been ever found out, and being unaware of this we women were following big and famous fashionatas fashion fad like a crazy. Somewhere down the line it is believed that women were responsible somewhere towards submissive – masochistic design. They were willing to resign to this design that is why they were forced to. This is especially seen in the Victorian women.

As we divulge information about corset as an artefact as a fossil from the Pleistocene Era. Fashion designer and high store brands are coming up with new trends and style for this Era: Gender-Neutral or Gender-free, clothes that can be worn by either men or women both bringing equality between both the sexes. Before we raise a toast to a world of post-gender fashion, it is important to differentiate between merchandise and actual breakthrough towards gender equality. To be sure, fashion can advocate for social change. There is a long antiquity of gender lines being vague in clothing as a way to exhibit equality of the sexes or freedom from sexual roles.

Founded in 1824, the New Harmony Socialist Utopian Community let men and women both wear trousers. It was borderline-scandalous for the era, but representative of their vision of gender equality. In the late 19th century, women's rights advocate Amelia Bloomer famously argued for the right of women to wear pants – called bloomers – under their shortened dresses. During filming for the countercultural road movie Easy Rider in parts of the South, actors Peter Fonda and Dennis Hopper discovered that men who grew their hair long were often asked whether they were a boy or a girl – and not in a friendly way. These real-life experiences were incorporated into the film's violent ending.

When hip-hop became a nationwide cultural phenomenon in the 1980s, male and female breakdancers – also known as b-boys and b-girls – wore tracksuits and other athletic clothing while they performed, blurring gender roles for a shared physical ability. They show how people – especially those on the margins – adapt and remix the clothes that are available to them, fashioning new styles and new meanings in a process that anthropologist Claude Levi-Strauss has called "bricolage."

The fashion industry's current attraction to unisex or gender-free clothing may be similar. While transgender models like Andreja Pejic and Hari Nef walk the runway and appear in fashion magazines, the real difficulties facing transgender individuals are often ignored. This is doubly true for transgender women of colour who are the victims of shocking amounts of violence. Probably more than any other daily act we engage in, clothes are how we convey our identity to the world. For that reason, they are important. They can be used in radical, subversive ways. But before we congratulate the fashion industry for making gender distinction a thing of the past, it's important to understand its motivations, its practices and its limitations and should make a move towards understanding and supporting transgender issues on a run way.[29]

As we move forward in twenty seventeen situation has some how changed but "patriarchy" is still in search of predicament by which women can be declared as a submissive beings or else can be slowed down with their progress. Women took charge for their clothing long back in 20s and now are surviving the era with little restriction now and then with every single step they take towards the horizon of grabbing equality. As we survive 2017 clothes are not only which catches our attention, but a trend revival of 90s is back with it's sexy, hip, bold-women statement that is – Choker, making every women going gaga over it and patriarchy finds yet another contrivance for bringing women and her accessory in limelight. Choker is basically a jewellery worn around neck a 90s trend which has found its way back in 2017.

Recalling one of my example: Sitting among a big bunch of friends on weekend is a thing that we all indulge in, at of this instance I was questioned by one of my male friend: What's up with the thin line jewellery on your neck? That's a choker I replied. I was interrupted by the other saying do you even know what does that symbolizes? He went on saying it's an animal thing, like a dog collar.

Notes

1. Helene E. Roberts, The Exquisite Slave: *The Role of Clothes in the Making of Victorian Women,* University of Chicago press, 1977, www.rci.rutgers.edu/~jemjones/Heleneroberts%20exquisiteslave.pdf
2. Henry Festing Jones, ed., *The Note-Books of Samuel Butler,* New York: E.P. Dutton & Co., 1917, p. 243.
3. John Keats, "Imitation of Spenser,“ in H. Buxton Formaned, *Poetical Works,* London: Oxford University Press, 1908, p. 23.
4. "Victorian Dress: Bodily Boundaries, Reform, and the Bloomer", *CSULA History of Costume*, 25 July 2016, csulaart204.wordpress.com/2016/04/25/victorian-dress-bodily-bounderies-reform-and-quaker-dress/
5. *Ibid,* p. 5.
6. *Ibid.*

7. *Ibid,* p. 4.
8. *Ibid,* p. 5.
9. *Ibid,* p. 557.
10. Margaret Oliphant, *Dress,* Philadelphia: Porter & Coats, 1879, pp. 73, 76, 90, 92.
11. Anthony Storr, *Sexual Deviation,* Harmondsworth: Penguin Books, 1964, pp. 43-48.
12. Victoria and Albert Museum, Online Museum, Web Team, webmaster@vam.ac.uk; "Restrictive Flamboyance and the Crinoline Craze: 1830-1860," Victoria and Albert Museum, Online Museum,London, 25 April 2013, www.vam.ac.uk/content/articles/c/corsets-and-crinolines-in-victorian-fashion/
13. *Ibid,* p. 5.
14. "Dressing the Indian woman through history." *BBC News*, BBC, 06 December 2014, www.bbc.com/news/magazine-30330693; Roberts, n. 1.
15. "The 10 Best Corset Wearing Characters of All Time,"Atomic Jane Clothing: Your Quick Guide To 1950's Fashion!, atomicjaneclothing.com/blogs/news/44870913-the-10-best-corset-wearing-characters-of-all-time.
16. Thomas Carlyle, *Sartor Resartus,* London: Chapman & Hall, 1896, pp. 27, 40, 49.
17. Clair Hughes, *Henry James and the Art of Dress*, London: Palgrave, 2001.
18. Charlotte Perkins Gilman, "The Dress of Women," *The Forerunner,* no. 6, issue 1915, p. 20.
19. Ribeiro, however, thinks that "true utopian dress is a contradiction in terms [...] it cannot be contemplated in terms of an unknown future" (Aileen Ribeiro, "Utopian Dress," *Chic Thrills: A Fashion Reader*, p. 226).
20. http://wps.prenhall.com/wps/media/objects/107/110026/ch18_a2_d2.pdf
21. "History of clothing in India", *Wikipedia*, 16 June 2017, en.wikipedia.org/wiki/History_of_clothing_in_India#Mauryan_period
22. "Dressing the Indian woman through history", *BBC News*, 06 December 2014, www.bbc.com/news/magazine-30330693
23. Sumedha Verma Ojha, "Fashions of the Past: Haute Couture And More From Ancient India," *Swarajya Read India Right ATOM*, 20 October 2016, swarajyamag.com/culture/fashions-of-the-past-haute-couture-and-more-from-ancient-india
24. AttireClub, "Menu," *Clothing As Symbols | Attire Club by Fraquoh and Franchomme*, attireclub.org/2013/05/19/clothing-as-symbols/
25. "7 ways your clothes change the way you think," *Brain Fodder*, 17 June 2016, brainfodder.org/psychology-clothes-enclothed-cognition/
26. Matthew HutsonTori Rodriguez, "Dress for Success: How Clothes Influence Our Performance," *Scientific American*, www.scientificamerican .com/article/dress-for-success-how-clothes-influence-our-performance/.
27. Charlotte Hilton Andersen, "How Your Clothes Affect Your Mood and Emotions," *Reader's Digest*, www.rd.com/advice/work-career/clothes-affect-mood/

28. n. 12.

29 "Runway Revolution: Can We Tie Unisex Fashion Trends to Gender Equality?," CNN, 14 January 2016, edition.cnn.com/style/article/unisex-fashion-gender-equality/index.html.

Authors' Profile

Binod C. Agrawal is an Anthropologist and former Vice Chancellor of Himgiri Zee University, Dehradun, India.

Nidhi Arora manages the Abjee Infosolution Pvt. Ltd., Ahmedabad, Gujarat. Dr Arora is a technophile with expertise in web technologies. Her research focuses on Artificial Intelligence and its application areas.

Pradeep Mallik is Adjunct Professor of Mass Communication at the School of Liberal Studies of Pandit Deendayal Petroleum University, Gujarat. As a communication teacher with more than 25 years of experience in print, broadcast and new media, Dr Mallik has worked with leading media houses and his last job was with Ahmedabad Mirror as its Deputy Resident Editor.

Mihir Bholey is a Senior Faculty of Interdisciplinary Design Studies at National Institute of Design (NID), Ahmedabad, Gujarat.

Harmik Vaishnav is Assistant Professor of Literature at the School of Liberal Studies of Pandit Deendayal Petroleum University, Gujarat. Dr Vaishnav is a professional with two decades of experience both in corporate and academics. He has worked in core HR, Operations and Core Management in various companies.

Supriya Pal is Lecturer in the School of Liberal Studies of Pandit Deendayal Petroleum University, Gujarat. She specializes in Strategic Human Resource, Organization Behaviour, Work Life Balance, HRIS, Talent Management, etc.

Swati Gupta is an adjunct faculty at Jain University, Bangalore, India.

Nausheen Nizami is Assistant Professor of Economics at the School of Liberal Studies of Pandit Deendayal Petroleum University, Gujarat. Dr Nizami is a labour economist with sound knowledge of SPSS for data-analysis.

Shilpa Parasuramparia is a PhD Candidate in the School of Liberal Studies (SLS) of Pandit Deendayal Petroleum University (PDPU), Gujarat.

Reshmi Kazi is Associate Professor at the Nelson Mandela Centre for Peace and Conflict Studies, Jamia Millia Islamia, New Delhi. Previously Dr Kazi was an Associate Fellow at the Institute of Defence Studies and Analysis (IDSA), New Delhi.

Manisha Chaurasia is a PhD Candidate at the Centre for International Politics, Organization and Disarmament, Jawaharlal Nehru University, New Delhi.

E. Dilipraj is Associate Fellow at the Centre for Air Power Studies (CAPS), New Delhi.

Parvathy Poornima is an Assistant Professor at the St. Joseph's College (Autonomous), Bangalore, India. Previously, Dr Poornima was a Visiting Faculty at the School of Liberal Studies (SLS) of Pandit Deendayal Petroleum University (PDPU), Gujarat.

Aanchal Jha is a PhD Candidate in the School of Liberal Studies (SLS) of Pandit Deendayal Petroleum University (PDPU), Gujarat. She is also English Language Trainer and Content Developer at the Knowledge Consortium of Gujarat.

Index

X

Y

Z